BLACKS IN THE AMERICAN WEST

Editors

Richard Newman
Marcia Renée Sawyer

The involvement of blacks at every point in the exploration, history, and ongoing life of the American West remains a little-known story. The books—both fiction and nonfiction—in this series aim to preserve these stories and to celebrate the achievement and culture of early African-American westerners.

Very truly Yours,
M. W. Gibbs

SHADOW AND LIGHT

AN AUTOBIOGRAPHY

WITH REMINISCENCES OF THE LAST AND PRESENT
CENTURY

BY
MIFFLIN WISTAR GIBBS

WITH AN INTRODUCTION BY
BOOKER T. WASHINGTON

Introduction to the Bison Books Edition
by Tom W. Dillard

A Fatherless Boy, Carpenter and Contractor, Anti-Slavery
Lecturer, Merchant, Railroad Builder, Superintendent of
Mine, Attorney-at-Law, County Attorney, Municipal Judge
Register of United States Lands, Receiver of Public Monies
for U.S., United States Consul to Madagascar—Prominent
Race Leaders, etc.

University of Nebraska Press
Lincoln and London

Introduction to the Bison Books Edition © 1995 by the University of Nebraska Press
All rights reserved
Manufactured in the United States of America

⊖ The paper in this book meets the minimum requirements of American National Standard for Information Sciences—Permanence of Paper for Printed Library Materials, ANSI Z39.48-1984.

First Bison Books printing: 1995
Most recent printing indicated by the last digit below:
10 9   8   7   6   5   4   3   2   1

Library of Congress Cataloging-in-Publication Data
Gibbs, Mifflin Wistar.
Shadow and light: an autobiography with reminiscences of the last and present century / by Mifflin Wistar Gibbs; with an introduction by Booker T. Washington; introduction to the Bison books edition by Tom W. Dillard.
p. cm.—(Blacks in the American West)
Reprinted from an original 1902 edition inscribed by the author.
Includes bibliographical references.
ISBN 0-8032-7050-X (alk. paper)
1. Gibbs, Mifflin Wistar. 2. Afro-Americans—History. 3. Afro-Americans—Biography. I. Title. II. Series.
E185.97.G44A3 1995
973′.0496073′0092—dc20
[B]
95-4568 CIP

Reprinted from an original 1902 edition inscribed by the author.

INTRODUCTION TO THE BISON BOOKS EDITION

Tom W. Dillard

Mifflin Wistar Gibbs is little known in African-American history. Even in Arkansas, where he spent most of his life, his name is mostly associated with the Little Rock elementary school named in his honor at the turn of the century. But to nineteenth-century black Americans, he was a man widely known for his substantial accomplishments and diverse interests. He was a leader of his race, and much more than that. He was an adventurous spirit, ready to join Frederick Douglass as a youthful orator on the abolitionist speaking circuit, or seek a fortune in Gold Rush California, or campaign for the first black municipal judgeship in America, or serve as the American consul in Madagascar, or start a bank at the ripe old age of eighty.

Students of American history are fortunate that Gibbs published his autobiography, *Shadow and Light: An Autobiography with Reminiscences of the Last and Present Century*, in 1902. While the writing is tinged with the flowery style typical of the Victorian era, and while much of Gibbs's long life remained to be lived (he did not die until 1915, at age ninety-two), this autobiography chronicles a great swath of African-American history.

Perhaps the main reason M. W. Gibbs is so interesting historically is that he serves as a wonderful window from which to look out upon practically the entire panorama of nineteenth-century African-American history. As a child in 1820s Philadelphia, he experienced race riots that engulfed many American cities with large black populations. As an apprentice carpenter, he helped build a new home for Bethel

African Methodist Episcopal Church, the birthplace of the A.M.E. denomination and known as "Mother Bethel." During the evenings Gibbs visited the developing black literary societies, where he came into contact with libraries and—more importantly—with the emerging black leadership elite.

Among the black leaders that Gibbs met was the great Frederick Douglass, who soon took his charge into the antislavery crusade. Gibbs had already become a "shrewd, active agent" in the "underground railroad." Soon he was traveling with Douglass on the antislavery lecture circuit; for Gibbs speaking out formed an "epoch in my life's history" (32). While on this trip with Douglass, Gibbs learned of the discovery of gold in California, and he was off to the West where he hoped to do "some great thing" (37).

Once in California, Gibbs quickly found an economic niche for himself—not as a miner but as a merchant. Going into business with another recent black immigrant, Peter Lester, Gibbs at last found economic security in the Pioneer Boot and Shoe Emporium. What California offered in economic opportunity, it took away in racial antagonism and confrontation. Within a year of his landing in San Francisco, he and other black leaders published a series of resolutions protesting the discriminatory practices common in the state. Next he helped create the Franchise League, and in 1855 Gibbs participated in a general meeting of black leaders from across the state. The following year he helped establish the first black newspaper in California, *The Mirror of the Times*, a weekly that he served as a publisher and occasional contributor. The newspaper grew out of the work of the San Francisco Atheneum Institute, which Gibbs helped establish and which served as the headquarters for the black intelligentsia of San Francisco.

A famous fugitive slave case, involving a slave named Archy Lee, caused Gibbs and other black leaders to organize opposition to slavery in California. The ferocity of the black protest offended many white Californians, and antago-

nism between the races grew much worse. Gibbs was especially active in fighting the California poll tax, a business
tax that was particularly galling to blacks because payment
of it in no way allowed them to vote. In 1858, when a bill
was introduced in the state legislature to limit black immigration, Gibbs struck back, writing that the African-
American's "right to the benefit of just government is as
good as that of his pale face brother who clamors for his
expatriation."[1] The situation reached the boiling point when
blacks were ordered to remove their children from the public schools. With their world collapsing about them, Gibbs
and several hundred other black Californians fled the United
States altogether, settling in the British possession of
Victoria, British Columbia.[1]

Victoria impressed Gibbs as a "whirlpool of excitement,"
and he immediately notified the San Francisco press that
British Columbia is "a country good enough for me."[3] Having already learned that he could make more money from
miners than mining, Gibbs and Peter Lester resumed their
retail business in Victoria. Soon Gibbs diversified his business undertakings by venturing into the real estate business, where he achieved financial success. Of all his business undertakings, none was more breathtaking in its scope
than his dealings with the Queen Charlotte Coal Mining
Company. In the spring of 1868, Gibbs was awarded a contract by the company to open a coal mine in the Queen
Charlotte's Islands north of Victoria. In May 1870, Gibbs
sailed back to Victoria, taking with him the first shipment
of anthracite coal ever mined on the Pacific coast. He arrived as a local hero. Now recognized as a wealthy man, he
had fulfilled his goal of going west and "doing some great
thing."

Although busy building his fortune, Gibbs took time out
in 1859 to begin a family. Why he waited until he was thirty-
six years of age before marrying is a puzzle. An intelligent,
handsome man with a warm sense of humor, he obviously

was not unattractive to women. His wife, Maria Alexander, a native of Kentucky and a student at Oberlin College in Ohio, was a suitable mate for a socially prominent and successful businessman. In quick succession they had five children. But Victoria was no paradise for the young family.

At first the black immigrants were well received, but as large numbers of white American gold miners rushed into the area, race relations deteriorated. An 1861 attempt by local white ruffians to expel Gibbs and his pregnant wife from a Victoria theater resulted in a fisticuff, with Gibbs being hauled into court and fined five pounds. Next came the denial of jury service to blacks, and in 1864 the local black militia company was disbanded. Still, black British Columbians could vote and stand for public office, as they could not in the United States.

Gibbs took his first step toward voting in 1859 when he registered, and two years later he and fifty-two other blacks applied for British citizenship. (Gibbs left Victoria before gaining citizenship.) In August 1862, Gibbs announced his candidacy for the newly incorporated Victoria City Council. He failed to win election by four votes, but four years later he handily won election to the Council. When his term ended, Gibbs won reelection without opposition. In 1868 he was elected a delegate to a convention to consider union between the colony of British Columbia and the Dominion of Canada, a cause Gibbs stoutly supported. His tenure on the Victoria City Council ended when his work kept him away from the city.[4]

Without warning, in 1870 Gibbs left Victoria and settled in Oberlin, Ohio. He probably left for a variety of reasons, one being his dissatisfaction with the "totally unfitted" government of British Columbia. Another reason was the relocation of his wife and children to Oberlin in 1867, so that the children could attend the fine school associated with Oberlin College, Mrs. Gibbs's alma mater. But, M. W. Gibbs never spent much time with his family, so it must not have surprised Mrs. Gibbs when he remained in Ohio only a brief time before seeking new adventure, and again without his family. On a warm Sunday morning in May 1871, he crossed the Arkansas River into Little Rock, Arkansas, a town that only a few years earlier had been freed of slavery.

Gibbs always seemed to be seeking opportunities in newly opened, frontier regions—first California, then British Columbia, then finally the Reconstruction-era South. His brother, Jonathan Gibbs, was already making a name for himself as the secretary of state in Reconstruction Florida. A man of economic means if not wealth, Gibbs took time to read law upon settling in Arkansas. Without reluctance, he threw himself into the bruising political wars then raging in Reconstruction Arkansas.[5]

Gibbs arrived in Arkansas just as the state Republican organization was splitting into warring factions of regulars and reformers. The new immigrant, with his freshly minted law license, joined the reform faction. Later the two factions united after a regular Republican named Elisha Baxter won the governorship and then proceeded to make a complete *rapprochement* with the Democrats. Gibbs became a close and loyal ally of United States Senator and former Governor Powell Clayton, an alliance that allowed Gibbs to run for police judge of Little Rock. His election victory in 1873 made Gibbs the first elected black municipal judge in American history. With the Democrats back in control by 1875, when he stood for reelection, Gibbs was defeated. But this defeat did not remove him from Republican politics.

For most of the remaining four decades of his life, Gibbs played an active role in the Arkansas GOP. He was a delegate to every Republican national convention but one from 1876 to 1904; from 1887 to 1897 he was secretary of the state's Republican central committee. During most of this time Gibbs was a member of the political organization of Powell Clayton. Clayton controlled the state GOP through a network of lieutenants who quashed dissent before it could get organized. Gibbs, then, played the game of "clientage politics," a process involving a small group of blacks who fashioned close associations with powerful whites, becoming clients of the white leaders in exchange for various rewards. Gibbs was rewarded for his loyalty to the GOP leadership with a variety of federal appointments. In 1877 President Rutherford B. Hayes named Gibbs registrar of the Little Rock land office, and he was reappointed by President Chester A. Arthur. President Benjamin Harrison named Gibbs receiver of public monies in Little Rock in 1889. Gibbs capped off his long career of presidential appointments in October 1897, when President William McKinley named him United States Consul to Tamatave, Madagascar.

The Madagascar appointment was not a choice diplomatic patronage plum, a fact that Gibbs recalled in his memoirs. Tamatave was a small, mosquito-plagued town, and the consular salary was a mere $2,000. Still, he was one of a handful of blacks to receive presidential appointments during the generally regressive 1890s, and he sailed for Madagascar with his usual optimism still intact. He arrived on the scene just as the French were consolidating their control over the island. He soon discovered that his duties were mostly to show the American flag, as the United States had almost no economic or governmental relations with Madagascar. His major accomplishment as consul was to reestablish good will between the consulate and the local French authorities, a relationship that had been strained during the tenure of Gibbs's two predecessors. Concluding that "Madagascar was a good place to *come from*" (321), Gibbs resigned as consul in 1901 and returned to Little Rock. Though an old man, Gibbs still had plans for his life.

In the years following his service in Madagascar, Gibbs turned his attention away from politics. Actually, blacks were practically disfranchised in Arkansas and most of the South during the 1890s, so politics offered little hope to African-Arkansans. More and more Gibbs gave his energies to advancing the economic standing of his race. He seemed to be the perfect man to promote black entrepreneurship, given his many economic successes. In 1903 Gibbs started a bank in Little Rock, his last great venture. It turned out to be a dismal failure and a stain on his reputation.

The Capital City Savings Bank, formed 1 January 1903 with Gibbs as president, was the second black-owned bank in Arkansas history. It must have seemed a propitious time to start a new bank in Little Rock. On the very day Gibbs started his bank, the local newspapers reported that 1902 bank clearings increased $13 million over the previous year. Until the very day the bank folded, it appeared that Capital City Savings Bank was in good fiscal condition. By 1905 deposits amounted to $100,000. The bank's officers and board were made up of the black elite of Little Rock. No one suspected that the bank was ill-managed, but on 18 June 1908, with scores of angry depositors nervously waiting to withdraw their deposits, the bank closed. As soon as the receiver audited the bank's books, word got out that the bank had been mismanaged and probably fraudulently so. The general economic panic at the time did not help matters. A leading black lawyer, Scipio A. Jones, filed numerous suits in circuit court seeking a total of $28,000 in claims against Gibbs. Still worse news came on 21 January 1909, when grand jury indictments were returned against Gibbs and other bank officials. Gibbs was arrested and released on bond, and his personal estate, valued at $100,000, was sequestered. He escaped prosecution by reaching an out-of-court settlement, and in so doing he also saved the bulk of his personal fortune. M. W. Gibbs could never again be viewed as the Horatio Alger of the black race.[6]

At age eighty-six Gibbs finally seemed ready to retire. He still had a large home to manage, investments to look after, and charities to assist. Since his wife and children never moved to Little Rock, he spent his years in Arkansas without close family support. His children did occasionally visit him, and on one occasion his daughter gave a recital in Arkansas. His most prominent child, Harriet Gibbs Marshall was a well-known musician who, with financial assistance from him, established the Washington Conservatory of Music in the District of Columbia. It appears that Gibbs did not have grandchildren.[7]

At the age of ninety-two, Mifflin Wistar Gibbs died at his home in Little Rock on 11 July 1915 after several months of declining health. Accompanied by mourners in fourteen black carriages, his remains were buried in the all-black Fraternal Cemetery on Confederate Boulevard in Little Rock.

GIBBS'S PLACE IN HISTORY

It is easy for students of African-American history, when thinking of black leaders, to concentrate on Frederick Douglass or Booker T. Washington or W. E. B. DuBois. Though never as nationally significant as any of these men, M. W. Gibbs does serve as an illuminating mirror of the times. Chronologically, he was contemporary with both Douglass and Washington as well as the early years of DuBois. Born while the American nation was still in its adolescence, Gibbs came to manhood during those years when Douglass was leading the fight against slavery. In some respects, Gibbs is representative of that group of aggressive black leaders— men such as Martin Delaney and Robert Purvis—who emerged quite early in American black history. These were men who came to view themselves as born leaders of the black race. Eventually, this select cadre evolved into a black leadership elite. Although the Civil War and emancipation brought reforms that this elite group had long sought, the war also resulted in the birth of a new type of black leader: the emancipated slave.

The death of slavery freed thousands of potential black leaders from the bonds of servitude. New leaders, men such as Booker T. Washington, began to emerge. Washington proved to be effective competition to the old black elite. Following the death of Douglass in 1895, Washington and his allies created a near cartel of race leaders. The old black elite, although severely overshadowed by Washington, survived and occasionally, through such men as Monroe Trotter, challenged the "Wizard of Tuskegee." However, the birth of the twentieth century brought a new force to black America in the person of William E. B. DuBois, who was born into an upper-class Massachusetts family. The arrival of DuBois on the scene signaled the reemergence of the old black leadership elite. The ensuing struggle between the confrontational DuBois and the accommodationist Washington symbolized, as historians have noted, an effort by the black elite to regain ideological control of black leadership.

Never one to lose his equilibrium, Gibbs managed to adapt to each of these phases. In some respects he acted as a bridge between the factions. As a former functionary in the Pennsylvania antislavery effort, Gibbs saw himself as an old comrade of Douglass. Yet, their similarity went further. Both men shared a firm faith in the eventual successful integration of African-Americans into national society and government. Like Douglass, Gibbs firmly believed in the essential correctness of American political democracy, if not in the existing political process.

When Booker T. Washington, immaculate in his black coat, marched onto the platform at the Atlanta Exposition on 18 September 1895, a new leader for America's blacks was born. African-Americans were in need of a new national leader since Douglass's death seven months earlier. That Washington would be a leader far different from Douglass was to be expected given the vastly different demeanor of the Tuskegeean. But, more than that, America had changed drastically during the last two decades of the nineteenth century. The uneasy racial truce of the post–Civil War years gave way to severe antagonism between black and white. Jim Crow segregation was expanding into more and more areas of national life. Disfranchisement of the black voter was proceeding apace throughout the South. Observing these changes in race relations, Booker T. Washington concluded that complete integration of the African-American into national society was impossible and that the only alternative to perpetual racial confrontation was to play the game by the rules of the white majority. Washington did not, however, completely capitulate to the racists. He believed that African-Americans, by making themselves indispensable in the Southern labor force, could come to terms with the South.

M. W. Gibbs was a solid link between the hopeful dreams of Frederick Douglass and the cold reality of Booker T. Washington. Like Douglass, Gibbs remained active in politics until his final days. Yet, like Washington, Gibbs came to believe that politics would not answer all the problems of his race. In "industrial education" these two men found a common denominator. Actually, Gibbs was a pioneer in the field of vocational training for blacks. Ten years before Washington urged the blacks at the Atlanta Exposition to "cast down your buckets where you are," Gibbs helped organize a black trade school conference. A man who had been a successful retailer in California, who had opened the first anthracite coal mine on the west coast, and who owned considerable property and investments in Arkansas would naturally endorse black business as a racial panacea.

If Gibbs and Washington agreed on the question of black business, the situation was quite different in politics. The Tuskegeean used politics as a tool to consolidate his power in the African-American world. On the other hand, Gibbs saw the franchise as a right which every American should exercise. Although both men viewed the Republican Party as the natural home of the black man, Gibbs, especially late in his life, grew to distrust its white leadership, and on at least one occasion abandoned the party of Lincoln.

It was on the question of black political independence that Gibbs most resembled the rising young black intellectual, W. E. B. DuBois. Gibbs and DuBois shared a mutual heritage, both coming from old free Northern families. Although Gibbs had almost no formal education, he shared DuBois's intellectual bent, as *Shadow and Light* makes clear. Both men read widely and both were literary craftsmen; DuBois wrote with a modern biting sharpness while Gibbs employed a more traditional and relaxed, yet effective, style. One can imagine that DuBois, had he known Gibbs, would have been especially impressed with the old man's long record on behalf of his race.

DuBois would have found it difficult to locate M. W. Gibbs within the matrix of African-American history. Unlike other black leaders, such as Washington or DuBois himself, Gibbs made no effort to preserve his personal papers, the means by which one gains historical immortality. It is true that Gibbs wrote his autobiography, but it was self-published and made its way into a mere handful of libraries. Mrs. Gwendolyn McConico Floyd, whose father was an associate of Gibbs, recalls that most of the copies of *Shadow and Light* languished unsold in the Gibbs home. The respected old man, always deferentially referred to by whites and blacks alike as "Judge Gibbs," was forgiven for his tendency to give the autobiography as a gift for every occasion. It was not until 1968 that a reprint of the volume was issued, although the Library of Congress did offer a microform copy.[8]

Gibbs was apparently prompted to write his autobiography by the realization that he had lived a different kind of life, one full of varied activities and peopled with characters as diverse as Chinese immigrant gold miners in California, a newspaper editor in Victoria with the unusual name of Amor de Cosmos, and President Ulysses S. Grant. It was probably during his tiresome service as American consul in Madagascar that Gibbs began his autobiography, for on at least one occasion he asked the French governor of the island colony to critique the manuscript (306–7). A close reading of the book demonstrates that Gibbs did not write completely from memory. On several occasions, he quotes from old documents, such as his citation of the resolutions he presented to the Colored Men's Convention in Little Rock in 1883 (175).

The book is surprisingly detailed, but occasionally the author omits important activities of his life, such as the important role he played in waging the effort to free the slave Archy Lee in California. The most glaring omission is Gibbs's almost complete refusal to write about his wife. Although married to a well-educated, cultured woman and the father of five children, he remained aloof from his family. His wife, Maria, even after the children completed their education, remained in Oberlin. In his autobiography Gibbs barely makes reference to his wife, and his children are mentioned only slightly more often.

Even with its limitations, *Shadow and Light* is an important historical document. More importantly, it is a heartfelt remembrance by a man of great drive and fortitude, a man of perseverance and determination. Perhaps the black journalist Ralph W. Tyler characterized Gibbs best when he called him "our Moses of the west."[9] Although Gibbs was never able to find a promised land for his people, he never stopped searching.

NOTES

1. *San Francisco Daily Evening Bulletin*, 5 April 1858.

2. An excellent account of the whole era is found in Rudolph M. Lapp, *Blacks in Gold Rush California* (New Haven: Yale University Press, 1977).

3. *San Francisco Daily Evening Bulletin,* 23 June 1858.

4. Robin W. Winks, *Blacks in Canada* (New Haven: Yale University Press, 1971), especially chapter 9.

5. Tom W. Dillard, " 'Golden Prospects and Fraternal Amenities': Mifflin W. Gibbs' Arkansas Years." *Arkansas Historical Quarterly,* 35 (winter 1976): 307–33.

6. The bank imbroglio is summarized in Tom W. Dillard, "The Black Moses of the West: A Biography of Mifflin Wistar Gibbs,

1823–1915," masters thesis, University of Arkansas, 1975.

7. The high social status of the Gibbs family is discussed in Willard B. Gatewood, *Aristocrats of Color: The Black Elite, 1880–1920* (Bloomington: Indiana University Press, 1990), 92–95, 268–71.

8. Reprint by Arno Press (New York: 1968).

9. *Washington Bee*, 7 February 1914.

PREFACE.

During the late years abroad, while reading the biographies of distinguished men
who had been benefactors, the thought occurred that I had had a varied career,
though not as fruitful or as deserving of re-
nown as these characters, and differing as
to status and aim. Yet the portrayal might
be of benefit to those who, eager for advancement, are willing to be laborious students to attain worthy ends.

I have aimed to give an added interest to
the narrative by embellishing its pages
with portraits of men who have gained distinction in various fields, who need only to
be seen to present the career of those now
living as worthy models, and the record of
the dead, who left the world the better for
having lived. To enjoy a life prominent
and prolonged is a desire as natural as
worthy, and there have been those who
sought to extend its duration by nostrums
and drinking-waters said to bestow the virtue of "perpetual life." But if "to live in
hearts we leave behind is not to die," to be
worthy of such memorial we must have
done or said something that blessed the
living or benefited coming generations.
Hence autobiography is the record, for
"books are as tombstones made by the liv-

ing, but destined soon to remind us of the dead."

Trusting that any absence of literary merit will not impair the author's cherished design to "impart a moral," should he fail to "adorn a tale."

Little Rock, Ark., January, 1902.

INTRODUCTION.

By BOOKER T. WASHINGTON.

It is seldom that one man, even if he has lived as long as Judge M. W. Gibbs is able to record his impressions of so many widely separated parts of the earth's surface as Judge Gibbs can, or to recall personal experiences in so many important occurrences.

Born in Philadelphia, and living there when that city—almost on the border line between slavery and freedom—was the scene of some of the most stirring incidents in the abolition agitation, he was able as a free colored youth, going to Maryland to work, to see and judge of the condition of the slaves in that State. Some of the most dramatic operations of the famous "Underground Railroad" came under his personal observation. He enjoyed the rare privilege of being associated in labor for the race with that man of sainted memory, the Hon. Frederick Douglass. He met and heard many of the most notable men and women who labored to secure the freedom of the Negro. As a resident of California in the exciting years which immediately followed the discovery of gold, he watched the development of lawlessness there and its results. A few years later he went to British Columbia to live, when that colony was practically an unknown country. Returning to the United States, he was a witness to the exciting events connected with the years of Reconstruction in Florida, and an active participant in the events of that period in the State of Arkansas. At one time and another he has met many of the men who have been prominent in the direction of the affairs of both the great political parties of the country. In more recent years he has been able to see something of life in Europe, and in his official capacity as United States Consul to Tamatave, Madagascar, adjoining Africa, has resided for some time in that far-off and strange land.

It would be difficult for any man who has had all these experiences not to be entertaining when he tells of them. Judge Gibbs has written an interesting book.

Interspersed with the author's recollections and descriptions are various conclusions, as when he says: "Labor to make yourself as indispensable as possible in all your relations with the dominant race, and color will cut less figure in your upward grade."

"Vice is ever destructive; ignorance ever a victim, and poverty ever defenseless."

"Only as we increase in property will our political barometer rise."

It is significant to find one who has seen so much of the world as Judge Gibbs has, saying, as he does: "With travel somewhat extensive and diversified, and with residence in tropical latitudes of Negro origin, I have a decided conviction, despite the crucial test to which he has been subjected in the past, and the present disadvantages under which he labors, that nowhere is the promise along all the lines of opportunity brighter for the American Negro than here in the land of his nativity."

I bespeak for the book a careful reading by those who are interested in the history of the Negro in America, and in his present and future.

BOOKER T. WASHINGTON.

CONTENTS.

CONTENTS.

ILLUSTRATIONS.

SHADOW AND LIGHT

CHAPTER I.

In the old family Bible I see it recorded that I was born April 17, 1823, in Philadelphia, Pa., the son of Jonathan C. Gibbs and Maria, his wife. My father was a minister in the Wesleyan Methodist Church, my mother a "hard-shell" Baptist. But no difference of religious views interrupted the even tenor of their domestic life. At seven years of age I was sent to what was known as the Free School, those schools at that time invaluable for colored youth, had not graded studies, systematized, and with such accessories for a fruitful development of the youthful mind as now exist. The teacher of the school, Mr. Kennedy, was an Irishman by birth, and herculean in proportions; erudite and severely positive in enunciation. The motto "Spare the rod and spoil the child" had no place in his curriculum. Alike with the tutors of the deaf and the blind, he was earnest in the belief that learning could be impressively imparted through the sense of feeling. That his manner and means were impressive you may well believe, when I say that I yet have a vivid recollection of a bucket with an inch or two of water in it near his desk. In it stood an assortment of rattan rods, their size when selected for use ranging in

the ratio of the enormity of the offence or
the age of the offender.

Among the many sterling traits of character possessed by Mr. Kennedy was economy; the frequent use of the rods as he
raised himself on tiptoe to make his
protest the more emphatic—split and
frizzled them—the immersion of the
tips in water would prevent this, and
add to the severity of the castigation, while
diminishing the expense. A policy wiser
and less drastic has taken the place of corporal punishment in schools. But Mr. Kennedy was competent, faithful and impartial. I was not destined to remain long
at school. At eight years of age two events
occurred which gave direction to my after
life. On a Sunday in April, 1831, my father
desired that the family attend his church;
we did so and heard him preach, taking as
his text the 16th verse of Chapter 37 in
Genesis: "I seek my brethren; tell me, I
pray thee, where they feed their flocks."

On the following Sunday he lay before
the pulpit from whence he had preached,
cold in death, leaving my mother, who had
poor health, with four small children, and
little laid by "for a rainy day." Unable to
remain long at school, I was "put out" to
hold and drive a doctor's horse at three
dollars a month, and was engaged in similar employment until I reached sixteen
years of age. Of the loving devotion and
self-sacrifice of an invalid mother I have
not words to express, but certain it is, that

should it ever appear that I have done anything to revere, or aught to emulate, it
should be laid on the altar of her Christian
character, her ardent love of liberty and intense aspiration for the upbuilding of the
race. For her voice and example was an
educator along all the lines of racial progress.

Needing our assistance in her enfeebled
condition, she nevertheless insisted that my
brother and myself should learn the carpenter trade. At this period in the career of
youth, the financial condition of whose parents or sponsors is unequal to their further
pursuit of scholastic studies, it is not without an anxious solicitude they depart from
the parental roof. For the correct example
and prudent advice may not be invulner-
abel to the temptation for illicit pleasures
or ruinous conduct. Happy will he be who
listens to the admonitions of age. Unfortunately by the action of response, sad in
its humor, too often is: I like the advice
but prefer the experience.

The foundation of the mechanical knowledge possessed by the Negro was laid in the
Southern States. During slavery the master selecting those with natural ability, the
most apt, with white foremen, had them
taught carpentering, blacksmithing, paint-
ing, boot and shoe making, coopering, and
other trades to utilize on the plantations,
or add to their value as property. Many of
these would hire themselves by the year
from their owners, contract on their own

account, and by thrift purchase their freedom, emigrate and teach colored youths of Northern States, where prejudice continues to exclude them from the workshops, while at the South the substantial warehouse and palatial dwelling from base to dome, is often the creation of his brain and the product of his handiwork.

James Gibbons, of the class above referred to, and to whom we were apprenticed, was fat, and that is to say, he was jolly. He had ever a word of kind encouragement, wise counsel or assistance to give his employees. Harshness, want of sympathy or interest is often the precursor and stimulator to the many troubles with organized labor that continue to paralyze so many of our great industrial concerns at the present time, resulting in distress to the one and great material loss to the other. Mr. Gibbons had but a limited education, but he possessed that aptitude, energy, and efficiency which accomplishes great objects, that men call genius, and which is ofttimes nothing more than untiring mental activity harnessed to intensity of purpose. These constituted his grasp of much of the intricacies of mechanical knowledge. His example was ever in evidence, by word and action, that only by assidious effort could young men hope to succeed in the battle of life.

Mr. Gibbons was competent and had large patronage. We remained with him until we reached our majority. During a religious revival we both became converted and joined the Presbyterian Church. My brother entered Dartmouth College, under the auspices of the Presbyterian Assembly, graduated and ministered in the church at Philadelphia.   After a brief period as a journeyman, I became a contractor and builder on my own account.   It is ever a source of strength for a young person to have faith in his or her possibilities, and as soon as may be, assume mastership.

While remaining subject to orders, the stimulus is lacking for that aggressive energy, indispensable to bring to the front. Temporary failure you may have, for failure lies in wait for all human effort, but sneaks from a wise and unconquerable determination.   We read of the military prisoner, alone, dejected, and despairing, looking to the walls of his cell; he watches a score of attempts and failure of a spider to scale the wall, only to renew an attempt crowned with success.   The lesson was fruitful for the prisoner.

Mr. Gibbons built several of the colored churches in Philadelphia, and in the early forties, during my apprenticeship, he was a bidder for the contract to build the first African Methodist Episcopal brick church of the connection on the present site at Sixth and Lombard streets in Philadelphia. A wooden structure which had been transformed from a blacksmith shop to a meeting house was torn down to give place to the new structure.   When a boy I had often been in the old shop, and have heard the founder, Bishop Allen, preach in the

wooden building. He was much reverenced.
I remember his appearance, and his feeble,
shambling gait as he approached the close
of an illustrious life.

The A. M. E. Church was distinctively
the pioneer in the career of colored
churches; its founders the first to typify
and unflinchingly assert the brotherhood of
man and the Fatherhood of God. Dragged
from their knees in the white churches of
their faith, they met exclusion by cohesion;
ignorance by effort for culture, and poverty by unflinching self-denial; justice and
right harnessed to such a movement, who
shall declare its ultimatum.

Out from that blacksmith shop went an
inspiration lifting its votaries to a self-
reliance founded on God, a harbinger of
hope to the enslaved.

From Allen to Payne, and on and on
along lines of Christian fame, its missionaries going from triumph to triumph in
America, and finally planting its standard
on the isles of the sea.

A distinct line is ever observable between
civilization and barbarism, in the regard
and reverence for the dead, the increase of
solicitude is evidence of a people's advancement. Until the year 1848 the colored people of Philadelphia used the grounds, always limited, in the rear of their churches
for burial. They necessarily became crowded, with sanitary conditions threatening,
without opportunity to fittingly mark and
adorn the last resting place of their dead.

WILLIAM LLOYD GARRISON.
"The Great Liberator."
"I Will not Excuse, I Will Not Retreat a Single Inch; I Will Be Heard"—
"Emancipation the Right of the Slave and Duty of the Master"—"He
Made Every Single Home, Press, Pulpit, and Senate Cham-
ber a Debating Society with His Right and
Wrong for the Subject."

In the above year G. W. Gaines, J. P. Humphries, and the writer purchased a tarct of land on the north side of Lancaster turnpike, in West Philadelphia, and were incorporated under the following act by the Legislature of the State of Pennsylvania: "An Act to incorporate the Olive Cemetery Company," followed by the usual reservations and conditions in such cases provided. Among reasons inducing me to refer to this are, first, to give an idea of the propriety and progress of the race fifty years ago, and secondly, for the further and greater reasons, as the following will show, that the result of the project was not only a palladium for blessed memory of the dead, but was the nucleus of a benefaction that still blesses the living.

The land was surveyed and laid out in lots and avenues, plans of gothic design were made for chapel and superintendent's residence, and contract for construction was awarded the writer. The project was not entirely an unselfish one, but profit was not the dominating incentive. After promptly completing the contract with the shareholders as to buildings and improvements of the ground, the directors found themselves in debt, and welcomed the advent of Stephen Smith, a wealthy colored man and lumber merchant, to assist in liquidating liabilities. To him an unoccupied portion of the ground was sold, and in his wife's heart the conception of a bounteous charity was formed. The "Old

Folks' Home," so beneficent to the aged poor of Philadelphia, demands more than a passing notice.

"The Harriet Smith Home for Aged and Infirm Colored Persons" is a continuation of a charity organized September, 1864, and the first board of managers (a noble band of humanitarians) elected. The preamble was as follows: "For the relief of that worthy class of colored persons who have endeavored through life to maintain themselves, but who, from various causes, are finally dependent on the charity of others, an association is hereby organized." The work of this home was conducted in a large dwelling house on South Front street until the year 1871, when, through the munificence of Stephen Smith and his wife, the land on the corner of Belmont and Girard avenues, previously purchased from the Olive Cemetery Company, together with a large four-story building, valued at $40,000, was given to the Board. In 1871 it was opened as the "Harriet Smith Home," where it still stands as an enduring monument to the original donors, and other blessed friends of the race, who have continued to assist with generous endowments. Edward T. Parker, who died in 1887, gave $85,000 for an annex to the building. Colored people since its incipiency have given $200,000. The board is composed of white and colored persons. On a recent visit I found the home complete, convenient, and cleanly in all its ap-

purtenances, with an air of comfort and
contentment pervading the place. From
many with bent and decrepit bodies, from
wrinkled and withered faces, the sparkling
eye of gratitude could be seen, and prayer
of thankfulness read; for this product of a
benign clemency that had blessed both
the giver and receiver. There can be no one
with filial affection happy in the thought
that it is in their power to assuage the
pain or assist the tottering steps of their
own father or mother, but will recognize
the humanity, Christian character, and un-
selfishness of the men and women organized for giving the helping hand to the
"unfortunate aged, made dependent by
blameless conditions."

During my apprenticeship, aware of my
educational deficiencies, having been unable to pursue a consecutive course of study
in earlier life, I spent much of the night and
odd times in an endeavor to make up the
loss. In joining the Philadelphia Library
Company, a literary society of colored men,
containing men of such mental caliber as
Isaiah C. Wear, Frederick Hinton, Robert
Purvis, J. C. Bowers, and others, where
questions of moment touching the condition of the race were often discussed with
acumen and eloquence, I was both benefited and stimulated. It was a needed
help, for man is much the creature of his
environments, and what widens his horizon
as to the inseparable relations of man to
man and the mutuality of obligation,

strengthens his manhood in the ratio he embraces opportunity.

Pennsylvania being a border State, and Philadelphia situated so near the line separating the free and slave States, that city was utilized as the most important adjunct or way-station of the "underground railroad," an organization to assist runaway slaves to the English colony of Canada. Say what you will against old England, for, like all human polity, there is much for censure and criticism, but this we know, that when there were but few friends responsive, and but few arms that offered to succor when hunted at home, old England threw open her doors, reached out her hand, and bid the wandering fugitive slave to come in and "be of good cheer."

As one of the railroad company mentioned, many cases came under my observation, and some under my guidance to safety in Canada. One of the most peculiar and interesting ones that came under by notice and attention, was that of William and Ellen Craft, fugitives from the State of Georgia. Summoned one day to a colored boarding house, I was presented to a person dressed in immaculate black broadcloth and silk beaver hat, whom I supposed to be a young white man. By his side stood a young colored man with good features and rather commanding presence. The first was introuecd to me as Mrs. Craft and the other as her husband, two escaped slaves.

They had traveled through on car and boat, paying and receiving first-class accommodations. Mrs. Craft, being fair, assumed the habit of young master coming north as an invalid, and as she had never learned to write, her arm was in a sling, thereby avoiding the usual signing of register on boat or at hotel, while her servant-husband was as obsequious in his attentions as the most humble of slaves. They settled in Boston, living very happily, until the passage of the fugitive slave law in 1850, when they were compelled to flee to England.

The civil war of 1861 and proclamation of freedom followed. In 1870, ariving in Savannah, Georgia, seeking accommodation, I was directed to a hotel, and surprised to find the host and hostess my whilom friends of underground railroad fame. They had returned to their old home after emancipation. The surprise was pleasant and recognition mutual.

One other, and I shall pass this feature of reminiscence. It was that of William Brown, distinguished afterward as William Box Brown, the intervening "Box" being a synonym of the manner of his escape. An agent of the underground railroad at Richmond, Virginia, had placed him in a box two feet wide and four feet long, ends hooped, with holes for air, and bread and water, and sent him through the express company to Philadelphia. On the arrival of the steamboat the box was roughly tumbled off as so much dead frieght on the wharf, but, unfortunately for Brown, on the end, with his feet up and head down. After remaining in such position for a time which seemed to him hours, he heard a man say to another, "Let's turn that box down and sit on it." It was done, and Brown found himself "right side up," if not "with care." I was called to the anti-slavery office, where the box was taken. It had been arranged that when he arrived at his destination, three slow and distinct knocks should be given, to which he was to respond. Fear that he was crippled or dead was depicted in the faces of Miller McKim, William Still and a few others that stood around the box in the office. Hence it was not without trepidation the agreed signal was given, and the response waited for. An "all right" was cheerily given; the lifting of suspense and the top of the box was almost simultaneous. Out sprang a man weighing near 200 pounds. Brown, though uneducated, it is needless to say, was imbued with the spirit of liberty, and with much natural ability, with his box he traveled and spoke of his experience in slavery, the novelty of his escape adding interest to his description. Many similar cases of heroism in manner of escape of men and women are recorded in William Still's "Underground Railroad."

CHAPTER II.

The immortal bard has sung that "there's a destiny that shapes our ends." At eight years of age, as already stated, two events occurred which had much to do in giving direction to my after life. The one the death of my father, as formerly mentioned; the other the insurrection of Nat Turner, of South Hampton, Virginia, in August, 1831, which fell upon the startled sense of the slaveholding South like a meteor from a clear sky, causing widespread commotion. Nat Turner was a Baptist preacher, who with four others, in a lonely place in the woods, concocted plans for an uprising of the slaves to secure their liberty. Employed in the woods during the week, a prey to his broodings over the wrongs and cruelties, the branding and whipping to death of neighboring slaves, he would come out to meetings of his people on Sunday and preach. impressing much of his spirit of unrest. Finally he selected a large number of confederates, who were to secretly acquire arms of their masters. The attack concocted in February was not made until August 20, when the assault, dealing death and destruction, was made.

All that night they marched, carrying consternation and dread on account of the suddenness, determination and boldness of the atack. The whole State was aroused, and soldiers sent from every part. The blacks fought hand to hand with the whites, but were soon overpowered by numbers and superior implements of warfare. Turner and a few of his followers took refuge in the "Dismal Swamp," almost impenetrable, where they remained two or three months, till hunger or despair compelled them to surrender. Chained together, they were taken to the South Hampton Court House and arraigned. Turner, it is recorded, without a tremor, pleaded not guilty, believing that he was justified in the atempt to liberate his people, however drastic the means. His act, which would have been heralded as the noblest heroism if perpetrated by a white man, was called religious fanatacism and fiendish brutality.

Turner called but few into his confidence, and foolhardy and unpromising as the attempt may have been, it had the ring of an heroic purpose that gave a Bossarius to Greece, and a Washington to America. A purpose "not born to die," but to live on in every age and clime, stimulating endeavors to attain the blessings of civil liberty.

It was an incident as unexpected in its advent as startling in its terrors. Slavery, ever the preponderance of force, had hitherto reveled in a luxury heightened by a

sense of security. Now, in the moaning of
the wind, the rustling of the leaves or the
shadows of the moon, was heard or seen a
liberator. Nor was this uneasiness confined to the South, for in the border free
States there were many that in whole or in
part owned plantations stocked with
slaves.

In Philadelphia, so near the line, excitement ran high. The intense interest depicted in the face of my mother and her
colored neighbors; the guarded whisper-
ings, the denunciations of slavery, the hope
defeated of a successful revolution keenly
affected my juvenile mind, and stamped
my soul with hatred to slavery.

At 12 years of age I was employed at the
residence of Sydney Fisher, a prominent
Philadelphia lawyer, who was one of the
class above mentioned, living north and
owning a plantation in the State of Maryland. Over a good road of 30 miles one
summer's day, he took me to his plantation.
I had never before been that distance from
home and had anticipated my long ride
with childish interest and pleasure. After
crossing the line and entering "the land of
cotton and the corn," a new and strange
panorama began to open, and continued to
enfold the vast fields bedecked in the snowy
whiteness of their fruitage. While over
gangs of slaves in row and furrough were
drivers with their scourging whip in hand.
I looked upon the scene with curious wonder. Three score of years and more have

passed, but I still see that sad and hum'bled
throng, working close to the roadway, no
head daring to uplift, no eye to enquiringly
gaze. During all those miles of drive that
bordered on plantations, as machines they
acted, as machines they looked. My
curiosity and youthful impulse ignoring
that reticence becoming a servant, I said:
"Mr. Fisher, who are these people?" He
said, "They are slaves." I was startled but
made no reply. I had not associated the ex-
hilaration of the drive with a depressing
view of slavery, but his reply caused a tu-
mult of feeling in my youthful breast. The
Turner episode of which I had heard so
much, the narratives of whippings received by fugitives, slaves that had
come to my mother's house, the sun
dering of family ties on the auction
block, were vividly presented to my
mind. I remained silent as to speech, as
to feelings belligerent. A few moments
elapsed and Mr. Fisher broke the silence
by saying, "Mifflin, how would you like to
be a slave?" My answer was quick and
conformed to feeling. "I would not be a
slave! I would kill anybody that would
make me a slave!" Fitly spoken. No
grander declaration I have ever made. But
from whom did it come—from almost childish lips with no power to execute. I little
thought of or knew the magnitude of that
utterance, nor did I notice then the effect
of its force. Quickly and quite sternly
came the reply: "You must not talk that

RIGHT REV. RICHARD ALLEN.

First Bishop of the A. M. E. Church.
Founder of that Faith That Once Nestled in a Blacksmith Shop, But Now
Encircles the World.

way down here." I was kept during our
stay in what was known during slavery
as the "great house," the master's residence, and my meals were eaten at the
table he had quit, slept in the same house,
and had, if desired, little or no opportunity
to talk or mingle with the slaves during
the week's visit. I did not understand at
that time the philosophy of espionage, but
in after years it became quite apparent that
from my youthful lips had came the "open
sesame to the door of liberty," "resistance
to oppression," the slogan that has ever
heralded the advent of freedom.

As I passed to manhood the object lesson
encountered on the Maryland plantation
did much to intensify my hatred of slavery
and to strengthen my resolution to ally myself with any effort for its abolition. The
burning of Pennsylvania Hall by a mob in
Philadelphia, in 1838, built and used by
anti-slavery people, the ravages of what
was known as the "Moyamensing Killers,"
who burned down the churches and residences of the colored people and murdered
their occupants, did much to increase the
anti-slavery feeling.

Old Bethel Church, then the nursery of
the present great A. M. E. Church, was
guarded day and night by its devoted men
and women worshipers. The cobble street
pavement in front was dug up and the
stones carried up and placed at the
windows in the gallery to hurl at the mob.
This defense was sustained for several

weeks at a time. Every American should
be happy in the thought that a higher civilization is making such acts less and less
frequent. It is not strange that our present generation enjoying a large measure of
civil and political liberty can but faintly
comprehend the condition fifty years ago,
when they were persistently denied. The
justice of participation seems so apparent
it is not easy to fully conceive, when all
were refused, in quite all that were de-
nominated free States.

When street cars were first established
in Philadelphia "the brother in black" was
refused accommodations. He nevertheless
persisted in entering the cars. Sometimes
he would be thrown out, at others, after being "sized up" the driver with his horses
would leave his car standing on switch,
while its objectionable occupant was
"monarch of all he surveyed."

The "man and brother" finding his enemy
impervious to direct attack, commenced a
flank movement. As he was not allowed to
ride inside, he resolved to ride alongside;
bought omnibuses and stock and established a line on the car route at reduced rates.
The cars were not always on time, and
many whites would avail themselves of its
service. I remember one of this class accosting a driver: "What 'Bus is this?" The simple driver answered, "It is the colored peoples!" "I don't care whose in the —— it
is, does it go to the bridge? I am in a hurry
to get there," and in he got. I thought then

and still think what a useful moral the incident conveyed to my race. Labor to make
yourself as indispensable as possible in all
your relations with the dominant race and
color will cut less and less figure in your upward grade. The line was kept up for some
time, often holding what was called "omnibus meetings" in our halls, always largely
attended, make reports, hear spirited
speeches, and have a deal of fun narrating
incidents of the line, receiving generous
contributions when the horses or busses
needed replenishing. But the most exciting times were those when there had been
interference with the running of the "underground railroad," and the attempt to
capture passengers in transit, or at the different way-stations, of which as previously
stated, Philadelphia was the most prominent in forwarding its patrons to Canada.
    Before the passage of the fugitive slave
law, in 1850, if the fugitive was taken back
it was done by stealth—kidnapped and
spirited away by clandestine means. Sometimes by the treachery of his own color, but
this was seldom and unhealthy. The agent
of the owner was often caught in the act,
and by argument more emphatic than gentle, was soon conspicuous by his absence.
At others local anti-slavery friends would
appeal to the courts, and the agent would
be arrested. Slavery in law being local before the passage of the "Act of 1850," making it national, we were generally successful in having the fugitives released.

We were extremely fortunate in having for our chief counsel David Paul Brown, a leader of the Philadelphia bar, who, with other white friends, never failed to respond to our call; learned in Constitutional law, eloquent in expression, he did a yeoman's service in behalf of liberty.

The colored men of Pennsylvania, like their brethren in other Northern States, were not content in being disfranchised. As early as 1845 a committee of seven, consisting of Isaiah C. Wear, J. C. Bowers, and others, including the writer, were sent to the capitol at Harrisburg to lay a petition before the Legislature asking for enfranchisement and all rights granted to others of the commonwealth. The grant was tardy, but it came with the cannon's boom and musketry's iron hail, when the imperiled status of the nation made it imperative. Thus, as ever, with the immutable decrees of God, while battling for the freedom of the slave, we broadened our consciousness, not only as to the inalienable rights of human nature, but received larger conceptions of civil liberty, coupled with a spirit of determination to defend our homes and churches from infuriated mobs, and to contend for civil and political justice.

They were truly a spartan band, the colored men and women. The naming of a few would be invidious to the many who were ever keenly alive to the proscription to which they were subject, and ever on the alert for measures to awaken the moral sense of the border States.

Meetings were nightly held for counsel, protests and assistance to the fugitive, who would sometimes be present to narrate the woes of slavery. Sometimes our meetings would be attended by pro-slavery lookers-on, usually unknown, until excoriation of the Northern abettors of slavery was too severe to allow them to remain incognito, when they would reply: It is a sad commentary on a phase of human nature that the oppressed often, when vaulted into authority or greater equality of condition, become the most vicious of oppressors. It has been said that Negro drivers were most cruel and unsparing to their race. The Irish, having fled from oppression in the land of their birth, for notoriety, gain, or elevation by comparison, were nearly all pro-slavery. At one of our meetings during the narration of incidents of his life by a fugitive, one of the latter class interrupted by saying, "Aren't you lying, my man? I have been on plantations. I guess your master did not lose much when you left." Now, it is a peculiarrity of the uneducated, when, puzzled for the moment, by the tardiness of an idea, to scratch the head. Jacobs, the fugitive, did so, and out it came. "I dunno how much he lost, only what master said. I was the house boy, one day, and at dinner time he sent me to the well to get a cool pitcher of water. I let the silver pitcher drop in the well. Well, I knowed that pitcher had to be got out, so I straddled down and fished it up. Master was mad, 'cause I staid so long, so I up and tells him. He fairly jumped and said "Did you go down that well? Why didn't you come and tell me and I would made Irish Mike, the ditcher, go down. If you had drowned I'd lost $800. Don't you do that agin."

It is needless to say that this "brought down the house," and shortly the exit of the son of the Emerald Isle. At another time the interrupter said: "Will you answer me a question or two? Did you not get enough to eat?" "Yes." "A place to sleep?" "Yes." "Was your master good or bad to you?" "Marster was pretty good, I must say." "Well, what else did you want? That is a good deal more than a good many white men get up here." The man stood for a moment busy with his fingers in a fruitless attempt to find the fugitive ends of a curl of his hair, temporarily nonplussed at his palliating concessions, half apologetically said: "Well, I think it a heap best to be free." Then suddenly and gallantly strengthening his defense; "but, look here, Mister, if you think it so nice down there, my place is still open." The questioner good naturedly joined in the general merriment.

Very frequently we were enthused and inspired by Frederick Douglass, Henry Highland Garnett, Marten R. Delaney, and Charles L. Remond, an illustrious quartet of the hallowed band in the anti-slavery crusade, whose eloquence, devotion, and effectiveness stood unsurpassed.

There were few, if any, available halls for these meetings. The only resort was the colored churches. Those under the auspices of white denominations had members who objected to their use for such a purpose. Craven and fawning, content with the crumbs that fell from these peace-loving Christians, who deprecated the discussion of slavery while they ignored the claim of outraged humanity, these churches were more interested in the physical excitement of a "revival" than in listening to appeals in behalf of God's poor and lonely. Their prototypes that "passed by on the other side" have been perpetuated in many climes, in those who believe that it is the formalities of contact with the building that blesses a people and not the Godliness and humanity of the worshippers that give glory and efficacy to the church. An antagonism thus created resulted in a crusade against such churches styled "Come-Outerism," and many left them on account of such apathy to carry on the warfare amid congenial association.

It has been said that citizenship was precipitated upon the Negro before he was fit for its exercise. Without discussing the incongruity of this, when applied to the ignorant native Negro and not to the ignorant alien emigrant, it may be conceded that keeping them in abject bondage with no opportunity to protest, made slavery anything but a preparatory school for the exercises of civic virtues, or the assumption of their responsibilities. It was not true, however, with the mass in the free, or many in the slave States. Always akin and adjunct are the yearnings indestructible in human nature for equal rights. And in every age and people the ratio of persistency and sacrifice have been the measure of their fitness for its enjoyment. During 25 years preceding the abolition of slavery the colored people of the free States, though much proscribed, were active in their protests against enslavement, seizing every chance through press and forum "to pour the living coals of truth upon the nation's naked heart," setting forth in earnest contrast the theory upon which the government was founded with its administration as practiced.

In 1848 Philadelphia Square, whereon the old State House of historic fame still stands, was made resonant by the bell upon whose surface the fathers had inscribed "Proclaim liberty throughout the world and to all the inhabitants thereof," and was bedecked with garlands and every insignia of a joyful people in honor of the Hungarian patriot, Louis Kossuth. Distinctive platforms had been erected for speakers whose fatherland was in many foreign lands. Upon each was an orator receiving the appreciation and plaudits of an

audience whose hearts beat as one for success to the "Great Liberator." The "unwelcome guests," the colored men present,
quickly embraced the opportunity, utilizing
for a platform a dry goods box, upon which
I was placed to give the Negro version of
this climax of inconsistency and quintes-
sence of hypocrisy. This was the unexpected. All the people, both native and
foreign, had been invited and special
places provided for all except the
Negro, and on the native platform
he was not allowed space. The novelty of the incident and curiosity to hear what
the colored man had to say quickly drew a
crowd equal to others of the occasion.
Then, as now, and perhaps forever, there
was that incalculable number of non-com-
mittals whose moral sense is disturbed by
popular wrong, but who are without courage of conviction, inert, waiting for a leader
that they may be one of the two that take
place behind him, or one of three or four, or
ten, who follow in serried ranks, that constitute the wedge-like motor that splits as-
sunder hoary wrong, proximity to the
leader being in ratio to their moral fibre.
Most of the audience listened to the utterance of sentiments that the allurements of
trade, or the exactions of society, forbade
them to disseminate.

The occasion was an excellent one to
demonstrate the heartlessness of the
projectors, who, while pretending to
glorify liberty in the distance, were

treating it with contumely at home, where 3,000,000 slaves were held in bondage, and feeling keenly the ostracism of the slave as beyond the pole of popular sympathy or national compassion, with words struggling for utterance,I spoke as best I could, receiving toleration, and a quiet measure of approbation, possibly on the supposition, realized in the fruition of time, that such discussion might eventuate in the liberation of white men from the octopus of subserviency to the dictum of slavery which permeated every ramification of American society. I heard Hon. Cassius M. Clay, of Kentucky, sometime in the forties, while making a speech in Philadelphia, say: "Gentlemen, the question is not alone whether the Negroes are to remain slaves, but whether we white men are to continue free." So bitter was the onslaught on all, and especially on white men, politically and socially, who dared denounce slavery.

CHAPTER III.

An event that came under my notice of startling character, attracting national attention, was the arrival of the schooner "Amistad" at Philadelphia in 1840. This vessel had been engaged in the slave trade. With a cargo of slaves from Africa was destined for one of the West India Islands. Cinguez, one of, and at the head of the captives, rebelled while at sea, killing a number of the crew and taking possession of the ship.

In the concluding scene of the foregoing drama, Mr. Douglass was an actor, I an observer. After the decision giving them their liberty, the anti-slavery society, who had been vigilant in its endeavors to have them liberated ever since their advent on American shores, held a monster meeting to receive them.

Frederick Douglass introduced "Cinguez" to the meeting. I cannot forget or fail to feel the inspiration of that scene. The two giants locked in each others embrace, looked the incarnation of heroism and dauntless purpose, equal to the achievement of great results. The one by indomitable will had shaken off his own shackles and was making slavery odius by his matchless and eloquent arraignment; the other, "a leader of men," had now written his protest with the blood of his captors. Cinguez, with unintelligable utterance in African dialect with emphatic gesture, his liberty loving soul on fire, while burning words strove for expression, described his action on the memorable night of his emancipation, with such vividness, power, and pathos that the audience seemed to see every act of the drama and feel the pulsation of his great heart. Through an interpreter he afterwards narrated his manner of taking the vessel, and how it happened to reach American shores. How, after taking the ship, he stood by the tiller with drawn weapon and commanded the mate to steer back to Africa. During the day he complied, but at night took the opposite course. After sometime of circuitous wandering the vessel ran into Long Island Sound and was taken possession of by the United States authorities. Cinguez, as hero and patriot, enobled African character.

When majority and the threshold of man's estate is attained, the transition from advanced youth to the entry of manhood is liable to casualties; not unlike a bark serenely leaving its home harbor to enter unfrequented waters, the crew exhilarated by fresh and invigorating breezes, charmed by a genial sky, it moves on "like a thing of beauty" with the hope

of "joy forever." The chart and log of
many predecessors may unheeded lie at
hand, but the glorious present, cloudless
and fascinating, rich in expectation, it
sails on, fortunate if it escapes the rocks
and shoals that ever lie in wait. It is unreasonable to expect a proper conception,
and the happiest performance of life's
duties at such a period, especially from
those with easy and favorable environments, or who have been heedless of parental restraint, for even at an advanced
stage in life, there have been many to ex-
claim with a poet:
"Ne'er tell me of evening serenely adorning
The close of a life richly mellowed by time,
Give me back, give me back the wild fresh-
        ness of morning
Her smiles and her tears are worth even-
        ing's best light."
    Twenty-one years of age found me the
possessor of a trade, an attainment, and a
capital invaluable for a poor young man
beginning the race of life. For whether
seen smutted by the soot of the blacksmith
shop, or whitened by the lime of the
plasterer or bricklayer; whether bending
beneath tool box of the carpenter or
ensconced on the bench of the shoemaker,
he has a moral strength, a consciousness
of acquirement, giving him a dignity of
manhood unpossessed by the menial and
those engaged in unskilled labor. Let it
never be forgotten that as high over in importance as the best interest of the race is

to that of the individual, will be the uplifting influence of assiduously cultivating a
desire to obtain trades. The crying want
with us is a middle class. The chief com-
ponent of our race today is laborers unskilled. We will not and cannot compete
with other races who have a large and influential class of artisans and mechanics,
and having received higher remuneration
for labor, have paved the way for themselves or offsprings from the mechanic to
the merchant or to the professional. These
three factors, linked and interlinked, an
ascending chain will be strong in its relation, as consistent in construction.

In 1849 Frederick Douglass, Charles
Lenox Remond and Julia Griffith, an English lady prominent in reform circles in
England, attended the National Anti-
slavery Convention held in Philadelphia,
and presided over by that apostle of liberty, Wm. Lloyd Garrison. At its close
Mr. Douglass invited me to accompany
him to his home at Rochester, and then to
join him in lecturing in the "Western Reserve."

Without salary, poor in purse, doubtful
of useful ability, dependent for sustenance
on a sentiment then prevailing, that for
anti-slavery expression was as reserved as
the "Reserve" was Western. I have often
thought of my feelings of doubt and fear
to go with Mr. Douglass, as an epoch in my
life's history. The parting of the ways,
the embarkation to a wider field of action,

HON. FREDERICK DOUGLASS.
"Sage of Anacostia."

The Most Distinguished Negro of the Race—As Statesman, Editor, Orator. Phil-
anthropist He Left an Indelible Mark on the Page of His Country's
History—Born in 1817 at Tuckahoe, Maryland—Died Febru-
ary, 1895—He was Author of "My Bondage and My
Freedom," "Life and Times of Frederick
Douglass," and Others.

the close connection between obedience to
an impulse of duty (however uninviting or
uncertain the outcome), and the ever
moral and often material benefit.
Rochester proved to be my pathway to
California. Western New York, 50 years
ago, then known as the "Western Reserve," was very unlike the present as to
population, means of travel, material developments, schools of learning, and
humanizing influences. Mr. Douglass, in
the Baptist Church in Little Rock, Ark., a
short time before his death, told how, in
1849, we there traveled together; that
where now are stately cities and villages
a sparsely settled wilderness existed; that
while we there proclaimed abolition as the
right of the slave, the chilling effect of
those December days were not more cold
and heartless than the reception we met
when our mission as advocates for the
slave became known; churches and halls
were closed against us. Stables and blacksmith shops would sometimes hold
audiences more generous with epithets
and elderly eggs than with manly de-
corum. God be thanked, Douglass, the
grandest of "our grand old men," lived to
see "the seeds of mighty truth have their
silent undergrowth, and in the earth be
wrought." A family, however poor, striving as best they may to give the rudiments
of knowledge to their children, should
have, if but few, books descriptive of the
hopes and struggles of those no better

situated, who have made impress on the
age in which they lived. We seldom remember from whence we first received the
idea which gave impulse to an honorable
action; we received it, however, most
probably from tongue or pen. For impressible youth such biography should be
as easy of access as possible.

It has been said that " a man's noblest
mistake is to be born before, his time."
This will not apply to Frederick Douglass.
His "Life and Times" should be in the
front rank of selection for blessing and
inspiration. A blessing for the high moral
of its teaching; an inspiration for the poor-
est boy; that he need not "beg the world's
pardon for having been born," but by fostering courage and consecration of purpose "he may rank the peer of any man."

Frederick Douglass, born a slave, ham-
pered by all the depressing influences of
that institution; by indomitable energy
and devotion; seizing with an avidity that
knew no obstacle every opportunity, cultivated a mind and developed a character
that will be a bright page in the history of
noble and beneficent achievements.

For the conditions that confronted him
and the anti-slavery crusade, have been
well and eloquently portrayed by the late
George William Curtis. That how terri-
bly earnest was the anti-slavery agitation
this generation little knows. To understand is to recall the situation of the country. Slavery sat supreme in the White

House and made laws at the capitol. Courts of Justice were its ministers, and legislators its lackeys. It silenced the preacher in the pulpit; it muzzled the editor at his desk, and the professor in his lecture-room. It sat a price on the heads of peaceful citizens; robbed the mails, and denounced the vital principles of the declaration of independence as treason. In the States where the law did not tolerate slavery, slavery ruled the club and drawing room, the factory and the office, swaggered at the dinner table, and scourged with scorn a cowardly society. It tore the golden rule from the school books, and from the prayer books the pictured benignity of Christ. It prohibited schools in the free States for the hated race; hunted women who taught children to read, and forbade a free people to communicate with their representatives."

It was under such conditions so pungently and truthfully stated that Douglass appeared as a small star on the horizon of a clouded firmament; rose in intellectual brilliancy, mental power and a noble generosity. For his devotion was not only to the freedom of the slave with which he was identified, but for liberty and the betterment of humanity everywhere, regardless of sex or color. His page already luminous in history will continue to brighten, and when statuary, now and hereafter, erected to his memory, shall have crumbled "neath the beatings of time;" the good fame of his name, high purpose and unflinching integrity to the highest needs of humanity, will remain hallowed "foot prints in the sands of time." Eminently fit was the naming of an institution in Philadelphia "The Frederick Douglass Hospital and Freedman's School;" the assuaging of suffering and the giving of larger opportunity for technical instruction were cherished ideals with the sage of Anacostia; also the lives of Harriet Beacher Stowe, Lucretia Mott and Francis E. Harper, and the noble band of women of which they were the type, who bravely met social ostracism and insult for devotion to the slave, will ever have a proud place in our country's history. Of this illustrious band was Julia Griffith, hitherto referred to, a grand representative of those renowned women, who at home or abroad, did so much to hasten the downfall of slavery and encourage the weak and lowly to hope and effort. Thackery has said that, "Could you see every man's career, you would find a woman clogging him, or cheering him, or beckoning him on."

Having finished my intended tour with Mr. Douglass, and returned to Rochester, the outlook for my future, to me, was not promising. The opportunities for advancement were much, very much less than now. With me ambition and dejection contended for the mastery, the latter often in the ascendant. To her friendly inquiry I gave reasons for my depression. I shall never forget the response; almost imperious in manner, you could already anticipate the magnitude of an idea that seemed to struggle for utterance. "What! discouraged? Go do some great thing." It was an inspiration, the result of which she may never have known. We are assured, however, that a kind act or helpful word is inseparably connected with a blessing for the giver. To earnest youth I would bequeath the excelsior of the "youth mid snow and ice," and the above injunction, "upward and onward;" "go do some great thing."

The war with Mexico, discovery of gold in California in 1848, the acquisition of new territory, and the developments of our hitherto undeveloped Western possessions, stimulated the financial pulse, and permeated every avenue of industry and speculative life. While in New York State I met several going and returning gold seekers, many giving dazzling accounts of immense deposits of gold in the new Eldorado; and others, as ever the case with adventurers, gave gloomy statements of peril and disaster. A judicious temperament, untiring energy, a lexicon of endeavor, in which there is no such word as "fail," is the only open sesame to hidden opportunities in a new country. Fortune, in precarious mood, may sometime smile on the inert, but she seldom fails to surrender to pluck, tenacity and perseverance. As the Oxford men say it is the one pull

more of the oar that proves the "beefiness
of the fellow;" it is the one march more
that wins the campaign; the five minutes
more persistent courage that wins the
fight.

I returned to Philadelphia, and with
some friendly assistance, sailed, in 1850,
from New York, as a steerage pas-
senger for San Francisco. Arriving at
Aspinwall, the point of debarkation, on
the Atlantic side, boats and boatsmen
were engaged to transport passengers and
baggage up the "Chagress," a small and
shallow river. Crossing the Isthmus to
Panama, on the Pacific side, I found Panama very cosmopolitan in appearance, for
mingled with the sombrero-attired South
American, could be seen denizens from
every foreign clime. Its make up was a
combination of peculiar attributes. It was
dirty, but happy in having crows for its
scavengers; sickly, but cheery; old, but
with an youthful infusion. The virtues
and vices were both shy and unblushing.
A rich, dark foliage, ever blooming, and
ever decaying; a humid atmosphere; a rot-
ting vegetation under a tropical sun,
while fever stalked on from conquest to
conquest.

The sudden influx, the great travel from
ocean to ocean, had given much impetus to
business as well as to local amusements.
For the latter, Sunday was the ideal day,
when bull and cock fights secured the attendance of the elite, and the humble, the
priest and the laity.

The church, preaching gentleness and peace in the morning, in the afternoon her minister, with sword spurred "bolosed" bantams under their arms, would appear on the scene eager for the fray.

After recovering from the Panama fever I took passage on the steamship "Golden Gate" for San Francisco. Science, experience, and a greatly increased demand have done much during the intervening fifty years to lessen risk and increase the comfort of ocean travel. Yet it is not without a degree of restless anticipation that one finds himself and baggage finally domiciled on an ocean-going steamer. Curiosity and criticism, selfishness and graciousness each in turn assert themselves. Curiosity in espionage, criticism in observation, while selfishness and graciousness alternate. You find yourself in the midst of a miniature world, environed, but isolated from activities of the greater, an epitome of human proclivities. A possible peril, real, imaginary or remote; a common brotherhood tightens the chain of fellowship and gradually widens the exchange of amenities.

We had a stormy passage, making San Diego with the top of smoke stack encrusted with the salt of the waves, paddle wheel broken and otherwise disabled, finally arriving at San Francisco in September.

CHAPTER IV.

Having made myself somewhat pre-
sentable upon leaving the steerage of the
steamer, my trunk on a dray, I proceeded
to an unprepossessing hotel kept by a
colored man on Kearny street. The
cursory view from the outside, and the
further inspection on the inside, reminded
me of the old lady's description of her
watch, for she said, "it might look pretty
hard on the outside, but the inside works
were all right." And so thought its jolly
patrons. Seated at tables, well supplied
with piles of gold and silver, where numerous disciples of that ancient trickster
Pharoah, being dubious perhaps of the
propriety of adopting the literal ortho-
graphy of his name, and abbreviated it to
Faro.

Getting something for nothing, or risk-
ing the smaller in hope of obtaining the
greater, seems a passion inherent in
human nature, requiring a calm survey of
the probabilities, and oftimes the baneful
effects to attain a moral resistance. It is
the "ignus fatus" that has lured many
promising ones and wrecked the future of
many lives.

The effervescent happiness of some of

the worshipers at this shrine was conspicuous. The future to them seemed cloudless. It was not so with me. I had a secret not at all complacent, for it seemed anxious to get out, and while unhappy from its presence, I thought it wise to retain it.

When I approached the bar I asked for accommodation, and my trunk was brought in. While awaiting this preparatory step to domicile, and gazing at the prints and pictures more or less "blaser" that adorned the bar, my eye caught a notice, prominently placed, in gilt letters. I see it now, "Board twelve dollars a week in advance." It was not the price, but the stipulation demanded that appalled me. Had I looked through a magnifying glass the letters could not have appeared larger. With the brilliancy of a search light they seemed to ask "Who are you and how are you fixed?" I responded by "staring fate in the face," and going up to the bar asked for a cigar. How much? Ten cents. I had sixty cents when I landed; had paid fifty for trunk drayage, and I was now a moneyless man— hence my secret.

Would there be strict enforcement of conditions mentioned in that ominous card. I was unacquainted with the Bohemian "song and dance" parlance in such extremities, and wondered would letting my secret come out let a dinner come in. Possibly, I may have often been deceived when appealed to, but that experience has often been fruitful to friendless hunger.

Finally the bell rang, and a polite invitation from the landlord placed me at the table. There is nothing so helpful to a disconsolate man as a good dinner. It dissipates melancholy and stimulates persistency. Never preach high moral rectitude or the possibilities of industry to a hungry man. First give him something to eat, then should there be a vulnerable spot to such admonition you will succeed. If not, he is an incorrigible.

After dinner I immediately went out, and after many attempts to seek employment of any kind, I approached a house in course of construction and applied to the contractor for work. He replied he did not need help. I asked the price of wages. Ten dollars a day. I said you would much oblige me by giving me, if only a few days' work, as I have just arrived. After a few moments thought, during which mayhap charity and gain held conference, which succumbed, it is needless to premise, for we sometimes ascribe selfish motives to kindly acts, he said that if I choose to come for nine dollars a day I might. It is unnecessary for me to add that I chose to come.

When I got outside the building an appalling thought presented itself; whoever heard of a carpenter announcing himself ready for work without his tools. A minister may be without piety, a lawyer without

clients, a politician impolitic, but a carpenter without tools, never! It would be
prima facia evidence of an imposter. I
went back and asked what tools I must
bring upon the morrow; he told me and I
left. But the tools, the tools, how was I to
get them. My only acquaintance in the
city was my landlord. But prospects were
too bright to reveal to him my secret. I
wended my way to a large tent having an
assortment of hardware and was shown
the tools needed. I then told the merchant
that I had no money, and of the place I
had to work the next morning. He said
nothing for a moment, looked me over, and
then said: "All right take them." I felt
great relief when I paid the merchant and
my landlord on the following Saturday.

Why do I detail to such length these
items of endeavor; experiences which have
had similarity in many lives? For the reason that they seem to contain data for a
moral, which if observed may be useful.
Never disclose your poverty until the last
gleam of hope has sunk beneath the
horizon of your best effort, remembering
that invincible determination holds the
key to success, while advice and assistance
hitherto laggard, now with hasty steps
greets you within the door.

I was not allowed to long pursue carpentering. White employees finding me at
work on the same building would "strike."
On one occasion the contractor came to
me and said, "I expect you will have to

stop, for this house must be finished in the' time specified; but, if you can get six or eight equally good workmen, I will let these fellows go. Not that I have any special liking for your people. I am giving these men all the wages they demand, and I am not willing to submit to the tyrany of their dictation if I can help it. This episode, the moral of which is as pertinent today as then, and more apparent, intensifies the necessity of greater desire upon the part of our young men and women to acquire knowledge in skilled handicraft, reference to which I have hitherto made. But my convictions are so pronounced that I cannot forbear the reiteration. For while it is enobling to the individual, giving independence of character and more financial ability, the reflex influence is so helpful in giving the race a higher status in the industrial activities of a commonwealth. Ignorance of such activities compel our people mostly to engage in the lower and less remunerative pursuits. I could not find the men he wanted or subsequent employment of that kind.

All classes of labor were highly remunerative, blacking boots not excepted.

I after engaged in this, and other like humble employments, part of which was for Hon. John C. Fremont, "the path-finder overland to California."

Saving my earnings, I joined a firm already established in the clothing business. After a year or more so engaged, I became

BOOKER T. WASHINGTON.
"The Sage of Tuskegee."

The Leader of Leaders For Negro Advancement.

a partner in the firm of Lester & Gibbs,
importers of fine boots and shoes.   Just
here a thought occurs which may be of advantage to ambitious but impecunious
young men.   Do not hesitate when you are
without choice to accept the most humble
and menial employment.   It will be a
source of pleasure, if by self-denial, saving
your earnings, you keep a fixed intent to
make it the stepping stone to something
higher.

The genius of our institutions, and the
noblest of mankind will estimate you by
the ratio of distance from the humblest
beginning to your present attainment; the
greater the distance the greater the luster;
the more fitting the meed of praise.

Our establishment on Clay street,
known as the "Emporium for fine boots and
shoes, imported from Philadelphia, London and Paris," having a reputation for
keeping the best and finest in the State,
was well patronized, our patrons extending to Oregon and lower California.   The
business, wholesale and retail, was profitable and maintained for a number of
years.   Mr. Lester, my partner, being a
practical bootmaker, his step to a merchant in that line was easy and lucrative.

Thanks to the evolution of events and
march of liberal ideas the colored men in
California have now a recognized citizenship, and equality before the law.   It was
not so at the period of which I write. With

thrift and a wise circumspection financially, their opportunities were good; from
every other point of view they were ostra-
cised, assaulted without redress, disfranchised and denied their oath in a court
of justice.

One occasion will be typical of the condition. One of two mutual friends (both our
customers) came in looking over and ad-
miring a display of newly arrived stock,
tried on a pair of boots, was pleased with
them, but said he did not think he needed
them then; lay them aside and he would
think about it. A short time after his
friend came in, was shown the pair the
former had admired; would he like such a
pair? He tried on several and then asked
to try on his friend's selection; they only
suited, and he insisted on taking them; we
objected, but he had them on, and said we
need not have fear, he would clear us of
blame, and walked out. Knowing they
were close friends we were content. Possibly, in a humorous mood, he went
straight to his friend, for shortly they both
came back, the first asking for his boots;
he would receive no explanation (while the
cause of the trouble stood mute), and with
vile epithets, using a heavy cane, again
and again assaulted my partner, who was
compelled tamely to submit, for had he
raised his hand he would have been shot,
and no redress. I would not have been allowed to attest to "the deep damnation of
his taking off."

The Magna Charter, granted by King John, at Runney Mead, to the Barons of England, in the twelfth century, followed by the Petition of Right by Charles I, has been rigidly preserved and consecrated as foundation for civil liberty. The Continental Congress led the van for the United States, who oftimes tardy in its conservatism, is disposed to give audience to merit and finally justice to pertinacity of purpose.

In 1851, Jonas P. Townsend, W. H. Newby, and other colored men with myself, drew up and published in the "Alto California," the leading paper of the State, a preamble and . resolutions protesting against being disfranchised and denied the right of oath, and our determination to use all moral means to secure legal claim to all the rights and privileges of American citizens.

It being the first pronouncement from the colored people of the State, who were supposed to be content with their status, the announcement caused much comment and discussion among the dominant class. For down deep in the heart of every man is a conception of right. He cannot extinguish it, or separate it from its comparative. What would I have others do to me? Pride, interest, adverse contact, all with specious argument may strive to dissipate the comparison, but the pulsations of a common humanity, keeping time with the verities of God never ceased to

trouble, and thus the moral pebble thrown
on the bosom of the hitherto placid sea of
public opinion, like its physical prototype,
creating undulations which go on and on
to beat against the rock and make sandy
shores, so this our earnest but feeble protest contributed its humble share in the re-
building of a commonwealth where "a
man's a man for all that."

The committee above named, with G. W.
Dennis and James Brown, the same
year formed a company, established
and published the "Mirror of the Times,"
the first periodical issued in the State for
the advocacy of equal rights for all Americans. It has been followed by a score of
kindred that have assiduously maintained
and ably contended for the rights and
privileges claimed by their zealous leader.

State conventions were held in 1854,
'55 and '57, resolutions and petitions passed and presented to the Legislature of
Sacramento. We had friends to offer
them and foes to move they be thrown out
the window. It is ever thus, "that men go
to fierce extremes rather than rest upon
the quiet flow of truths that soften hatred
and temper strife." There was that unknown quantity, present in all legislative
bodies, composed of good "little men"
without courage of conviction, others of
the Dickens' "devilish sly" type, who put
out their plant-like tendrils for support;
others "who bent the pliant servile knee
that thrift may follow fawning"—all

these the make-weight of a necessary con-
stituent in representative government conservatism. The conservative majority laid
our petition on the table, most likely with
the tacit understanding that it was to be
"taken up" by the janitor, and as such action on his part is not matter for record,
we will in this happier day with "charity
to all," over this episode on memory's leaf,
simply wrote "lost or stolen."

Among the occasions continually occur-
ring demanding protests against injustice
was the imposition of the "poll tax." It
was demanded of our firm, and we refused
to pay. A sufficient quantity of our goods
to pay tax and costs were levied upon, and
published for sale, and on what account.

I wrote with a fervor as cool as the circumstances would permit, and published
a card from a disfranchised oath-denied
standpoint, closing with the avowal that
the great State of California might annually confiscate our goods, but we would
never pay the voters tax. The card attracted attention, the injustice seemed
glaring, the goods were offered. We learned that we had several friends at the sale,
one in particular a Southern man. Now
there was this peculiarity about the Southern white man, he would work a Negro for
fifty years for his victuals and clothes, and
shoot a white man for cheating the same
Negro, as he considered the latter the
height of meanness. This friend quietly
and persistently moved through the

crowd, telling them why our goods were there, and advising to give them a "terrible letting alone." The auctioneer stated on what account they were there, to be sold, asked for bidders, winked his eye and said "no bidders." Our goods were sent back to our store. This law, in the words of a distinguished Statesman, was then allowed to relapse "into innocuous desuetude." No further attempts to enforce it upon colored men were made.

BISHOP HENRY M. TURNER.

Born in Newberry, S. C.—Ordained Bishop in 1880—President of Bishop Council,
Home and Foreign Missionary Society and Sunday School Union of the
A. M. E. Church—From Slave to Statesman—As Soldier, Editor,
Author, Legislator, Orator, and African Explorer—For Vitality
and Ability, Courage and Fidelity, Along so Many
Lines, He Stands Without a Peer.

CHAPTER V.

A rush to newly discovered gold fields
bring in view every trait of human character. The more vicious standing out in bold
relief, and stamping their impress upon
the locality. This phase and most primitive situation can be accounted for partly
by the cupidity of mankind, but mainly
that the first arrivals are chiefly adventurers. Single men, untrammeled by family
cares, traders, saloonists, gamblers, and
that unknown quantity of indefinite quality, ever present, content to allow others
to fix a status of society, provided they do
not touch on their own special interests,
and that other, the unscrupulous but active
professional politician, having been dis-
honored at home, still astute and determined, seeks new fields for booty, obtain
positions of trust and then consummate
peculation and outrage under the forms of
law. But the necessity for the honest administration of the law eventually asserts
itself for the enforcement of order.

It was quaintly said by a governor of
Arkansas, that he believed that a public
official should be "reasonably honest."
Even should that limited standard of official integrity be invaded the people with

an honest ballot need not be long in rectifying the evil by legal means. But cannot something be said in palliation of summary punishment by illegal means, when it is notorious and indisputable that all machinery for the execution of the law and the maintenance of order, the judges, prosecuting attorneys, sheriff and drawers of jurors, and every other of court of law are in the hands of a despotic cabal who excessively tax, and whose courts convict all those who oppose them, and exonerate by trial the most farcical, the vilest criminal, rob and murder in broad day light, often at the bidding of their protectors. Such a status for a people claiming to be civilized seems difficult to conceive, yet the above was not an hypothesis of condition, but the actual one that existed in California and San Francisco, especially from 1849 to 1855. Gamblers and dishonest politicians from other States held the government, and there was no legal redress. Every attempt of the friends of law and order to elect honest men to office was met at the polls by vituperation and assault.

One of the means for thinning out the ranks of their opponents at the polls they found very efficient. It was to scatter their "thugs" along the line of waiting voters and known opposers, and quickly and covertly inject the metal part of a shoemaker's awl in the rear but most fleshy part of his adversary's anatomy, making sitting unpleasant for a time.

There was usually uncertainty as to the
point of compass from which the hint
came to leave, but none as to the fact of
its arrival. Hence the reformer did not
stand on the order of his going, but generally left the line. These votes, of course,
were not thrown out, for the reason they
never got in. It diminished, but did not
abolish the necessity of stuffing ballot
boxes. In the West I once knew an old
magistrate named Scott, noted for his impartiality, but only called Judge Scott by
non-patrons of his court, who had never
came within the purview of his administration, to others he was known as "old
Necessity," for it was said he knew no
law. Revolutions, the beneficial results of
which will ever live in the history of mankind, founded as they were on the rights
of human nature and desire for the establishment and conservation of just government, have ever been the outgrowth of
necessity.

Patient in protest of misgovernment,
men are prone to "bear the ill they have"
until, like the accumulation of rills on
mountain side, indignation leaps the
bounds of legal form and prostrate law to
find their essence and purpose in reconstruction. At the time of which I write,
there seemed nothing left for the friends of
law, bereft as they were of all statutary
means for its enforcement, but making a
virtue of this necessity by organizing a

"vigilance committee" to wrench by physical strength that unobtainable by moral right. There had been no flourish of trumpets, no herald of the impending storm, but the pent up forces of revolution in inertion, now fierce for action, discarded restraint. Stern, but quiet had been the preparation for a revolution which had come, as come it ever will, with such inviting environments. It was not that normal status, the usual frailties of human nature described by Hooker as "stains and blemishes that will remain till the end of the world, what form of government, soever, may take place, they grow out of man's nature." But in this event the stains and blemishes were effaced by a common atrocity.

Sitting at the back of my store on Clay street a beautiful Sunday morning, one of those mornings peculiar to San Francisco, with its balmy breezes and Italian skies, there seemed an unusual stillness, such a quiet as precedes the cyclone in tropical climes, only broken occasionally by silvery peals of the church bells. When suddenly I heard the plank street resound with the tramp of a multitude. No voice or other sound was heard but the tramp of soldiery, whose rhymth of sound and motion is ever a proclamation that thrills by its intensity, whether conquest or conservation be its mission. I hastened to the door and was appalled at the sight. In marching

column, six or eight abreast, five thousand
men carrying arms with head erect, a reso-
lute determination born of conviction depicted in linament of feature and expression.

Hastily improvised barracks in large
storehouses east of Montgomery street,
fortified by hundreds of gunny sacks filled
with sand, designated "Fort Gunney," was
the quarters for committee and soldiers.
The committee immediately dispatched
deputies to arrest and bring to the Fort
the leaders of this cabal of misgovernment. The effort to do so gave striking
evidence of the cowardice of assassins.
Men whose very name had inspired terror,
and whose appearance in the corridors of
hotels or barrooms hushed into silence the
free or merry expression of their patrons,
now fled and hid away "like damned
ghosts at the smell of day" from the popular uprising of the people. The event which
precipitated the movement—the last and
crowning act of this oligarchy—was the
shooting of James King, of William, a
banker and publisher of a paper dedicated
to the exposure and denunciation of this
ring of dishonest officials and assassins. It
was done in broad daylight on Montgomery Street, the main thoroughfare of the
city. Mr. King, of William County, Maryland, was a terse writer, a gentleman
highly esteemed for integrity and devotion
to the best interests of his adopted State.

Many of the gang who had time and opportunity hid on steamers and sailing vessels to facilitate escape, but quite a number were arrested and taken to Fort Gunny for trial. One or two of the most prominent took refuge in the jail—a strong and well-appointed brick building—where, under the protection of their own hirelings in fancied security considered themselves safe. A deputation of the committee from the fort placed a cannon at proper distance from the entrance to the jail. With a watch in his hand, the captain of the squad gave the keepers ten minutes to open the doors and deliver the culprits. I well remember the excitement that increased in intensity as the allotted period diminished; the fuse lighted, and two minutes to spare; the door opened; the delivery was made, and the march to Fort Gunny began. A trial court had been organized at which the testimony was taken, verdict rendered, and judgment passed. From a beam projecting over an upper story window, used for hoisting merchandise, the convicted criminals were executed.

The means resorted to for the purification of the municipality were drastic, but the ensuing feeling of personal safety and confidence in a new administration appeared to be ample justification. Much has been said and written in defense and in condemnation of revolutionary methods for the reformation of government. It cannot but be apparent that when it is impossible to execute the virtuous purposes of government, the machinery having passed to notorious violators, who use it solely for vicious purpose, there seems nothing left for the votaries of order than to seize the reins with strong right arm and restore a status of justice that should be the pride and glory of all civilized people.

But what a paradox is presented in the disregard for law and life today in our common country, including much in our Southland! It is a sad commentary on the weakness and inconsistences of human nature and often starts the inquiry in many honest minds, as a remedial agency, is a republican form of government the most conducive in securing the blessings of liberty of which protection to human life is the chief?

For the actual reverse of conditions that existed in California in those early days are present in others of our States today. All the machinery and ability for the just administration of the law are in the hands of those appointed mainly by the ballot of the intelligence and virtue of these States, who, if not participants, are quite as censurable for their "masterly inactivity" in having allowed thousands of the most defenceless to be lynched by hanging or burning at the stake. That there have been cases of assault on women by Negroes for which they have been lynched, it is needless to deny. That they have been lynched for threatening to do bodily harm to white

men for actual assaults on the Negro wife
and daughter is equally true. The first
should be denounced and arrested (escape
being impossible) and by forms of law suffer its extreme penalty. The other for the
cause they were murdered should have the
highest admiration and the most sincere
plaudits from every honest man. Is it true
that "he is a slave most base whose love
of right is for himself and not for all the
race," and that the measure you mete out
to others—the same shall be your portion.
All human history verifies these aphor-
isms; and that the perpetrators and silent
abettors of this barbarism have sowed to
the winds a dire penalty, already being
reaped, is evidenced by disregard of race
or color of the victim when mob law is in
the ascendant. And further, as a salvo for
their own acts, white men are allowing bad
Negroes to lynch others of their kind without enforcing the law.

The Negro, apish in his affinity to his
prototype in a "lynching bee," is beneath
contempt.

HON. GEORGE H. WHITE.

Born at Rosedale, North Carolina—Graduate from Howard University in 1877—
Practiced Law in all the Courts of his State—Member of House of Repre-
sentatives in 1880 and of Senate in 1884—Eight Years Prosecuting
Attorney—Elected Member of the Fifty-fifth Congress as a
Republican, With a Record Unimpeachable.

CHAPTER VI.

Early in the year 1858 gold was discovered on Fraser River, in the Hudson Bay Company's territory in the Northwest. This territory a few months later was organized as the Colony of British Columbia and absorbed; is now the western outlook of the Dominion of Canada. The discovery caused an immense rush of gold seekers, traders, and speculators from all parts of the world. In June of that year, with a large invoice of miners' outfits, consisting of flour, bacon, blankets, pick, shovels, etc., I took passage on steamship Republic for Victoria. The social atmosphere on steamers whose patrons are chiefly gold seekers is unlike that on its fellow, where many have jollity moderated by business cares, others reserved in lofty consciousness that they are on foreign pleasure bent. With the gold seeker, especially the "tenderfoot," there is an incessant social hilarity, a communion of feeling, an ardent anticipation that cannot be dormant, continually bubbling over. We had on board upward of seven hundred, comprising a variety of tongues and nations. The bustle and turmoil incident to getting off and being preperly domiciled; the confusion of tongues and peculiarity of temperament resembled the Babel of old. Here the mercurial Son of France in search of a case of red wine, hot and impulsive, belching forth "sacres" with a velocity well sustained. The phlegmatic German stirred to excitability in quest of a "small cask of lager and large box of cheese;" John Chinaman "Hi yah'd" for one "bag lice all samee hab one Melican man," while a chivalric but seedy-looking Southerner, who seemed to have "seen better days," wished he "might be—if he didn't lay a pe-yor of boots thar whar that blanket whar." Not to be lost in the shuffle was a tall canting specimen of Yankeedom perched on a water cask that "reckoned ther is right smart chance of folks on this 'ere ship," and "kalkerlate that that boat swinging thar war a good place to stow my fixin's in." The next day thorough system and efficiency was brought out of chaos and good humor prevailed.

Victoria, then the capital of British Columbia, is situated on the southern point of Vancouver's Island. On account of the salubrity of its climate and proximity to the spacious land-locked harbor of Esquimault it is delightful as a place of residence and well adapted to great mercantile and industrial possibilities. It was the headquarters of the Hudson Bay Company, a very old, wealthy, and influential English trading company. Outside the company's fort, enclosing immense storehouses, there were but few houses. The

nucleus of a town in the shape of a few
blocks laid out, and chiefly on paper maps,
was most that gave promise of the populous city of Victoria of the present. On
my arrival my goods were sold at great advance on cost, an order for more sent by
returning steamer. I had learned prior to
starting that city lots could be bought for
one hundred dollars each, and had come
prepared to buy two or three at that price.
A few days before my arrival what the authorities had designated as the "land office" had been subjected to a "Yankee
rush," which had not only taken, and paid
for all the lots mapped out, but came near
appropriating books, benches, and window
sashes; hence the office had to close down
and haul off for repairs, and surveyed lots,
and would not be open for business for ten
days. Meanwhile those that were in at the
first sale were still in, having real estate
matters their own way. Steamers and sailing craft were constantly arriving, dis-
charging their human freight, that needed
food, houses, and outfits for the mines, giving an impetus to property of all kinds that
was amazing for its rapidity. The next
afternoon after the day of my arrival I
had signed an agreement and paid one
hundred dollars on account for a lot and
one-story house for $3,000—$1,400 more in
fifteen days, and the balance in six months.
Upon the arrival of my goods ten days later
I paid the second installment and took possession. Well, how came I to take a responsibility so far beyond my first intended

investment? Just here I rise to remark:
For effective purposes one must not be unduly sensitive or overmodest in writing autobiography—for, being the events and
memoirs of his life, written by himself,
the ever-present pronoun "I" dances in
such lively attendance and in such profu-
sion on the pages that whatever pride he
may have in the events they chronicle is
somewhat abashed at its repetition.

Addison truly says: "There is no passion which steals into the heart more im-
perceptible and covers itself under more
disguises than pride." Still, if in such memoirs there be found landmarks of precept
or example that will smooth the rugged-
ness of Youth's pathway, the success of its
mission should disarm invidious criticism.
For the great merit of history or biography
is not alone the events they chronicle, but
the value of the thought they inspire. Previous to purchasing the property I had calculated the costs of alteration and estimated the income. In twenty days, after
an expenditure of $200 for improvements,
I found myself receiving a rental of $500
per month from the property, besides a
store for the firm. Anyone without mechanical knowledge with time and opportunity to seek information from others
may have done the same, but in this case
there was neither time nor opportunity;
it required quick perception and prompt
action. The trade my mother insisted I
should learn enabled me to do this. Get

a trade, boys, if you have to live on bread
and apples while attaining it. It is a good
foundation to build higher. Don't crowd
the waiters. If they are content, give
them a chance. We received a warm welcome from the Governor and other officials of the colony, which was cheering.
We had no complaint as to business patronage in the State of California, but there
was ever present that spectre of oath denial and disfranchisement; the disheart-
ening consciousness that while our existence was tolerated, we were powerless to
appeal to law for the protection of life or
property when assailed. British Columbia
offered and gave protection to both, and
equality of political privileges. I cannot
describe with what joy we hailed the opportunity to enjoy that liberty under the
"British lion" denied us beneath the pinions of the American Eagle. Three or four
hundred colored men from California and
other States, with their families, settled in
Victoria, drawn thither by the two-fold inducement—gold discovery and the assurance of enjoying impartially the benefits
of constitutional liberty. They built or
bought homes and other property, and by
industry and character vastly improved
their condition and were the recipients of
respect and esteem from the community.

An important step in a man's life is his
marriage. It being the merging of dual
lives, it is only by mutual self-abnegation

that it can be made a source of contentment and happiness. In 1859, in consummation of promise and purpose, I returned
to the United States and was married to
Miss Maria A. Alexander, of Kentucky,
educated at Oberlin College, Ohio. After
visits to friends in Buffalo and my friend
Frederick Douglass at Rochester, N. Y.,
thence to Philadelphia and New York
City, where we took steamship for our long
journey of 4,000 miles to our intended
home at Victoria, Vancouver Island. I
have had a model wife in all that the term
implies, and she has had a husband migratory and uncertain. We have been
blessed with five children, four of whom
are living—Donald F., Horace E., Ida A.,
and Hattie A. Gibbs; Donald a machinist,
Horace a printer by trade. Ida graduated
as an A. B. from Oberlin College and is
now teacher of English in the High School
at Washington, D. C.; Hattie a graduate
from the Conservatory of Music at Oberlin,
Ohio, and was professor of music at the
Eckstein-Norton University at Cave
Springs, Ky., and now musical director of
public schools of Washington, D. C.

In passing through the States in 1859 an
unrest was everywhere observable. The
pulsebeat of the great national heart quickened at impending danger. The Supreme
Court had made public the Dred Scott decision; John Brown had organized an insurrection; Stephen A. Douglass and

Abraham Lincoln at the time were in exciting debate; William H. Seward was proclaiming the "irrepressible conflict." With
other signs portentous, culminating in secession and events re-enacting history—
for that the causes and events of which
history is the record are being continuously re-enacted from a moral standpoint
is of easy observation. History, as the narration of the actions of men, with attendant results, is but a repetition. Different
minds and other hands may be the instru-
ments, but the effects from any given
course involving fundamental principles
are the same. This was taught by philoso-
phers 2,000 years ago, some insisting that
not only was this repetition observable in
the moral world, but that the physical
world was repeated in detail—that every
person, every blade of grass, all nature,
animate and inanimate, reappeared upon
the earth, engaged in the same pursuits,
and fulfilling the same ends formerly accomplished.

However skeptical we may be as to
this theory of the ancients, the student of modern history has accomplished little if he fails to be impressed
with the important truth standing out on
every page in letters of living light—that
this great world of ours is governed by a
system of moral and physical laws that are
as unerring in the bestowal of rewards as
certain in the infliction of penalties. The
history of our own country is one that

will ever be an exemplification of this pre
eminent truth. The protests of the victims of oppression in the old world resulted in a moral upheaval and the establishment by force of arms of a Republic in
America. The Revolutionary Congress, of
which, in adopting the Federal Constitution, closed with this solemn injunction:
"Let it be remembered that it has been the
pride and boast of America that the rights
for which she contended were the rights of
human nature." And it was reserved for
the founders of this nation to establish in
the words of an illustrious benefactor, "a
Government of the people, for the people,
and by the people"—a Government deriv-
ing all its powers from the consent of the
governed, where freedom of opinion,
whether relating to Church or State, was
to have the widest scope and fullest expression consistent with private rights
and public good—where the largest indi-
viduality could be developed and the patri-
cian and plebeian meet on a common level
and aspire to the highest honor within the
gift of the people.

This was its character, this its mission. How it has sustained the character, how fulfilled the mission upon
which it entered, the impartial historian
has indited, every page of which is redo-
lent with precept and example that point
a moral.

With the inauguration of republican
government in America the angel of

freedom and the demon of slavery wrestled for the mastery. Tallyrand has beautifully and forcibly said: "The Lily and Thistle may grow together in harmonious proximity, but liberty and slavery delight in the separation." The pronounced policy of the best minds at the adoption of the Federal Constitution was to repress it as an institution inhuman in its character and fraught with mischief. Foretelling with accuracy of divine inspiration, Jefferson "trembled for his country" when he remembered that God was just and that "His justice would not sleep forever." Patrick Henry said "that a serious view of this subject gives a gloomy prospect to future times." So Mason and other patriots wrote and felt, fully impressed that the high, solid ground of right and justice had been left for the bogs and mire of expediency.

They died, leaving this heritage growing stronger and bolder in its assumption of power and permeating every artery of society. The cotton gin was invented and the demand for cotton vaulted into the van of the commerce of the country. Men, lured by the gains of slavery and corrupted by its contact, sought by infamous reasoning and vicious legislation to avert the criticism of men and the judgment of God. In the words of our immortal Douglass, "To bolster up and make tolerable what was intolerable; to make human what was inhuman; to make divine

what was infernal." To make this giant
wrong acceptable to the moral sense it was
averred and enacted that slavery was
right; that God himself had so predeter-
mined in His wisdom; that the slave could
be branded and sold on the auction block;
that the babe could be ruthlessly taken
from its mother and given away; that a
family could be scattered by sale, to meet
no more; that to teach a slave to read was
punishable with death to the teacher. But
why rehearse this dead past—this terrible
night of suffering and gloom? Why not
let its remembrance be effaced and forgotten in the glorious light of a happier day?
I answer, Why?

All measure of value, all estimates of
greatness, of joy or sorrow, of health or
suffering, are relative; we judge by comparison, and if in recalling these former
depths we temper unreasonable criticism
of waning friendships, accelerate effort as
we pass the mile-stones of achievement,
and stimulate appreciation of liberty in
the younger generation, the mention will
not be fruitless.

But to the resume of this rapid statement of momentous events: Meanwhile,
the slave, patient in his longings, prayed
for deliverance. Truly has it been said by
Elihu Burrit that "you may take a man
and yoke him to your labor as you yoke
the ox that worketh to live, and liveth to
work; you may surround him with ignorance and cloud him over with artificial

night. You may do this and all else that will degrade him as a man, without injuring his value as a slave; yet the idea that he was born to be free will survive it all. 'Tis allied to his hope of immortality—the ethereal part of his nature which oppression cannot reach. 'Tis the torch lit up in his soul by the omnipotent hand of Deity Himself." The true and tried hosts of freedom, represented and led by Garrison, Douglass, Lovejoy, Phillips, Garnet, Harriet Beecher Stowe, and Frances Ellen Harper, and others—few compared to the Indifferent and avowed defenders of slavery, welcoming outrage and ostracism, by pen and on forum, from hilltop and valley, proclaimed emancipation as the right of the slave and the duty of the master. The many heroic efforts of the anti-slavery phalanx were not without effect, and determined resistance was made to the admission of more slave territory which was in accordance with the "Proviso" prohibiting slavery in the Northwest. Slavery controlled the Government from its commencement, hence its supporters looked with alarm upon an increasing determination to stay its progress.

California had been admitted as a free State, after a struggle the most severe. Its admission John C. Calhoun, the very able leader of the slave power, regarded as the death-knell of slavery, if the institution remained within the union and counseled secession. Washington, Jefferson, and Mad-

ison, in despair at the growth of slavery;
Calhoun at that of freedom. But how
could this march of moral progress and national greatness be arrested? Congress
had, in 1787, enacted that all the territory
not then States should forever be reserved
to freedom. The slave power saw the
"handwriting on the wall" surround it
with a cordon of free States; increase
their representatives in Congress advocat-
ing freedom, and slavery is doomed. The
line cherished by the founders, the Gibraltar against which slavery had dashed
its angry billows, must be blotted out, and
over every rod of virgin soil it was to be
admitted without let or hindrance.

Then came the dark days of compromise,
the era of Northern fear of secession, and,
finally, opinion crystallizing into legislation non-committal, viz: That States ap-
plying for admission should be admitted
as free or slave States, as a majority of
their inhabitants might determine. Then
came the struggle for Kansas. Emigration
societies were fitted out in the New England and Northern States to send free
State men to locate who would vote to
bring in Kansas as a free State. Similar
organizations existed in the slave States
for the opposite purpose.

It is not pleasant to dwell nor fitly por-
tray the terrible ordeal through which the
friends of freedom passed. In 1859 they
succeeded; right and justice were triumphant, the beneficial results of which will

HON. JOHN M. LANGSTON.

Born in Louisa Country, Va.—Educated at Oberlin, Ohio—Member Board of
Health, District of Columbia in 1871—Minister Resident and Consul-
General to Port-au-Prince, Hayti, 1877—Elected to Congress
from Fourth Congressional District of Virginia in
1890—Author of "Freedom and Citizenship"
and "From the Virginia Plantation
to the National Capitol."

reach remotest time. It was in this conflict that the heroism of John Brown developed. It was there he saw his kindred
and his friends murdered, and there registered his vow to avenge their blood in
the disenthralment of the slave. The com-
peers of this "grand old man" or people of
the nation could have scarcely supposed
that this man, hitherto obscure, was to be
the instrument of retributive justice, to inaugurate a rebellion which was to culmi-
nate in the freedom of 4,000,000 slaves.
John Brown, at the head of a few devoted
men, at Harper's Ferry, struck the blow
that echoed and re-echoed in booming gun
and flashing sabre until, dying away in
whispered cadence, was hushed in the joy-
ousness of a free nation. John Brown was
great because he was good, and good because he was great, with the bravery of a
warrior and the tenderness of a child, loving liberty as a mother her first born, he
scorned to compromise with slavery. Virginia demanded his blood and he gave it,
making the spot on which he fell sacred
for all time, upon which posterity will see
a monument in commemoration of an effort, grand in its magnanimity, to which
the devotees of liberty from every clime
can repair to breathe anew an inspiration
from its shrine—

"For whether on the gallows high
    Or in the battle's van,
The noblest place for man to die
    Is where he dies for man."

The slave power, defeated in Kansas, fearful of the result of the vote in other territories to determine their future status, found aid and comfort from Judge Taney, a Supreme Judge of the United States. Bancroft, the historian, has said: "In a great Republic an attempt to overthrow a State owes its strength to and from some branch of the Government." 'Tis said that this Chief Justice, without necessity or occasion, volunteered to come to the rescue of slavery, and, being the highest court known to the law, the edict was final, and no appeal could lie, save to the bar of humanity and history. Against the memory of the nation, against decisions and enactments, he announced that, slaves being property, owners could claim constitutional protection in the territories; that the Constitution upheld slavery against any act of a State Legislature, and even against Congress. Slavery, previous to 1850, was regulated by municipal law; the slave was held by virtue of the laws of the State of his location or of kindred slave States. When he escaped that jurisdiction he was free. By the decision of Judge Taney, instead of slavery being local, it was national and freedom outlawed; the slave could not only be reclaimed in any State, but slavery could be established wherever it sought habitation.

Black laws had been passed in Northern States and United States Commissioners appointed in these States searched for

fugitives, where they had, in fancied security, resided for years, built homes, and
reared families, seizing and remanding
them back into slavery, causing an era of
terror, family dismemberment, and flight,
only to be remembered with sadness and
horror. For had not the heartless dictum
come from a Chief Justice of the United
States—the "Jeffry of American jurisprudence," that it had been ruled that black
men had no rights a white man was bound
to respect?

The slave power, fortified with this dec
laration, resolved that if at the approaching election they did not *succeed* they
would *secede*. Lincoln was elected, and the
South, true to its resolve, prepared for the
secession of its States. Pennsylvania is
credited with having then made the last
and meanest gift to the Presidency in the
person of James Buchanan. History tells
of a Nero who fiddled while Rome burned.
The valedictory of this public functionary
breathing aid and comfort to secession,
was immediately followed by South Carolina firing on Fort Sumter, and Southern
Senators advised their constituents to
seize the arsenals and ports of the nation.
Rebellion was a fact.

CHAPTER VII.

Abraham Lincoln, the President-elect, was the legitimate outgrowth of American institutions; in him was presented choice fruit, the product of republican government. Born in a log cabin, of poor, uneducated parents, his only aids untiring industry, determination, and lofty purpose. Hewing out his steps on the rugged rocks of poverty, climbing the mountains of difficulty, and attaining the highest honor within the gift of the nation—"truly a self-made man, the Declaration of Independence," says a writer, "being his daily compendium of wisdom, the life of Washington his daily study, with something of Jefferson, Madison, and Clay." For the rest, from day to day, he lived the life of the American people; walked in its light; reasoned with its reason: thought with its powers of thought, and felt the beatings of its mighty heart." In 1858 he came prominently forward as the rival of Stephen A. Douglass, and, with wealth of argument, terseness of logic, and enunciation of just principles, took front rank among sturdy Republicans, battling against the extension of human slavery, declaring that

ABRAHAM LINCOLN,
The Emancipator.

The Embodiment of Patriotism and Justice. "I hope peace will come to stay, and then there will be some colored men who can remember that they helped mankind to this great consummation."

"the nation could not endure half free and half slave."

On the 4th of March, 1861, he took the oath of office and commenced his Administration. With confidence and doubt alternating, our interest as a race became intensified. We knew the South had rebelled; we were familiar with the pagan proverb "Those whom the gods would destroy they first made mad." We had watched the steady growth of Republicanism, when a tinge on the political horizon "no bigger than a man's hand," increase in magnitude and power and place its standard-bearer in the White House. But, former Presidents had professed to hate slavery. President Fillmore had, yet signed the fugitive slave law; Pierce and Buchanan had both wielded the administrative arm in favor of slavery. We had seen Daniel Webster, Massachusetts' ablest jurist, and the most learned constitutional expounder—the man of whom it was said that "when he speaks God's own thunder can be seen pent up in his brow and God's own lightning flash from his eye"—a man sent by the best cultured of New England to represent the most advanced civilization of the century—we had seen this brilliant star of anti-slavery Massachusetts "pale his ineffectual fires" before the steady glare, the intolerance, blandishment, and corrupting influences of the slave power—and tell the nation they must compromise with slavery.

When Daniel O'Connell, Ireland's states-man and philanthropist, was approached in Parliament by West India planters with promises of support for measures for the relief of Ireland if he would vote in the interest of slavery in British colonies, he said: " 'Tis true, gentlemen, that I repre-sent a poor constituency—God only knows how poor; but may calamity and afflic-tion overtake me if ever I, to help Ireland, vote to enslave the Negro." A noble ut-terance! Unlike the Northern representa-tives sent to Congress, who "bent the pli-ant, servile knee that thrift might follow fawning." What wonder our race was keenly alive to the situation? The hour had arrived—was the man there?

For Abraham Lincoln impartial history will answer "Nor memory lose, nor time im-pair" his nobility of character for human-ity and patriotism that will ever ennoble and inspire. Mr. Lincoln was slow to be-lieve that the rebellion would assume the proportions that it did, but he placed him-self squarely on the issue in his inaugural address: "That he should, to the extent of his ability, take care that the laws of the nation be faithfully executed in all the States; that in doing it there would be no bloodshed unless it was forced upon the national authority." His patriotism and goodness welling up as he said: "We are not enemies, but friends, though we may have strained, it must not break our bonds of affection. The mystic chords of memory, stretching from every battlefield and hearthstone, will yet swell the chorus of the Union when again touched by the better angels of our nature."

"But the die was cast;
Ruthless rapine righteous hope defied."

The necessity for calling the nation to arms was imminent on the 15th of April, 1861; the call for 75,000 men rang like a trumpet blast, startling the most apathetic. The response from the Northern and portions of the Southern States was hearty and prompt. The battle at Bull Run dispelled the President's idea that the war was to be of short duration. Defeat followed defeat of the national forces; weeping and wailing went up from many firesides for husbands and sons who had laid down on Southern battlefields to rest. The great North, looking up for succor, saw the "national banner drooping from the flagstaff, heavy with blood," and typical of the stripes of the slave. For 200 years the incense of his prayers and tears had ascended. Now from every booming gun there seemed the voice of God, "Let my people go"—

"They see Him in watch fires
Of a hundred circling camps;
They read His righteous sentence
By the dim and flaring lamps."

The nation had come slowly but firmly up to the duty and necessity of emancipation. Mr. Lincoln, who was now in accord with Garrison, Phillips, Douglass, and their adherents, had counseled them to continue urging the people to this demand, now pressing as a miltary necessity. The 1st of January, 1863, being the maturity of the proclamation, lifted 4,000,000 of human beings from chattels to freemen, a grateful, praying people. Throughout the North and wherever possible in the South the colored people, on the night of December 31, assembled in their churches for thanksgiving. On their knees in silence—a silence intense with suppressed emotion—they awaited the stroke of the clock. It came, the thrice-welcomed harbinger of freedom, and as it tolled on, and on, the knell of slavery, pent-up joy could no longer be restrained. "Praise God, from whom all blessings flow," from a million voices, floated upward on midnight air. While some shouted "Hallelujah," others, with folded arms, stood mute and fixed as statuary, while "Tears of joy like summer raindrops pierced by sunbeams" fell.

When Robespierre- and Danton disenthralled France, we learn that the guillotine bathed in blood was the emblem of their transition state, from serfs to freemen. With the Negro were the antithesis of anger, revenge, or despair, that of joy, gratitude, and hope, has been memory's most choice trio.

This master stroke of policy and justice came with telling effect upon the consciousness of the people. It was now in deed and in truth a war for the Union coeval with freedom; every patriot heart beat a responsive echo, and was stirred by a new inspiration to deeds of heroism. Now success followed success; Port Hudson, Vicksburg, Chattanooga, Gettysburg, and the Mississippi bowed in submission to the national power. The record of history affirms subsequent events that during the ensuing twelve months war measures more gigantic than had been witnessed in modern times were inaugurated; how the will of the people to subdue the rebellion crystallized as iron; that General Grant, planting himself before Richmond, said he would "fight it out on that line if it took all summer," and General Sherman's memorable march fifty thousand strong from Atlanta to the sea. General Grant's campaign ended in the surrender of General Lee, and Peace, with its golden pinions, alighted on our national staff.

Abraham Lincoln was again elected President, the people seeming impressed with the wisdom of his quaint phrase that "it was best not to swap horses while crossing a stream." Through all the vicissitudes of his first term he justified the unbounded confidence of the nation, supporting with no laggard hand, cheering and inspiring the citizen soldier with noble example and kindly word. The reconstruction acts, legislation for the enrollment of

the colored soldier, and every other measure of enfranchisement received his hearty
approval, remarking at one time, with
much feeling, that "I hope peace will come
to stay, and there will be some black men
that can remember that they helped mankind to this great consummation."

Did the colored troops redeem the
promise made by their friends when
their enlistment was determined? History records exhibitions of bravery and
endurance which gave their survivors
and descendants a claim as imperishable as eternal justice. Go back to
the swamps of the Carolinas, the Savan-
nahs of Florida, the jungles of Arkansas,
or on the dark bosom of the Mississippi.
Look where you may, the record of their
rugged pathway still blossoms with deeds
of noble daring, self-abnegation and a holy
devotion to the central ideas of the war—
the freedom of the slave, a necessity for
the salvation of free government.

The reading of commanders' reports bring
no blush of shame. At the terrific assault
on Fort Hudson, General Banks reported
they answered "every expectation; no troops
could have been more daring." General
Butler tells of his transformation from a
war Democrat to a radical. Riding out at
early morn to view the battlefield, where
a few hours before shot and shell flew thick
and fast, skillfully guiding his horse, that
hoofs should not profane the sacred dead,
he there saw in sad confusion where lay

BISHOP W. B. DERRICK.

Born July, 1843, Antique, Bristol, West Indies—Educated at Graceville, W. I.—
Ordained Deacon in 1868, and now one of the Foremost Bishops of the
A. M. E. Church—Noted for Wisdom of Counsel and Great Ability.

the white and black soldier, who had gone
down together. The appeal, though mute,
was irresistible. Stopping his horse and
raising his hand in the cold, grey light to
heaven, said: "May my tongue cleave to
the roof of my mouth and my right hand
forget its cunning if I ever cease to insist
upon equal justice to the colored man."
It was at the unequal fight at Milliken's
Bend; it was at Forts Wagner and Pillow,
at Petersburg and Richmond, the colored
troops asked to be assigned the posts of
danger, and there before the iron hail of
the enemy's musketry "they fell forward
as fits a man." In our memory and affections they deserve a fitting place "as those
long loved, and but for a season gone."

Slavery, shorn of its power, nurtured revenge. On the 14th day of April, 1865,
while sitting with his family at a public
exhibition, Abraham Lincoln was assassinated, and the nation was in tears. Never
was lamentation so widespread, nor grief
so deep; the cabin of the lowly, the lordly
mansion of wealth, the byways and high-
ways, gave evidence of a people's sorrow.
"Men moved about with clinched teeth and
bowed-down heads; women bathed in tears
and found relief, while little children
asked their mothers why all the people
looked so mournful," and we, as we came
up out of Egypt, lifted up our voices and
wept. Our friend was no more, but intrenched in the hearts of his countrymen

(6)

a's one who did much "to keep the jewel of liberty in the family of nations."

Since that eventful period the Negro has had a checkered career, passing through the reconstruction period, with its many lights and shadows, despite the assaults of prejudice and prescription by exclusion from most of the remunerative callings and avocations, partiality in sentencing him to the horrors of the chain-gang, lynching, and burning at the stake. Despite all these he has made progress—a progress often unfairly judged by the dominant race. Douglass has pithily said: "Judge us not from the heights on which you stand, but from the depths from whence we sprung." So, with a faith and hope undaunted, we scan our country horizon for the silver lining propitious of a happier day.

Regarding that crime of crimes, lynching by hanging and burning human beings, a barbarity unknown in the civilized world save in our country, it is cheering to observe an awakening of the moral sense evidenced by noble and manly utterance of leading journals, notably those of Arkansas; the Governor of Georgia, and other Southern Governors and statesmen, have spoken in derogation of this giant crime.

When others of like standing and State influence shall so pronounce, this hideous blot upon the national escutcheon will disappear. It is manly and necessary to protest when wronged. But a subject class or race does but little for their ameliora-

tion when content with its denouncement.
Injustice can be more effectually arraigned
by others than the victim; his mere proclamation, however distinct and unanswer-
able, will be slow of fruition. A measure
of relief comes from the humane sympathies of the philanthropist, but the inherent attraction of forces (less sympathetic,
perhaps, though indispensable) for his real
uplifting and protection will be in the ratio
of his morality, learning, and wealth. For
vice is ever destructive; ignorance ever a
victim, and poverty ever defenceless. Morality should be ever in the foreground of
all effort, for mere learning or even wealth
will not make a class of brave, honest men
and useful citizens; there must be ever an
intensity of purpose based upon convictions of truth, and "the inevitable oneness
of physical and moral strength." St. Pierre
de Couberton, an eminent French writer
on education and training, has pertinently
said: "Remember that from the cradle to
the grave struggle is the essence of life,
as it is the unavoidable aim, the real life
bringer of all the sons of men. Existence
is a fight, and has to be fought out; self-de-
fence is a noble art, and must be practiced.
Never seek a quarrel, but never shun one,
and if it seeks you, be sure and fight to
the last, as long as strength is given you
to stand, guard your honesty of purpose,
your good faith; beware of all false seeming, of all pretence, cultivate arduous
tasks, aspire to what is difficult, and do

persistently what is uncomfortable and unpleasant; love effort passionately, for without effort there can be no manliness; therefore acquire the habit of self-restraint, the habit of painful effort, physical pain, is a useful one." With such purpose the Negro should have neither servility, bitterness, nor regret, but "instinct with the life of the present rise with the impulse of the age."

CHAPTER VIII.

My election to the Common Council of the City of Victoria, Vancouver Island, in 1866, was my first entry to political life, followed by re-election for succeeding term.

The exercise of the franchise at the polls was by "viva voce," the voter proclaiming his vote by stating the name of the candidate for whom he voted in a distinct voice, which was audited on the rolls by clerks of both parties.

Alike all human contrivances, this mode of obtaining the popular will has its merits and demerits. For the former it has the impossibility of ballot-stuffing, for the bystander can keep accurate tally; also the opportunity for the voter to display the courage of his conviction, which is ever manly and the purpose of a representative Commonwealth. On the other hand, it may fail to register the desire of the voter whose financial or other obligation may make it impolitic to thus openly antagonize the candidate he otherwise would with a secret ballot, "that falls as silently as snow-flakes fall upon the sod" and (should) execute a freeman's will as lightning doth the will of God." This is its mission, the faithful execution of its fiat, the palladium of liberty for all the people. Opposition to the exercise of this right in a representative government is disintegrating by contention and suicidal in success. It has been, and still is, the cause of bitter struggle in our own country. Disregard of the ultimatum of constitutional majorities, the foundation of our system of government, as the cause of the civil war, the past and ever-occurring political corruption in the Northern and the chief factor in the race troubles in the Southern States, where the leaders in this disregard and unlawful action allow the honors and emoluments of office to shut out from their view the constitutional rights of others; and by the criminality of their conduct and subterfuge strive to make selfish might honest right.

That slavery was a poor school to fit men to assume the obligations and duties of an enlightened citizenship should be readily admitted; that its subjects in the Elysium of their joy and thankfulness to their deliverers from servitude to freedom, and in ignorance of the polity of government, should have been easy prey to the unscrupulous is within reason. Still the impartial historian will indite that, for all that dark and bloody night of reconstruction through which they passed, the record of their crime and peculation will "pale its ineffectual rays" before the blistering blasts of official corruption, murder,

and lynching that has appalled Christen-
dom since the government of these Southern States has been assumed by their
wealth and intelligence. The abnormal
conditions that prevailed during reconstruction naturally produced hostility to
all who supported Federal authority,
among whom the Negro, through force of
circumstances, was prominent and most
vulnerable for attack, suffered the most
physically, and subsequently became easy
prey for those who would profit by his disfranchisement.

The attempt to justify this and condone
this refusal to allow the colored American
exercise of civil and constitutional rights
is based on caste, hatred, and alleged ignorance—conditions that are world-wide—
and the measure of a people's Christianity
and the efficiency of republican institutions can be accurately determined by the
humanity and zeal displayed in their amelioration, not in the denial of the right, but
zealous tuition for its proper exercise.

During the civil war the national conscience, hitherto sluggish, was awakened
and great desire prevailed to award the
race the full meed of civil and political
rights, both as a measure of justice and recognition of their fealty and bravery in support of the national arm.

The Freedman's Bureau, Christian and
other benevolent agencies were inaugurated to fit the freedman for the new obligations. Handicapped as he has been in

many endeavors, his record has been inspiring. Four-fifths of the race for generations legally and persistently forbidden to
learn to read or write; with labor unrequited, a conservative estimate, in 1898,
little more than three decades from slavery, finds 340,000 of their children attending 26,300 schools and their property val-
uation $750,000,000, while in learned pro-
fessions, journalism, and mercantile pursuits their ability and efficiency command
the respect and praise of the potential
race.

When the amendments were being considered, opinion differed as to the bestowal of the franchise; many favored only
those who could read and write. The popularity of this phase of opinion was voiced
in the following interview with Hon.
Schuyler Colfax, afterward Vice President, who was at that time Speaker of the
lower house of Congress, and was said to
have the "Presidential bee in his bonnet."
While "swinging around the circle he
touched at Victoria, and the British Colonist of July 29, 1865, made the following
mention: "A committee consisting of Ab-
ner Francis and M. W. Gibbs called on
Hon. _Schuyler Colfax, Speaker of the
House of Representatives of the United
States, yesterday morning. On being introduced by the American Consul, Mr.
Gibbs proceeded to say that they were
happy to meet him and tender him on behalf of the colored residents of Vic

toria their esteem and regard. They were not unacquainted with the noble course he had pursued during the great struggle in behalf of human liberty in the land of their nativity. They had watched with intense interest the progress of the rebellion and rejoiced in the Federal success and sorrowed in its adversity. Now that victory had perched on the national standard—a standard we believe henceforth and forever consecrated to impartial liberty—they were filled with joy unspeakable. And he would allow them to say that it had afforded them the greatest pleasure to observe the alacrity with which the colored men of the nation offered and embraced the opportunity to manifest their devotion and bravery in support of the national cause.

They had full confidence in the magnanimity of the American people that in the reconstruction of the seceded States they would grant the race who had proved their claim by the most indisputable heroism and fidelity, equality before the law, upon the ground of immutable justice and importance of national safety. Without trespassing further on his valuable time they would only tender him, as the distinguished Speaker of the popular house of Congress, as well as the sterling friend of freedom, their sincere respect and esteem.

Mr. Colfax, in reply, said he was truly glad to see and meet the committee and felt honored by the interview.

For himself he had ever been an enemy of slavery. From his earliest recollections he had ever used his influence against it to the extent of his power; but its abolition was environed by so many difficulties that it seemed to require the overruling hand of God to consummate its destruction. And he did not see how it could have been brought about so speedily but for those who desired to perpetuate it by raising rebellious hands against the nation. Now, with regard to the last sentiment expressed, concerning reconstruction, he would say that it was occupying the earnest attention of the best and purest minds of the nation. Most men were in favor of giving the ballot to colored men; the question was to what extent it should be granted. Very many good men were disposed to grant it indiscriminately to the ignorant as well as the more intelligent. For himself he was not, but among the other class. If colored men generally were as intelligent as the gentleman who had honored him with this interview—for he considered the speech he had just listened to among the best he had heard on the coast—there would be no trouble; but slavery had made that impossible. He knew that the President—decidedly an anti-slavery man—was not in favor of bestowing the franchise on all alike, while Charles Sumner and others favored it.

The honorable gentleman closed his remarks by desiring the colored people not to consider the Administration inimical to their welfare, if in the adjustment the right of suffrage was not bestowed on all, for it was probable that reading and writing would be the qualification demanded. He paid a high tribute to the colored people of Washington, D. C., for their intelligence, moral worth, and industry, and said that it was probable that the problem of suffrage would be solved in the District of Columbia. After a desultory conversation on phases of national status succeeding the rebellion, both parties seeming well pleased with the meeting, the committee retired."

I did not then, nor do I now, agree with the views of that distinguished statesman. The benignity of the ballot lies in this: It was never devised for the protection of the strong, but as a guardian for the weak. It is not true that a sane man, although unlettered, has not a proper conception of his own interests and what will conserve them —what will protect them and give the best results for his labor. You may fool him some of the time, as you do the most astute, but he will be oftener found among those of whom Lincoln said "You could not fool all the time." William Lloyd Garrison, jr., "a worthy son of a noble sire," pointedly says: "Whoever laments the scope of suffrage and talks of disfranchising men on account of ignorance or poverty has as little comprehension of the meaning of self-government as a blind

man has of the colors of the rainbow. I
declare my belief that we are suffering not
from a too extended ballot, but from one
too limited and unrepresentative. We
enunciate a principle of government, and
then deny its practice. If experience has
established anything, it is that the interest
of one class is never safe in the hands of
another. There is no class so poor or ignorant in a Republic that it does not know
its own suffering and needs better than the
wealthy and educated classes. By the rule
of justice it has the same right precisely to
give them legal expression. That expression is bound to come, and it is wisest for it
to come through the ballot box than
through mobs and violence born of a feeling of misery and despair."

James Russell Lowell has said: "The
right to vote makes a safety valve of every
voter, and the best way to teach a man
to vote is to give him a chance to practice.
It is cheaper, too, in the long run to lift
men up than to hold them down. The ballot in their hands is less dangerous than a
sense of wrong in their heads."

BISHOP ALEXANDER WALTERS.

Born in Kentucky, August, 1858—Educated in the Common Schools of that State
—At Thirty-five Elected Bishop of the A. M. E. Zion Church, Taking
High Rank as a Theologian, Originator and First President
of the National Afro American Council - Thinker,
Orator and Leader.

CHAPTER IX.

Among the estimable friendships I made on the Pacific Coast forty years ago was Philip A. Bell, formerly of New York City, one of nature's noblemen, broad in his humanity and intellectually great as a journalist. As editor of The Elevator, a weekly newspaper still published in San Francisco, he made its pages brilliant with scintillations of elegance, wealth of learning, and vigor of advocacy. To his request for a correspondent I responded in a series of letters. I forbear to insert them here, as they describe the material and political status of British Columbia thirty-five years ago—being well aware that ancient history is not the most entertaining. But, as I read them I cannot but note, in the jollity of their introduction, the immature criticism, consciousness of human fallability, broadening of conclusions, mellowed by hope for the future that seemed typical of a life career. Like the horse in "Sheridan's Ride," their beginning "was gay, with Sheridan fifty miles away;" but if they were helpful with a truth-axiom or a moiety of inspiration—as a view of colonial conduct of a nation, with which we were then and are now growing in affinity—the purpose was attained.

At first the affairs of British Columbia and Vancouver were administered by one Governor, the connection was but nominal; Vancouver Island had control by a representative Parliament of its own; the future seemed auspicious. Later they, feeling it "in fra dig" to divide the prestige of government, severed the connection. But Vancouver finding it a rather expensive luxury, and that the separation engendered strife and rivalry, terminating in hostile legislation, determined to permanently unite with British Columbia.

But alas, for political happiness. Many afterward sighed for former times, when Vancouver Island, proud beauty of the North, sat laving her feet in the genial waters of the Pacific, her lap verdant with beautiful foliage and delicious fruits; her head raised with peerless majesty to brilliant skies, while sunbeams playing upon a brow encircled by eternal snows reflected a sheen of glorious splendor; when, conscious of her immense wealth in coal, minerals, and fisheries, her delightful climate and geographical position, she bid for commercial supremacy. It is said of States, as of women, they are "fickle, coy and hard to please." For, changed and governed from England's Downing Street, "with all its red tape circumlocution," "Tile Barncal," incapacity, and "how-not-to-do-it" ability that attached to that venerable institution, its people were sorely perplexed. During the discussion which the nature and inefficiency of the Government evoked several modes of relief from these embarrassments were warmly espoused, among them none more prominent than annexation to the United States. It was urged with much force that the great want of the country, immigration and responsible government, would find their fulfillment in such an alliance. All that seemed wanted was the "hour and the man." The man was considered present in Leonard McClure, editor of a local, and afterward on the editorial staff of the San Francisco Times. He was a man of rare ability, a terse writer, and with force of logic labored assiduously to promote annexation. But the "hour" was "non est." For while it was quite popular and freely discussed upon the forum and street, influential classes declined to commit themselves to the scheme, the primary step necessary before presentation to the respective Governments. Among the opposition to annexation, naturally, were the official class. These gentry being in no way responsible to the people, an element ever of influence, and believing that by such an alliance they would find their "occupation gone," gave it no quarter. Added to these was another possessed of the prestige and power that wealth confers—very conservative, timid, cautious, self-satisfied, and dreading innovations of popular rule, but especially republicanism. Amid these two classes, and sprinkled among the rank and file, was found a sentiment extremely patriotic, with those who saw nothing worth living for outside of the purview of the "tight little island."

There seems a destiny in the propriety of territory changing dominion. God seems to have given this beautiful earth, with its lands, to be utilized and a source of blessing, not to be locked by the promptings of avarice nor the clog of incapacity; that it should be occupied by those who, either by the accident of locality or superior ability, can make it the most efficient in development. There should be, and usually is, regard for acquired rights, save in the case of Africans, Indians, or other weak peoples, when cupidity and power hold sweet converse. Nor should we slightly estimate the feeling of loyalty to the land of birth and the hearths of our fathers, the impulse that nerves the arm to strike, and the soul to dare; that brings to our country's altar all that we have of life to repel the invader of our homes or the usurper of our liberties. That has given to the world a Washington, a Toussant, a Bozzaris—a loyalty that will ever stand with cloven helmet and crimson battle-ax in the van of civilization and progress. But, like other ennobling sentiments, it can be perverted, allowing it to permeate every view of government, finding its ultimatum in the conclusion that, if government is despotic or inefficient, it is to be endured and not removed. Such patriots are impressed with the conviction that the people were made for governments, and not governments for the people. A celebrated poet has said—

"Our country's claim is fealty,
I grant you so; but then
Before man made us citizens
Great Nature made us men."

Men with essential wonts and laudable aspirations, the attainment of which can be accelerated by the fostering love and enlightened zeal of a progressive government.

In 1859 at Esquimault, the naval station for British Columbia, I had a pleasant meeting with Lady Franklin, widow of Sir John Franklin, the Arctic explorer, who sailed in 1845 and was supposed to have perished in 1847. With a woman's devotion, after many years of absence, she was still in quest, hoping, from ship officer or seaman of her Majesty's service, some ray of light would yet penetrate the gloom which surrounded his "taking off" in that terra incognito of the North pole, whose attraction for the adventurer in search of scientific and geographical data in the mental world is akin to its magnetic attraction in the physical. To her no tidings

(7)

came, but still lingered "hope, the balm
and life-blood of the soul."

In 1868 the union of British Columbia
with the Dominion of Canada was the political issue, absorbing all others. But the
allurements of its grandeur and the magnitude of promised results were insufficient
to allay opposition, ever encountered on
proposal to change a constitutional polity
by those at the time enjoying official honors or those who benefit through contracts
or trade, and are emphatic in their protest;
these, however, constitute an element that
is unwittingly the safety valve of constitutional government. Wherever the people rule the public welfare is ever endan-
gered whenever radical changes are to be
introduced, unaccompanied with a vigorous opposition. A healthy opposition is
the winnowing fan that separates the politician's chaff from the patriot's wheat, presenting the most desirable of the substantial element needed. At the convention in
1868 at Fort Yale, called by A. Decosmos,
editor of The British Colonist, and others,
for the purpose of getting an expression of
the people of British Columbia regarding
union with the Dominion of Canada (and
of which the writer was a delegate), the re-
duction of liabilities, the lessening of taxation, increase of revenue, restriction of expenditure, and the enlargement of the people's liberties were the goal, all of which
have been attained since entrance to the
Dominion, which has become a bright

jewel in his Majesty's Crown, reflecting a civilization, liberal and progressive, of a loyal, happy people.

The "British American Act," which created the Dominion of Canada, differs from the Constitution of the United States in important particulars. It grants to the Dominional, as well as the provincial Legislatures the "want of confidence principle," by which an objectionable ministry can be immediately removed; at the same time centralizing the national authority as a guard against the heresy of "State rights" superiority. Among the terms stipulated, the Dominion was to assume the colonial debt of British Columbia, amounting to over two million dollars; the building of a road from the Atlantic to the Pacific within a stipulated time. The alliance, however, contained more advantage than the ephemeral assistance of making a road or the assumption of a debt, for with confederation came the abolition of the "one-man system of government" and in its place a responsible one, with freedom of action for enterprise, legislation to encourage development, and assist budding industries; the permanent establishment of schools, and the disbursement of revenue in accordance with popular will.

It is ever and ever true that "right is of no sex, and truth of no color." The liberal ideas, ever struggling for utterance and ascendancy under every form of government, are not the exclusive property of any community or nation, but the heritage of mankind, and their victories are ever inspiring. For, as the traveler sometimes ascends the hill to determine his bearings, refresh his vision, and invigorate himself for greater endeavors, so we, by sometimes looking beyond the sphere of our own local activities, obtain higher views of the breadth and magnitude of the principles we cherish, and perceive that freedom's battle is identical wherever waged, whether her sons fight to abolish the relics of feudalism or to possess the ballot, the reflex influence of their example is mutually beneficial.

But of the Dominion of Canada, who shall write its "rise, decline, and fall?" Springing into existence in a day, with a population of 4,000,000 people—a number larger than that possessed by the United States when they commenced their great career—its promise is pregnant with benign probabilities. May it be the fruition of hope that the banner of the Dominion and the flag of our Republic, locked and interlocked, may go forward in generous rivalry to bless mankind.

The most rapid instrumentalities in the development of a new country are the finding and prospecting for mineral deposits. The discovery of large deposits of gold in the quartz and alluvial area of British Columbia in 1858 was the incipiency of the growth and prosperity it now enjoys. But although the search for the precious is alluring, the mining of the grosser metals and minerals, such as iron, lead, coal, and others, are much more reliable for substantial results.

The only mine of importance in British Columbia previous to 1867 was at Naniamo, where there was a large output of bituminous coal. In that year anthracite was discovered by Indians building fire on a broken vein that ran from Mt. Seymour, on Queen Charlotte Island, in the North Pacific. It was a high grade of coal, and on account of its density and burning without flame, was the most valuable for smelting and domestic purposes. A company had been formed at Victoria which had spent $60,000 prospecting for an enduring and paying vein, and thereafter prepared for development by advertising for tenders to build railroad and wharfs for shipping. Being a large shareholder in the company, I resigned as a director and bid. It was not the lowest, but I was awarded the contract. The Hudson Bay Co. steamship Otter, having been chartered January, 1869, with fifty men, comprising surveyor, carpenters, blacksmiths, and laborers, with timber, rails, provisions, and other necessaries for the work I embarked at Victoria. Queen Charlotte Island was at that time almost a "terra incognito," sparsely inhabited solely by scattered tribes of Indians on the coast lines, which were only occasionally visited by her Majesty's ships for discovery and capture of small craft engaged in the whisky trade.

Passing through the Straits of Georgia, stopping at Fort Simpson, and then to Queen Charlotte Island, entering the mouth of Skidegate River, a few miles up, we reached the company's quarters, consisting of several wooden buildings for residence, stores, shops, etc. At the mouth and along the river were several Indian settlements, comprising huts, the sides of which were of rough riven planks, with roof of leaves of a tough, fibrous nature. At the crest was an opening for the escape of smoke from fires built on the ground in the center of the enclosure. As the ship passed slowly up the river we were hailed by the shouting of the Indians, who ran to the river side, got into their canoes and followed in great numbers until we anchored. They then swarmed around and over the ship, saluting the ship's company as "King George's men," for such the English are known and called by them. They were peaceful and docile, lending ready hands to our landing and afterward to the cargo. I was surprised, while standing on the ship, to hear my name called by an Indian in a canoe at the side, coupled with encomiums of the native variety, quite flattering. It proved to be one who had been a domestic in my family at Victoria. He gave me kind welcome, not to be ignored, remembering that

I was in "the enemy's country," so to speak. Besides, such a reception was so much the more desirable, as I was dependent upon native labor for excavating and transportation of heavy material along the line of the road. While their work was not despatched with celerity of trained labor, still, as is general with labor, they earned all they got. "One touch of nature makes the whole world kin." I found many apt, some stupid; honesty and dishonesty in usual quantities, with craft peculiar to savage life.

Their mode of stealing by stages was peculiar. The thing coveted was first hid nearby; if no inquiry was made for a period deemed sufficiently long the change of ownership became complete and its removal to their own hut followed, to be disposed of when opportunity offered. If you had a particle of evidence and made a positive accusation, with the threat of "King George's man-of-war," it was likely to be forthcoming by being placed secretly nearby its proper place. But through it we see the oneness of human frailty, whether in the watered stock of the corporation or that of its humble servitor the milkman, there is kinship. To get something for nothing is the "ignis fatuus" ever in the lead. My experience during a year's stay on the island, and constant intercourse with the natives, impressed me more and more with the conviction that we are all mainly the creatures of environments; yet through all the strata and fiber of human nature there is a chord that beats responsive to kindness —a "language that the dumb can speak, and that the deaf can understand."

The English mode of dealing with semi-civilized dependents is vastly different from ours. While vigorously administering the law for proper government, protection of life, and suppression of debauchery by un-scrupulous traders, they inspired respect for the laws and the love of their patrons. Uprisings and massacres among Indians in her Majesty's dominions are seldom, if ever, to be chronicled. Many of our Indian wars will remain a blot on the page of im-partial history, superinduced, as they were, by wanton murder or the covet of lands held by them by sacred treaties, which should have been as sacredly inviolate. Fol-lowed by decimation of tribes by toleration of the whisky trade and the conveyance of loathsome disease. The climate of the island was much more pleasant than expected. The warm ocean currents on the Pacific temper the atmosphere, rendering it more genial than the same degree of latitude on the Atlantic. A few inches of snow, a thin coat of ice on the river, were the usual attendants of winter. But more frequently our camp was overhung by heavy clouds, broken by Mt. Seymour, precipitating much rain.

After being domiciled we proceeded with the resident superintendent to view

HON. HENRY P. CHEATHAM,

Late Recorder of Deeds for the District of Columbia.
Born in North Carolina Forty Odd Years Ago—Educated in Public Schools and
"Shaw University"—Register of Deeds for his County—Elected to the
Fifty-first and Fifty-second Congress—Able and Progressive.

the company's property, comprising several thousand acres. Rising in altitude, and on different levels, as we approached Mt. Seymour, croppings of coal were quite frequent, the broken and scattered veins evidencing volcanic disturbance. The vein most promising was several hundred feet above the level of the sea, and our intended wharf survey was made, which showed heavy cuttings and blasting to obtain grade for the road. The work was pushed with all the vigor the isolated locality and climatic conditions allowed. Rain almost incessant was a great impediment, as well as were the occasional strikes of the Indian labor, which was never for more wages, but for more time. The coal from the croppings which had been at first obtained for testing, had been carried by them in bags, giving them in the "coin of the realm" so many pieces of tobacco for each bag delivered on the ship. There was plenty of time lying around on those trips, and they took it. On the advent of the new era they complained that "King George men" took all the time and gave them none, so they frequently quit to go in quest. The nativity of my skilled labor was a piece of national patchwork—a composite of the canny Scotch, the persistent and witty Irish, the conservative but indomitable English, the effervescent French, the plegmatic German, and the irascible Italian. I found this variety beneficial, for the usual national and race bias was sufficiently in evidence to preclude a combination to retard the work. I had three Americans, that were neither white nor colored; they were born black; one of them—Tambry, the cook—will ever have my grateful remembrance for his fatherly kindness and attention during an illness.

The conditions there were such that threw many of my men off their feet. Women and liquor had much the "right of way." I was more than ever impressed with the belief that there was nothing so conclusive to a worthy manhood as self-restraint, both morally and physically, and the more vicious and unrestraining the environment the greater the achievement. Miners had been at work placing many tons of coal at the mouth of the mine during the making of the road, the grade of which was of two elevations, one from the mine a third of the distance, terminating at a chute, from which the coal fell to cars on the lower level, and from thence to the wharf. After the completion of the road and its acceptance by the superintendent and the storage of a cargo of coal on the wharf, the steamer Otter arrived, was loaded, and despatched to San Francisco, being the first cargo of anthracite coal ever unearthed on the Pacific seaboard. The superintendent, having notified the directors at Victoria of his intention to return they had appointed me to assume the office. I was so engaged, preparing for the next shipment on the steamer.

CHAPTER X.

My sojourn on the island was not without its vicissitudes and dangers, and one of the latter I shall ever remember—one mingled, as it was, with antics of Neptune, that capricious god of the ocean, and resignation to what seemed to promise my end with all sublime things. The stock of oil brought for lubricating cars and machinery having been exhausted, I started a beautiful morning in a canoe with three Indians for their settlement at the mouth of Skidegate River for a temporary supply. After a few hours' paddling, gliding down the river serenely, the wind suddenly arose, increasing in force as we approached the mouth in the gulf. The high walls of the river sides afforded no opportunity to land. The storm continued to increase in violence, bringing billows of rough sea from the ocean, our canoe dancing like a feather, one moment on a high crest by its skyward leap, and in the next to an abyss deep, with walls of sea on either side, shutting out a view of the horizon, while I, breathless with anxious hope, waited for the succeeding wave to again lift the frail bark. The better to preserve

the equilibrium of the canoe—a conveyance treacherous at the best—wrapped in
a blanket in the bottom of the canoe I laid,
looking into the faces of the Indians, con-
torted by fright, and listened to their peculiar and mournful death wail, "while the
gale whistled aloft his tempest tune. "

I afterward learned that they had a su-
perstition based upon the loss of many of
their tribe under like conditions, that escape was impossible. The alarm and distrust in men, aquatic from birth, in their
own waters was to me appalling. I seemed
to have "looked death in the face"—and
what a rush of recollections that had been
long forgotten, of actions good and bad,
the latter seeming the most, hurried, serried, but distinct through my excited brain;
then a thought, bringing a calm content,
that "To every man upon this earth death
cometh soon or late;" and with a fervent
resignation of myself to God and to what I
believed to be inevitable; then a lull in the
wind, and, after many attempts, we were
able to cross the mouth of the river to the
other side—the place of destination.

In 1869 I left Queen Charlotte Island
and returned to Victoria; settled my business preparatory to joining my family, then
at Oberlin, Ohio. It was not without a
measure of regret that I anticipated my
departure. There I had lived more than a
decade; where the geniality of the climate
was excelled only by the graciousness of
the people; there unreservedly the frater-

nal grasp of brotherhood; there I had received social and political recognition;
there my domestic ties had been intensified
by the birth of my children, a warp and
woof of consciousness that time cannot
obliterate. Then regret modified, as love
of home and country asserted itself.

"Breathes there a man with soul so dead
  Who never to himself hath said:
    'This is my native land'—
  Whose heart has not within him burned
  As homeward footsteps he has turned
  From wandering on a foreign strand?"

En route my feelings were peculiar. A
decade had pasesd, fraught with momentous results in the history of the nation.
I had left California disfranchised and my
oath denied in a "court of justice" (?); left
my country to all appearances enveloped
in a moral gloom so dense as to shut out
the light of promise for a better civil and
political status. The star of hope glim-
mered but feebly above the horizon of contumely and oppression, prophetic of the
destruction of slavery and the enfranchisement of the freedman. I was returning,
and on touch of my country's soil to have
a new baptism through the all-pervading
genius of universal liberty. I had left politically ignoble; I was returning pano-
plied with the nobility of an American citizen. Hitherto regarded as a pariah, I had
neither rejoiced at its achievement nor sor-

rowed for its adversity; now every patriotic pulse beat quicker and heart throb warmer, on realization that my country gave constitutional guarantee for the common enjoyment of political and civil liberty, equality before the law—inspiring a dignity of manhood, of self-reliance and opportunity for elevation hitherto unknown.

Then doubt, alternating, would present the immense problems awaiting popular solution. Born in the seething cauldron of civil war, they had been met in the arena of fervid Congressional debate and political conflict. The amendments to the Constitution had been passed, but was their inscription a record of the crystallization of public sentiment? Subsequent events have fully shown that only to the magnanimity and justice of the American people and the fruition of time can they be commended. Not to believe that these problems will be rightfully solved is to doubt not only the efficacy of the basic principles of our Government, but the divinity of truth and justice. To these rounds of hope's ladder, while eager in obtaining wisdom, the Negro should cling with tenacity, with faith "a higher faculty than reason" unconquerable.

Having resolved to locate in some part of the South for the purpose of practicing law, I had while in Victoria read the English Common Law, the basis of our country's jurisprudence, under Mr. Ring, an English barrister. Soon after my arrival in Oberlin, Ohio, where my family, four years before, had preceded me, I entered the law department of an Oberlin business college, and after graduation proceeded South, the first time since emancipation. In an early chapter I described my first contact with and impressions of slavery, when a lad; then the hopelessness of abject servitude and consciousness of unrequited toil had its impress on the brow of the laborer. Now cheerfulness, a spirit of industry, enterprise, and fraternal feeling replaced the stagnant humdrum of slavery. Nor was progress observable only among the freedmen. Many evidences of kindness and sympathy were shown and expressed by former owners for the moral and mental advancement of their former bondsmen, which, to a great degree, unfortunately, was counterbalanced by violence and persecution.

My brother, Jonathan C. Gibbs, was then Secretary of State of Florida, with Governor Hart as executive. He had had the benefit of a collegiate education, having graduated at Dartmouth, New Haven, and had for some years filled the pulpit as a Presbyterian minister. The stress of reconstruction and obvious necessity for ability in secular matters induced him to enter official life. Naturally indomitable, he more than fulfilled the expectations of his friends and supporters by rare ability as a thinker and speaker, with unflinching fidelity to his party principles. I found him at Tallahassee, the capital, in a well-appointed residence, but his sleeping place in the attic contracted, and, as I perceived, considerable of an arsenal. He said that for better vantage it had been his resting place for several months, as his life had been threatened by the "Ku Klux," that band of midnight assassins whose deeds of blood and carnage darken so many pages of our national history, and was the constant terror of white and black adherents to the national Government's policy of enfranchisement. He was hopeful of better conditions in Florida, and introduced me to Governor Hart. Both urged me to locate in the State, promising me their support. I highly appreciated the affection of the one and the proffered friendship of the other. But the feeling paramount was that my brother had "won his spurs" by assiduity and fidelity through the scathing and fiery ordeal of those troublesome times; that it would ill become me to profit or serenely rest beneath the laurels he had won. It was the last interview or sight of my brother. Subsequently after a three hours' speech, he went to his office and suddenly died of apoplexy.

I continued my tour of observation, and, having been appointed a delegate from Ohio to a national convention to be held in Charleston, South Carolina, I attended. It was the first assembly of the kind at which I had been present since emancipation. I had hitherto met many conventions of colored men having for their object the amelioration of oppressive conditions. This gathering was unlike any similar meeting. The deliberations of the convention presented a combination of a strong intellectual grasp of present needs and their solution, with much uninformed groping and strife for prominence, features of procedure I have observed not confined to Negro assemblies.

The majority were unlettered, but earnest in their mental toiling for protection to life and equality before the law. Hitherto the purpose had been to make earnest appeals to the law-making power for such legislation as would abolish slavery and award equal justice—the first supported by the national conscience, but mainly as a military necessity, was a "fait accompli;" the other had been legislatively awarded, but for its realization much more was necessary than its simple indentification on the statute books of a nation, when public sentiment is law. More than a third of a century has now passed, enabling a view more dispassionate and accurate of the conditions surrounding the freedmen directly after emancipation and the instrumentalities designed for fitting him for citizenship.

It is not surprising, neither is he blameworthy, if in the incipiency of joy for freedom bestowed he could not properly estimate the factors necessary to form an homogenous citizenship. The ways for two

(8)

centuries had been divergent paths. The dominant claiming and exercising, as an heirloom, every civil and political right; the subordinate, with knowledge the most meager of their application or limits, by compulsion was made to concede the claim. Neither is it singular that participation in the exercise of these rights by the freedman should have created a determined opposition in a majority of the former, who claimed their fitness to rule as the embodiment of the wealth and intelligence (which are generally the ruling factors worldwide), and would have at an early date derived a just "power from the consent of the governed," did not history record the unnecessary and inhuman means resorted to to extort it, the obliquity of which can be erased only by according him the rights of an American citizen. Mutual hostility, opposition on the one hand to the assumption and exercise of these rights, and consequent distrust by the freedman, often fostered by unscrupulous leaders, have been alike detrimental to both classes, but especially so to the Negro, for his constant need in the Southland is the cordial friendship and helping hand of "his brother in white." He deserves it for his century of unrequited labor in peace and in war for fidelity to the tender ties committed to his care. Anti-revolutionist in his nature, he will continue to merit it and possibly save the industrial life in the South in the coming conflict of capital and labor.

That, as a class, they are in antagonism
to the prevailing political sentiment is the
legitimate result of the manner of their
emancipation and a commendable gratitude and kinship for the party through
which they obtained their freedom. But
Gibbon, in his "Decline and Fall of Rome,"
has said that "gratitude is expensive," and
so the Negro has found it, and is beginning
to echo the sentiment and would gladly
hail conditions and opportunity where he
could, after thirty-five years of blood and
fidelity, be less partisan and more frater
nal politically, conscious his united affiliation with his early alliance, and consequent ostracism of the opposition has
given him a "hard road to travel." Commendable as has been his devotion, he finds
commendation a limited currency and not
negotiable for the protection and benefits
that should accompany the paladium of
citizenship. While his treatment by the
Democratic party has made a continuous
political relation compulsory, it is unfortunate; for the political affinity of no other
class of American citizens is judged by the
accident of birth. It is detrimental to the
voter whose proclivity is thereby determined. Wherever the Negro vote, in the
estimation of any party, is an uncertain
quantity, its value as a factor will have increased, consolidated, and in numbers con-
trolling, it has been considered a menace
and vigorously eliminated.

This view has to an extent an auxiliary in certain Republican circles, where it is avowed that the party could get in the South a large accession of hitherto Democratic voters, giving it a commanding influence, but for its colored contingent, which is averred to be repellant. There may be difference of opinion as to the merit of such conclusions and the fitness of their rehearsal "to the marines;" but none as to the measure of welcome of those that hold them. However, given that they are correct. Self-respect and a desire to help the old party can go hand in hand, and when possible in a manly way, room should be made for such anticipated accession.

There is another phase of present conditions that deserves, and I have no doubt has claimed, attention. It is the emphatic trend of the national leaders of the party to conciliate the hitherto discordant elements in the South in the interest of national harmony, an object lesson of which was presented by the late President on his Southern tour. But few years have elapsed since no man seeking a renomination on the Republican ticket would have put on and worn a Confederate badge. This President McKinley did, receiving the indiscriminate applause and the concurrence of his own party. Such an act, which is not only allowable, but commendable, would formerly have been political suicide. This being a movement in the house of his political alliance, it is up to the Negro to consider which is his best interest, should the olive branch of political friendship be extended by those from whom he receives his chief support. Under like conditions, his white brother would have no hesitancy.

There is yet another phase which indicates the Negro in jeopardy on industrial lines. A few years hence the South will have ceased to be chiefly agricultural. Mills for cotton, iron, and other factories will have dotted hilltop and valley, and with them will come the Northern operative with his exclusive "unions" and trade prejudice, shutting the doors of mills and foundries against him. To meet this scramble for favor from the wealth and intelligence of the Southland —the ruling factors—he should avail himself of every appliance for fostering harmony and co-operation along all the lines of contact. In slavery and in his subsequent journey in freedom he has suffered much. But what nation or people have escaped that ordeal who have made mark in the world's history? There is now prospective unfriendly legislation in several Southern States; also the lowest of the whites, as they deem occasion may require, go, often undisturbed, on shooting and lynching expeditions.

The problem that continues to force itself for solution is, How the innocent are to receive immunity from these outrages or a fair trial, when accused of crime.

These being under the purview of State
sovereignty, the Federal arm is not only
powerless, but there exists no Northern
sentiment favoring drastic means for their
correction.   Hence it is evident that relief
can only come from those who fashion the
sentiment that crystallizes into law.   But
with the bitter is mingled the sweet; much
of his advancement along educational and
material lines is due to the liberality of the
white people of the South, who, it has been
computed, have contributed one hundred
millions of dollars since emancipation by
taxes and donations for his education, and
there are many evidences that the best
thought of the South is in line with Negro
employment and his educational advancement in the belief that the more general
the intelligence the greater the State's
progress, morally and materially.   This
conviction was emphatically expressed by
an overwhelming negative vote in the Arkansas Legislature recently, where a measure was introduced to abandon him to his
own taxable resources for education.   The
ratio of his moral and material product
will be the measure of his gratitude for
this great boon.   For, after all, many of
"our great dangers are not from without."

General ——, a leading Democrat of this
State, and an unmistakable friend of the
negro, referring to the above evidence of
good feeling, said he did not see why I,
and other reputed leaders, in view of such
evidences of friendship, did not induce our

EDWARD E. COOPER.
Editor and Publisher of "Colored American," Washington, D. C.

Founder of "Colored World" and "Indianapolis Freeman" Conspicuous as a
Leader and Enterprising as a Journalist.

people to be fraternal politically. I replied that the effort had once been made, but that the Democratic party, intrenched as it was in large majorities in the South, "by ways that are dark and tricks that are vain," its leaders say they "do not need, neither do they solicit, the colored vote; but if they choose, they may so vote." He said that certainly had a ringing sound of independence and was uninviting as an announcement—an independence, however, that will not forever outlive the vagaries of sound, for it is not unlikely that he will not only vote the ticket, but be earnestly solicited to do so. For it will happen, during the whirligig of time and action, in my party as well as others, that there will be a change of policies, new issues, local dissatisfaction, friction, contemplated antagonism and the political arithmetic sounded. But I cannot but believe that the clannishness of the Negro has been the boomerang that has knocked him out of much sympathy, being impractical as a political factor and out of harmony with the material policies of the Southern people."

I replied I had thought the highest ideal of patriotism was adherence to measures materially as well as politically that were for the benefit of the whole people.

He said: "I know your party preach that they have a monopoly of wisdom; but the fact is the wisest statesmen of the world are divided in opinion as to the benefits

claimed for the leading policies of your
party. But how do they benefit you, as a
dependent class? Your immediate need is
employment and good educational facilities. You should be less sentimental and
more practical. You may honestly believe
in a protective tariff, having for its object
the protection of the American working-
man, but does it help you when you know
that the doors of mills, foundries, and man-
ufactories are shut against you? As to
the currency, you are at a disadvantage
when you attempt to antagonize the financial views of your employers.

"It reminds me of an incident," he continued, "in my native town in Virginia, not
long after reconstruction. There had been
a drought and short crop, succeeded by a
pretty hard winter. My father, whose politics, you may well judge, I being 'a chip
of the old block,' without soliciting money
or favor, threw open his cellar, wherein
was stowed many bushels of sweet potatoes; invited all the destitute to come. It
is needless to say they came. In the spring
Tobey, the Negro minister of the Baptist
Church—a man illiterate, but with much
native sense—after morning service, said:
'Brethren, there's gwine to be a 'lection
here next week, and I wants you all to
vote in de light dat God has gin you to
see de light, but I spects to vote wid de
taters.' Now, this may seem ludicrous, but
Tobey, in that act, was a fit representative
of the white man in politics—for every

class of American citizens except the Negro divide their vote and put it where to them personally it will do the most good."

"Much," I replied, "that you have said is undoubtedly true. But can you wonder at the Negro's cohesion? Is it not a fact that his is the only class of citizens that your party deny equal participation in the franchise, and unjustly discriminate against in the application of the laws? Where better could a change of conduct which you would admire and he so happily embrace, be inaugurated than within your own political household; where could nobility of character be more grandly displayed than by the abolition of these vicious hindrances to the uplifting of the weak and lowly?"

"Be that as it may," he replied, "your race is not in a condition to make friends by opposing the prevailing local policies of their environments."

I have narrated this interview for the reason that it is a fitting type of the views of friends of the Negro of the South who somehow fail to see the difficulty in his fraternizing with them in the midst of so much political persecution and bodily outrage. I referred in the above interview to an effort of colored leaders to assimilate with Southern politics.

CHAPTER XI.

In 1876 (twenty-five years ago) I was President of a National Convention held at Nashville, Tenn, and of which H. V. Redfield, an able correspondent of the "Cincinnati Commercial," made the following unduly flattering mention: "Mifflin W. Gibbs, of Arkansas, was selected as President. It may be interesting to know that Gibbs is strongly in favor of Bristoe, now an aspirant for the Presidency. He will likely be a delegate from Arkansas to the National Republican Convention at Cincinnati. He is a lawyer, one of the foremost of his race in Arkansas. He is rather slender and a genteel-looking man, with something in his features that denotes superiority" ("Though poor in thanks," Redfield, yet I thank thee.) "His speech upon taking the chair, was another event. It was the third good speech of the day and calculated to leave the believers of internal inferiority in something of a muddle.

"He made a manly plea for equal rights for his race. All they wanted was an equal chance in the battle of life. They did not desire to hinder any man for exercising his political rights as he saw fit, and all they claimed was liberty of thought and action for themselves. He was sorry there was occasion for a convention of black men to consider black men's status. The fact alone was evidence that the race had not been accorded right and justice. Of the treatment of his race in Arkansas he had little to complain of, but spoke bitterly of the murders at Vicksburg, Miss. He gave the Republican party, as administered at Washington, several blows under the chin. He complained of bad treatment of colored men by that party, notwithstanding all its professions. He made the bold declaration that all the whites of the South need do to get their votes was to promise equal and exact justice and stand to it. All they wanted was their rights as American citizens and would go into the party that would secure them. He said the question primarily demanding the attention of the convention were educational and political, and he hoped the proceedings would be so orderly as to convince the whites present that we were capable of self-control. His speech had a highly independent flavor and the particular independent passages were applauded by whites and blacks alike."

While the call for the convention was not distinctly political, that feature of the proceedings was the most pronounced. For at that early day, through an experience the most bitter, the lesson had been learned that politics was not the panacea, but that our affiliation with the Repub-

lican party was the main offence. Hence
a disposition to fraternize with Southern
politicians for race protection and opportunity had many adherents, and voiced by
Governor Pinchback and other prominent
leaders in the South, who, while preferring
to maintain their fealty to the Republican
party, were willing to sacrifice that allegiance if they could secure protection and
improve conditions for the race. Had the
leaders of Southern opinion met these
overtures, even part of the way, much of
the friction and turbulence of subsequent
years would have been avoided. But that
there will be a breaking up of the political
solidarity of the South, not on sentimental
but on material lines, at no distant day
all signs promise, and be its status what it
may, the Negro will benefit by comming-
ling with the respective parties in political fellowship. Laying down the "old
grudge" at the door of opportunity and
entering, should the premises be habitable,
he could "report progress and ask leave to
sit again."

It has been alleged to the discredit of
the Negro that he too soon forgets an injury. Nevertheless as a virtue it should
redound to his credit. He is swift to forgive and, if necessary, apologize for the
shortcomings of his adversary. But human nature seldom appreciates forgive-
ness, preceded as it is by censure, the subject of which usually repels, and another
melancholy phase is often apparent, for the

pricks of conscience for those we have wronged, we seek solace by hating. There are in both parties a fraction of saints, who, notwithstanding his immense contribution by unrequited labor to the wealth of the nation whilst a slave; his fidelity and bravery in every war of the Republic, have for him neither care nor regard; denounce him as an incapable and a bad legacy. He should, nevertheless, be patient, diligent, and hopeful, with appreciation for his friends and for his enemies a consciuosness expressed in the Irishman's toast to the Englishman—

"Here's to you, as good as you are;
    And here's to me, as bad as I am;
But as good as you are,
    And as bad as I am,
I'm as good as you are,
    As bad as I am."

Very ill considered is the opinion held and advocated by some, that he should defer or eschew politics—who say: "Let the Negro be deprived of this right of citizenship until he learns how to exercise it with wisdom and discretion." As well say to the boy, Do not go into the water until you learn to swim! The highest type of civilization is the evolution of mistakes. While education, business, and skilled labor should have the right of way and be primarily cherished, his right to vote and persistent desire to exercise it should never be abandoned, for he will yet enjoy its fullest fruition all over this, our God-blessed land.

Among the delegates I met at the South Carolina convention in 1871 were the Hon. William H. Grey, H. B. Robinson, and J. H. Johnson, of Arkansas, prominent planters and leaders in that State. I was much impressed with the eloquence of Grey, and the practical ideas advanced by Robinson, the one charmed, the other convinced. Learning that I sought a desirable place to locate in the South, they were enthusiastic in describing the advantages held out by the State of Arkansas. The comparative infancy of its development, its golden prospects, and fraternal amenities. Crossing the Arkansas River in a ferry-boat, in May, 1871, I arrived in Little Rock a stranger to every inhabitant. It was on a Sunday morning. The air refreshing, the sun not yet fervent, a cloudless sky canopied the city; the carol of the canary and mocking bird from treetop and cage was all that entered a peaceful, restful quiet that bespoke a well-governed city. The chiming church bells that soon after summoned worshipers seemed to bid me welcome. The high and humble, in their best attire, wended their way to the respective places of worship.

Little Rock at that date, not unlike most Western cities in their infancy, and bid for immigration, was extensively laid out, but thinly populated,

having less than 12,000 inhabitants. From
river front to Twelfth Street, on the south,
and to Chester on the west, it was but
sparsely settled. The streets were unimproved, but the gradual rise from river
front gave a natural drainage. Residences
and gardens of the more prominent, on
the outskirts, gave token of culture and refinement. The nom de plume "City of
Roses" seemed fittingly bestowed, for with
trellis or encircling with shady bower, the
stately doorway of the wealthy, or the
cabin of the lowly could be seen the rose,
the honeysuckle, or other verdure of per-
fume and beauty, imparting a grateful fra-
grance, while "every prospect pleases."
My first impressions have not been less-
ened by lapse of time; generous nature has
enabled human appliance to make Little
Rock an ideal city.

As knowledge of the local status of
a State, as well as common law,
must precede admission to the bar, I
applied and was kindly permitted to enter the law office of Benjamin & Barnes,
at that time the only building on the
square now occupied by the postoffice and
the Allis Block. In this for preparatory
reading I was very fortunate. I not only
found an extensive law library, but the
kindness and special interest shown by
Sidney M. Barnes was of incalculable benefit. Mr. Barnes was an able jurist, one
of nature's noblemen, genial, generous,
and patriotic. A wealthy slaveholder in

Kentucky, when the note of civil war was
sounded, called together his slaves, gave
them their freedom, and at an early date
had them enrolled in the Federal army,
and went forth himself to fight for the
Union. James K. Barnes, his son, now a
prominent citizen of Fort Smith, and the
able United States Attorney for the Western district of Arkansas, and whose fellowship and kindness has extended through
all my political career in Arkansas, is "a
worthy son of a noble sire," having courage
of conviction and eloquence in their enunciation. Among the young men then practicing law was Lloyd G. Wheeler, a graduate from a law school in Chicago, popular
and an able lawyer, with considerable
practice. In 1872 we joined, under the firm
name of Wheeler & Gibbs, opening an office in the Old Bank Building, corner Center and Markam Streets.

It is not without considerable trepidation that an infant limb of the
law shies his castor into the ring,
puts up his shingle announcing that A,
B, or C is an "Attorney and Counsellor
at Law." His cerebral column stiffens as,
from day to day, he meets members of the
bar, who congratulate him upon his advent, and feels his importance as he waits
from day to day for the visit of his first
client, but collapses when he arrives and
with ghostly dread salutes him and pre
pares to listen with a disturbed sense of
an awful responsibility he is about to un-

HON. JUDSON W. LYONS.

Present Register of the Treasury.
Born in Georgia—A Graduate of Howard University— Appointed by President
McKinley to the Above Position.

dertake. For, side by side with his client's statements there seem to appear in stately majesty all the adjuncts of the law: First, the inquisitive glance of the judge, like a judicial searchlight, scans him as he rises to defend Mr. Only Borrow, charged with larceny. Will he be able to think on his feet at the bar as he did in his chair in his office? Will he succeed or fail in stating his case, with eye and ear of every veteran of the bar intent on his first utterance? How about the jury, that unknown quantity of capricious predilections? Will they give him attention, or will their eyes find a more congenial resting place? Unbidden, the panorama insists on prominence. He attempts the most nonchalant air, tells Mr. B. to proceed and state his case. This was not the first time that he had been requested to perform this incipient step of the law's demand, and he does it with such astuteness and flippancy, and how he had been wronged and persecuted by the plaintiff, that tears, unbidden, are ready to glisten in your eyes. Injured innocence and your sworn duty to your profession inspire courage and induce you to take his case. Later on the tyro will have learned that it was highly probable that Mr. B. would not have called on him but for the fact that he was not only out of cash, but out of credit with able and experienced practitioners.

At the time of my examination for entry to the bar by the committee,

(9)

of which William G. Whipple was
one, I was instructed that the most important acquisition for a member of the
bar was ability to secure his fee. Having
noted all the points of defence for his honesty, the last, but not the least matter to
be considered was the fee, resulting in an
exchange of promises and his departure.
When the case was called, for reasons not
divulged, the plaintiff failed to appear. Mr.
Borrow was acquitted; I won my case and
am still wooing my fee. The study of the
law is not solely of advantage to those who
intend adopting it as a profession, for its
fundamental principles are interwoven
with the best needs of mankind in all his
undertakings, making it of value to the
preacher or laymen, the merchant or politician. For the young man intending the
pursuit of the latter it is quite indispensable. The condition in the South for a
quarter of a century giving opportunity for
colored men to engage in the professions
has not been neglected. In each of the
States there are physicians and lawyers
practicing with more or less success. With
equality of standing as to culture, ability
and devotion, the doctor has had the advantage for a growing and lucrative practice. This can be accounted for partly on
account of the private administrations of
the one and the public career of the other.
The physicians has seldom contact with his
professional brother in white and escapes
much of the difficulty that lies in wait for
the colored disciple of Blackstone.

During my practice I found the judges
eminently fair in summing up the evidence
produced, noting the points and impartially charging the jurors, who were also
fair when plaintiff and defendant were of
the same race, but who, alas, too often,
when the case had been argued by, or the
issue was between the representatives of
the two races, bowed to the prevailing bias
in their verdict. Bishop, in his introduction to his "Criminal Law," has fittingly
said: "The responsibilities which devolve
on judicial tribunals are admitted. But a
judge sitting in court is under no higher
obligation to cast aside personal motives
and his likes and dislikes of the parties litigant, and to spurn the bribe if proffered
than any other official person acting under
a jurisdiction to enforce laws not judicial.
Happy will be the day when public virtue
exists otherwise than in name." It often
happens with cases commanding liberal
fees and where the litigant has high regard for the legal learning and ability of
the colored lawyer, yet conscious of this
hindrance to a successful issue of his case,
very naturally goes elsewhere for legal assistance. Hence, as an advocate not having inducement for continued research and
opportunity for application of the more intricate elements of the law, confined to
petty cases with corresponding fee, he is
handicapped in his effort to attain eminence as a jurist. It has been said that
great men create circumstances. But cir-

cumstances unavoidably produce great
men. Henry Drummond is quoted as saying: "No matter what its possibilities may
be, no matter what seeds of thought or virtue lie latent in its breast, until the ap-
propriate environment presents itself, the
correspondence is denied, the development
discouraged, the most splendid possibilities of life remain unrealized, and thought
and virtue, genius and art, are dead."

It should be the solemn and persistent
duty of the race to contend for every right
the Magna Charta of the Republic has granted them, but it might assuage the pang of
deprivation and stimulate opportunity did
he fully know the stages of savagery, slavery, and oceans of blood through which the
Anglo-Saxon passed to attain the exalted
position he now occupies. Much of the
jurisprudence we now have responding to
and crystallizing the best needs of humanity were garnered in this sanguine and
checkered career. It is said that the law
is a jealous mistress, demanding intense
and entire devotion and unceasing wooing
to succeed in winning her favor, or profit-
ing by her decrees. Yet, for student or layman, the study is instructive and ennobling. It is an epitome of ages of human conduct, the products, the yearnings,
and strivings of the human heart, as higher
conceptions of man's relation to his fellow
found echo or inscription in either the
common or written law. Locality, nationality, race, sex, religion, or social manner

may differ, but the accord of desire for civil liberty—the "torch lit up in the soul by the omnipotent hand of Deity itself"— is ever the same. Constitutional law "was not attained by sudden flight," but it is the product of reform, with success and restraint alternating through generations. It is the ripeness of a thousand years of ever-recurring tillage, blushing its scarlet rays of blood and conquest ante-dating historic "Runny Meade."

It is well to occasionally have such reminiscent thought; it makes us less pessimistic and gives life to strive and spirit and hope. We cannot unmake human nature, but can certainly improve conditions by self-denial, earnest thought, and wise action.

CHAPTER XII.

Previous to my resolve to settle in the South I had read and learned much of politics and politicians; the first as being environed by abnormal conditions unstable and disquieting—the class that had established and controlled the enonomy of the Southern States; had been deposed in the wage of sanguinary battle on many well contested fields—deposed by an opponent equally brave, and of unlimited resources; defeated, but unsubdued in the strength of conviction in the rightfulness of their cause. A submission of the hand but not of the heart. New constitutions granting all born beneath the flag equality of citizenship and laws in unison adopted, and new officers alien to local feeling were the executors.

It is unnecessary here to remark that if a succession of love feasts had been anticipated, they had been indefinitely postponed.

For the officers of the new system were by their whilom predecessors ordered to go "nor stand upon˙ the order of their going," the bullet at times conveying the order. Assassinations, lynchings, and re-

prisals by both parties to the feud were of
daily occurrence. The future for life, liberty, and pursuit of happiness in busy city
or sylvan grove, was not alluring. My subsequent career makes it necessary for me
to arise to explain. Taking at the time a
calm survey of the situation, an addition to
the column of martyrs seemed to me unnecessary. I believed in the principles of
the Republican party and as a private I
was willing to vote, work, and be slightly
crippled; but had not reached the bleeding
and dying point. With such conclusions I
resolved to come, and confine myself
to the pursuit of my profession and give
politics a "terrible letting alone." Oh, if
abandoned resolutions were a marketable
commodity, what emporium sufficiently capacious and who competent to classify!

The organization of the Republican party
of Arkansas was on the eve of disruption.
Its headquarters were in the building and
over the law office of Benjamin & Barnes,
with whom I was reading. Violent disputes as to party policy, leadership, and
the distribution of the plums of office
were of frequent occurrence. I very distinctly remember the day when the climax was reached and "the parting of the
ways" determined. The adherents of Senator Clayton and the State administration
on the one part, and Joseph Brooks and
his followers on the other, coming down
the stairs—some with compressed lip and
flashing eye, others as petulent as the chil-

dren who say: "I don't want to play in your yard; I don't like you any more." It was the beginning of the overt act that extinguished Republican rule in Arkansas. The factions led by Powell Clayton and Joseph Brooks, respectively, were known as the "Minstrels" and "Brindle Tails."

Incongruity, being the prevailing force, possibly accounted for the contrary character of the names, for there was little euphony in the minstrelsy of the one or a monopoly of brindle appearance in the other, for each faction's contingent, were about equally spotted with the sons of Ham. My friends, Benjamin & Barnes, were prominent as Brindles, and I, being to an extent a novice in the politics of the State, in a position to hear much of the wickedness of the Minstrels and but little of the "piper's lay" in his own behalf, fidelity to my friends, appalled at the alleged infamy of the other fellows, susceptible to encomiums which flattered ambition, I became a Brindle, and an active politician minus a lawyer.

In 1873 I was appointed County Attorney for Pulaski, and after a few months' service resigned to assume the office of Municipal Judge of the City of Little Rock, to which I had been elected. I highly appreciated this, as exceedingly complimentary from a population of 16,000, a large majority of which were not of my race. I entered upon and performed the duties of the office until

some time after the culmination of the
Brooks and Baxter war in the State.   It
having been announced that I was the first
of my race elected to such an office in the
United States, it was not without trepidation that I assumed the duties that the
confidence of my fellow citizens had imposed upon me for the novelty of such an
administration attracted attention.

A judge who has to deal with and inflict
penalties for violation of law consequent
upon the frailties and vices of mankind en-
counters much to soften or harden his humanity, which may have remained normal
but for such contact. His sworn duty to ad-
minister the law as he finds it often con-
flicts with a sense of justice implanted in
the human soul, of which the law, imperfect man has devised is often the imperfect vehicle for his guidance; but nevertheless to which his allegiance must be
paramount, even when attempting to temper justice with mercy.

Nowhere is so plainly presented as
many of the various lights and shadows of human character.   Love and
faithlessness, sincerity and deceit, nobility and dishonor, kindness and ingratitude, morality and vice—all the virtues and their antitheses take their place
at the bar of the court of justice and await
the verdict, while truth and deception
strive for conquest; an honest son of toil
arrested in a den of infamy whither he has
been decoyed and his week's earnings

filched; his wife in tears before you; the
clash of prejudice when the parties litigant were of opposite races; the favorable
expectation of the rich, prominent, and influential when confronted by the poor and
lowly; humble and conscientious innocence
appalled when rigid law would mulct them
in fine and imprisonment; the high and
the haughty incensed at discharge of the
obscure and indigent. In cases slight,
where the justice of leniency was apparent
and yet the mandates of the law had to
be enforced, I would pronounce the penalty and suspend the fine during good behavior. But if the culprit returned, mercy
was absent.

An incident in relation to the suspen-
sion of the fine will show that I did to
others as I would have others do to me:
A member of the court was at times irri-
table and vexations. During a session there
was a misunderstanding, which, upon
adjournment, growing in intensity, resulted
in my committing an assault. The chasm,
however, was soon bridged with mutual
pledges. Nevertheless I requested the
chief of police to have charge entered upon
docket, to come up at next session of court,
whereupon the judge, after expressing regret that the law had been violated, fined
Citizen Gibbs and suspended the fine dur
ing good behavior, and, as the citizen was
not again arraigned, it may be presumed
that his conduct was reasonably good, however doubtful may be the presumption.

I was fortunate in having the confidence
of the community, always an important adjunct to the bench, for it is not always that
the executor of the law has to deal with
the humble of no repute. An old resident,
wealthy and prominent, was arrested and
was to appear before me for trial. During the interim it was several times suggested to me in a friendly way that I had
better give the case a letting alone by dismissal, as it would probably be personally
dangerous to enforce the law, as he was
known to be impulsive and at times violent. I heard the case, which had aggra-
vated features, together with resisting and
assaulting an officer, and imposed the highest penalty provided by law. Those who
had thought that such action would give
offence little knew the man. It being the
last case on the docket for the day, de-
scending from the bench and passing, I
saluted him, which he pleasantly returned,
without a murmur as to the justice of the
fine. Subsequently, on several occasions,
he placed me under obligations to him for
favors. Personally, insignificant as I may
have been to him, he recognized in me for
the time being a custodian of the majesty
of the law, which he knew he had violated.
When it shall happen as a rule and not as
the exception that men will esteem, applaud and sustain the honest administration of the law, irrespective of the administrator, a great step will have been taken
toward a better conservation of constitu-

tional liberty. In Arkansas the political cauldron continued to boil. In Powell Clayton were strongly marked the elements of leadership, fidelity to friends, oratorical power, honesty of purpose, courage of conviction, with unflinching determination to enforce them. The late Joseph Brooks, an ex-minister of the Methodist Church, and who secularized as a politician, was an orator to be reckoned with. Sincere, scathing, and impressive, his following was large and devoted. Senator Clayton, the present Ambassador to Mexico, has outlived the political bitterness that so long assailed him, and was lately guest of reception and banquet given him and largely attended by Democrats, chiefly his political opponents.

The divided Republicans held their State convention in 1872. The Clayton faction (the Minstrels) had for their nominee Elisha Baxter, a North Carolinian by birth, and hence to the Southern manor born. This, is was premised, would bring strength to the ticket. Joseph Brooks was the nominee of the Brindle wing of the party, and a battle royal was on. Although a minority of Democrats respectable in number joined the Brooks faction, the majority stood off with wish for "plague on both your houses," and awaited the issue. It was in my first of twenty-eight years of recurrent canvassing. Many districts of the State at that time being destitute of contact by railroads, made wagon and buggy travel a necessity.

HON. POWELL CLAYTON.
Embassador to Mexico.

Governor of Arkansas—United States Senator—Honest and Fearless, with a
Public and Private Life Beyond Reproach.

After nominations were made for the various State officers in convention, appointments were made and printed notices posted and read at church and schoolhouse neighborhoods, that there would be "speaking" at stated points.

The speakers, with teams and literature and other ammunition of political warfare known and "spiritually" relished by the faithful, would start at early morn from their respective headquarters on a tour of one or two hundred miles, filling ten or twenty appointments. Good judgment was necessary in the personal and peculiar fitness of the advocate. For he that could by historic illustration and gems of logic carry conviction in a cultured city would be "wasting his sweetness on the desert air" in the rural surroundings of the cabins of the lowly. I have heard a point most crudely stated, followed by an apposite illustrative anecdote, by a plantation orator silence the more profuse cultured and eloquent opponent.

As he was still at his lesson on the duties and responsibilities of citizenship, it was a study worthy the pencil of a Hogarth to watch the play of lineament of feature, while gleaning high ideals of citizenship and civil liberty amid the clash of debate of political opponents; cheerful acquiescence, cloudy doubt, hilarious belief, intricate perplexity, and want of comprehension by turns impressed the countenance. But trustful in the sheet anchor of liberty, they were worthy students, who strove to merit the great benignity. Canvassing was not without its humorous phases during the perilous times of reconstruction. The meetings, often in the woods adjoining church or schoolhouse, were generally at a late hour, the men having to care for their stock, get supper, and come often several miles; hence it was not unusual for proceedings to be at their height at midnight. I was at such a gathering in the lower part of the State, where Jack Agery, a noted plantation orator, was holding forth, denouncing the Democracy and rallying the faithful. He was a man of great natural ability and bristling with pithy anecdote. From a rude platform half a dozen candles flickered a weird and unsteady glare. Agery as a spellbinder was at his best, when a hushed whisper, growing into a general alarm, announced that members of the Ku Klux, an organization noted for the assassination of Republicans, were coming. Agery, a born leader, in commanding tones, told the meeting to be seated and do as he bid them. The Ku Klux, disguised and pistol belted, very soon appeared, but not before Agery had given out, and they were singing with fervor that good old hymn "Amazing Grace, How Sweet It Sounds to Save a Wretch Like Me." The visitors stood till the verse was ended, when Agery, self-controlled, called on Brother Primus to next lead in prayer.

Brother P. was soon hammering the bench and calling on the Lord to come on His "white horse, and to come this very minute." "Oh," said the chief of the night riders, "this is only a nigger prayer meeting. Come, let us go." Scouts were sent out and kept out to see that "distance lent enchantment to the view," and the political feature of the meeting was resumed.

The Negro is not without many of the prominent characteristics of the successful politician. He is aggressive, conservative, and astute, as occasion demands. Of the latter trait Hon. John Allen, ex-member of Congress from Mississippi, and said to have been the prince of story tellers, at his own expense gives this amusing incident. It was on the occasion of the Carmack-Patterson contested election case. In beginning his speech he called attention to Mr. Patterson's remarks. "Did any of you," he said, "ever hear anyone pronounce a more beautiful eulogy on himself than that just pronounced by Josiah Patterson? In listening to it I was reminded of what my friend Jake Cummings once said about me. It was in the great campaign of 1884. The Cleveland-Hendricks-Allen Club at Tupelo had a meeting, and Mr. Taylor and Mr. Anderson spoke to the club that night. As I chanced to be at home from my campaigning, I attended the club meeting. After the regular speakers I was called

for and submitted some remarks about myself and my campaign. After I had
spoken the crowd called for Jake Cummings, a long, black, slick old Negro carpenter, who lives in Tupelo. Jake's speech
ran about this way: "Well, gentlemen, it's
gettin' kinder late now. I don't know as
it's necessary for me to say anything.
You's heerd Mister Taylor and Mister Allen on the general politics of the day.
They's dun told you what sort of man
Blaine is, and what sort of a man Cleveland is. It don't look to me like no honest
man ought to have trouble in picking out
the fittinest man of them two. And then
you's heerd Mister Allen on hisself, and he
has ricommended hisself so much higher
than any the rest of us kin ricommend him
it ain't worth while for me to say nuthin'
about him."

CHAPTER XIII.

There is at present a lowering cloud on prospect of righteous rule in many of the Southern States, but the relative rights and responsibilities of equitable government, enunciated from desk in church, schoolhouse, or from stump in grove by the Republicans during and since reconstruction, have been an education to the poor whites, hitherto ignorant and in complete political thraldom to the landed class, and to the freedman a new gospel, whose conception was necessarily limited to his rights as a newly-fledged citizen. Nevertheless, they were the live kernels of equality before the law, that still "have their silent undergrowth," inducing a manhood and patriotism that is now and will more and more blossom with national blessing. Friends regretfully and foes despairingly sometimes speak of the tardiness of his progress. He will compare favorably, however, for all history records that it is slowly, through the crucible of physical and mental toiling, that races pass to an elevated status. For of serfs he was not the least in his appreciation of liberty.

Sir Walter Scott, in his note on English history during the reign of George III, of

the "colliers and salters, who were not Ne
groes," says: "The persons engaged in
these occupations were at the time bondsmen, and in case they left the ground of
the farms to which they belonged, and as
pertaining to which their services were
bought and sold, they were liable to be
brought back by a summary process. The
existence of this species of slavery being
thought irreconcilable with the spirit of
liberty, the "colliers and salters were declared free, and put on the same footing
with other servants by the act of George
III. But they were so far from desiring
or prizing the blessing conferred on them
that they esteemed the interest taken in
their freedom to be a mere decree on the
part of the proprietors to get rid of what
they called "head or harigold money" pay-
able to them when a female of their number, by bearing a child, made an addition
to the live stock of their master's property."

If the fitness for liberty is the measure of persecution sustained in an effort
for its enjoyment, of that disciplinary process the freedmen have not been deprived,
for ever since his maiden attempt to exercise the right of an American citizen he has
encountered intense opposition and physical outrage, all of which has been met
by non-resistance and manly appeal to the
American conscience for protection; first
from the "Ku Klux band" of murderers,
and subsequently against the vicious prac-

tices to deprive him of his political rights, should establish his claim. Nevertheless, after a third of a century of successful endeavor, educationally and materially, efforts are being made in Southern States for his disfranchisement and the curtailment of his education. On this attempt George C. Lormer, a noted divine and writer, in a late article in "The Watchman," under the head of "The Educational Solution of Race Problems," has this to say:

"But may it not be that this reactionary movement rather expresses a fear of education than a serious doubt of its power? We must remember that conditions are peculiar in the South, and, in some quarters, there exists a not unnatural apprehension that Negro supremacy may prevail. To avert this political catastrophe, extraordinary measures have been adopted. To the difficulties that beset the Southern people we cannot be indifferent, and neither should we assume that we would act very differently, were we similarly situated. But we think, in view of all the circumstances, that their position on this subject exposes them to the suspicion that it is the success of education they fear, and not its failure. This apparent misgiving reasonably awakens distrust in the soundness of their contention."

It is assumed by many who oppose the educational solution that inferior races are unassimilable in their nature to the higher civilization. Proof is sought for in the alleged decadence or disappearance of the Turanian people of Europe, the natives of South America, and the West India Islands. But what is this civilization that is so fatal in its operation? What do we mean by the term? What is that exalted something before which African and Asiatic must perish? Does it consist in armies, machinery, saloons, breweries, railways, steamboats, and certain commercial methods that are fatal to truth and honesty. Baron Russell, Lord Chief Justice of England, included none of these in his conception of its character. He is recorded as saying: "It's true, signs are thoughts for the poor and suffering, chivalrous regard and respect for women, the frank recognition of human brotherhood, irrespective of race or color, or nation or religion; the narrowing of the domain of mere force as a governing factor in the world, the love of ordered freedom, abhorrence of what is mean and cruel and vile, ceaseless devotion to the claims of justice. Civilization in its true, its highest sense, must make for peace."

Previous to the National Convention which nominated General Grant for a second term, there had been held a conference of colored leaders, who assembled at New Orleans to elicit opinion and divine the probable course of the colored delegates at that convention. It was there I first met that faithful, able, and invincible champion of the race, Governor P. B. S. Pinch-

HON. PINCKNEY B. S. PINCHBACK,
United States Senator.

Born May, 1837—Educated at Gilmon High School, Cincinnati, Ohio—Captain Co.
A. 2d Regiment, Louisiana Volunteers—Member of Constitutional
Convention of Louisiana—State Senator—Lieutenant-Gover-
nor—Editor and Lawyer—Able as a Statesman,
Eloquent as an Advocate, and Unflinch-
ing in Defense of Equal Justice.

back and Captain James Lewis, my fellow-member of the "Old Guard," who, true in peace as war, never surrendered. The conference, though not great numerically, was strong in its mental calibre and representative character, with Douglas, Langston, Cuney, and others who have since passed to the great beyond. The colored office holders at Washington under Grant were much in evidence and naturally eager for his endorsement.

There was much discussion, and while an ardent advocate for Brooks, I could not follow his supporters—the Brindle wing of the party in my State—in their choice of Horace Greely for President. My slogan in the State canvass had been Grant for President and Brooks for Governor. The wisdom of the conference determined upon a non-committal policy. It was thought unwise, in our peculiar condition, to hasten to proclaim in advance of the gathered wisdom of such an august body as a National Convention. Hence, the conference concluded by setting forth by resolutions, grievances, and a reaffirmation of fealty to the Republican party.

The result of the State election in Arkansas in 1872 was that Brooks got the votes and Baxter the office, whereupon a contest was inaugurated, terminating in civil war. The Baxter, or Minstrel, wing of the party, with the view of spiking the guns of the Brindles, had, in their overtures to the Democrats during

the campaign and in their platform at the
nominating convention declared in favor
of enfranchising the Confederates that
took part in the war against the Union.
Baxter's movement in that direction and
his appointment of Democrats to office created discontent in both wings of the Republican party, leading to their union and
determined steps for his removal and the
seating of Brooks, who, both factions now
declared, was elected. The doctrine of
estoppel "cutting no figure" with the Baxter contingent. A writ of ouster was obtained from Judge Vicoff, of the Circuit
Court, which Sheriff Oliver, accompanied
by Joseph Brooks, J. L. Hodges, General
Catterson, and one or two others, including
the writer, proceeding to the State House
and made service.

No notice of such action having preceded, Governor Baxter was ill-prepared for the announcement. After a
short parley with his private secretary,
General McCanany, escorted by the Sheriff
and General Catterson down the stairway,
they were met by Hon. J. N. Smithea, the
able editor of the "Arkansas Gazette."
Leaving the building, they went direct to
the Antony House, on East Markam Street.
Word was sent to A. H. Garland, U. B.
Rose, R. C. Newton, and other prominent
Democrats, who soon joined him in con-
sultation. Governor Baxter immediately
notified President Grant of the situation
and sent instructions to the custodian of

State arms at the U. S. Arsenal to honor
none but his order for delivery. Joseph
Brooks was sworn in, and the two Governors made immediate preparations for
siege and defence. Main Street south from
the river to the boundary line of the city
was the dividing line of the two factions,
Governor Baxter to the east on Markam
Street, and Governor Brooks, at the Antony House, to west; at the State House
established their respective quarers.

A condition of unrest had pervaded the
State for several months preceding
this event, and when the slogan of
war was sounded the respective adherents by hundreds from all over
the State hastened to the capital. On
the morning following the "coup d'etat"
a report reached the State House that a
company of colored men, commanded by
Gen. King White, from Pine Bluff, had
arrived and was quartered on Rock Street.
On the assumption that the men were mis-
informed as to the merits of the quarrel,
it was proposed that they be interviewed.
To do that was to cross the line and enter
the enemy's territory. It was not unlike
the query of the rats in the fable, Who
shall bell the cat? I was solicited, and,
learning I had friends in the company, consented to go. Going south on Center Street
to cross the line by a circuitous route, I
reached Rock Street, and nearly the ren-
dezvous. But the "best laid plans of men
and mice oft gang a glee." The emissary

had been discovered and reported. Approaching me at a rapid rate, mounted on a charger which seemed to me the largest, with an artillery of pistols peeping from holsters, rode General George L. Bashman, of the Baxter forces. Reining up his steed he said, not unkindly: "Judge Gibbs, I am instructed to order you to leave the lines immediately, or subject yourself to arrest." As formerly intimated, and not unlike Artemus Ward, I was willing that all my wife's relatives might participate in the glories and mishaps of war. Hence I bowed a submissive acquiescence and returned. I appreciated the amity expressed in the manner and delivery of the order—an amity of which I have been the recipient from my political opponents during the thirty years of my domocile in Arkansas.

General Rose, who held command at the Arsenal, and had received instructions from Washington to keep peace pending a settlement of the controversy, with a detail of soldiers, had erected a barricade opposite the City Hall on Markam Street and placed a piece of artillery on Louisiana Street, pointing to the river. In the afternoon of their arrival, General White's troops, headed by a brass band, marched on Markam Street to the Antony House. While so doing a report became current that they were preparing to attack the State House. General Rose attempted to investigate and, with his orderly, rode rapidly on Markam Street, across Main, to

ward the Antony House. At the moment a
shot, increasing into volleys, from combat-
ants on either side, who primarily were
the aggressors was never known. It resulted in several casualties. Colonel Shall
was killed in the Antony House, and others
within the precincts of the City Hall and
Metropolitan Hotel. Markam Street suddenly assumed a Sunday-like appearance,
the Brooksites seeking safety in the State
House and the Baxterites in the Antony.
The feet of General White's troops fought
bravely. Three hours later it was an
nounced that they had made the fifty miles
to Pine Bluff without a break, windless,
but happy. Each faction was deficient in
arms to equip their adherents. A company
of cadets from St. John's College had been
placed at the service of Baxter.

At the State University at Fayettesville
were stored rifles and ammunition, the property of the State. Thither Col. A. S. Fowler,
of the Brooks forces, proceeded, and, with
courage and diplomacy, succeeded in obtaining and placing a supply on a flat boat,
and commenced his trip down the river. Information of this movement having
reached the Antony House, the river
steamer Hallie, with a detachment of Baxter forces, was dispatched up the river to
intercept, and succeeded in passing the
State House without interference. The
circuitous character of the river enabled a
company from the State House, by quick
march, to overhaul it at a bend of the river,

a fusillade of whose rifle shots killed the captain, wounded several others, and disabled the steamer, which was captured and brought back to the State House. A restless quiet then ensued, occasionally broken by random shots.

In the meantime Governor Baxter had called an extraordinary session of his legislative adherents, vacancies of recalcitrant Republicans filled, the Brooks government denounced, and an appeal to the President for support. All the records and appurtenances of the Secretary of State's office, including the great seal of the State, were in possession of Brooks at the State House. Information that a duplicate had been made in St. Louis and was en route to the Antony House was received, whereupon General D. P. Upham made application for a search warrant to intercept it, a copy of which is as follows:

"I, D. P. Upham, do solemnly swear that one Elisha Baxter and his co-conspirators have ordered and caused to be made, as I am informed, a counterfeit of the great seal of the State of Arkansas, and that the same is now or soon will be in the express office of the city of Little Rock, as I am informed, and that the same is intended for the purpose of defrauding, counterfeiting, and forging the great seal of the State of Arkansas by the said Elisha Baxter and his co-conspirators, and to use the same for illegal and fraudulent purposes, against the peace and dignity of the State of Arkansas, and I ask that a search warrant may issue forthwith, according to law, to search for and seize said counterfeit seal, wherever or in whomsoever possession it may be found.

"(Signed.)   D. P. UPHAM.

"Subscribed and sworn to before me this 1st day of May, 1874.   M. W. GIBBS,

"City Judge."

The warrant was duly served and return made, with the seal. Baxter, having now ignored the men who placed him in power, called around him as supporters and advisers the brain and strength of the Democratic party. Meanwhile each party had representatives in Washington, urging their claims for recognition. As a party, the Republicans were at a disadvantage. When Brooks, being elected, was contesting Baxter's right to the Governorship, Baxter was supported by the leading and most prominent republicans of the State, who swore "by all the gods at once" that he and not Brooks was elected; but now they swore at once at all opposing gods, who said that Baxter was.

A committee of Brooks men, of whom the writer was one, was sent to Washington to present the claims and conditions to the President. When the train, en route, stopped at Alexandria a gentleman came hurriedly in and, accosting another, said: "What do you think? Grant has recognized Baxter." I

did not learn the thought or hear the response, being possessed immediately by a
feeling not unlike the boy whose "piece of
bread and butter falls with the butter side
down." We pursued our way to Washington to find the report true. We called at
the White House several times, but the
engagements of the President prevented
an interview. Late of an afternoon, sitting
in my room on I Street, I saw the President approaching slowly and alone. I put
on my hat, and was soon with him, and,
with becoming salute, addressed him.
General Grant, who was ever accessible to
the most humble, attentively listened, as
we walked, to my brief statement of our
case. He replied that his sympathies were
with us, for he believed that Brooks was
elected; but that his Attorney General had
given an opinion that the people, through
the expression of their last Legislature,
had endorsed Baxter, and that he must ac-
quiesce.

That this avowal was sincere was shown
by a subsequent message to Congress
on the subject, condemning the process by which the Democracy had vaulted
into power. When the dispatch from
Washington recognizing Baxter was received at the Antony House the faithful,
while making the welkin ring, made immediate preparations to take undisturbed
possession of the State House. The march
of Governor Baxter and his adherents to
the capital was made, as imposing as had

his former exclusion been humiliating. A band playing inspiring music not unlike "See, the Conquering Hero Comes," and stepping to the air came an array, led by General King White, on horseback, with flags flying, animated and exhilarated with all the pomp and circumstance of a victo-rious legion, entered and occupied the building which Brooks and his following, defeated and depressed, had vacated, in obedience to the President's mandate. The prospect for their rehabilitation seemed shadowy, but, with that hope said "to spring eternal in the human breast," they had resolved to carry their contest to Con-gress.

It may be properly said of Joseph Brooks, as of Charles II, "His fault—and no statesman can have a worse one—was that he never saw things as they really were. He had imagination and logic, but he was an idealist, and a theorizer, in which there might have been good if only his theories and ideals had not been out of relation with the hard duties of a day of storm."

There was opportunity for him to have secured the approval of the Poland Com-mittee. But the tenacity of his ideal of no concession allowed it to pass.

CHAPTER XIV.

In 1874 a constitutional convention was called and a new constitution adopted. At the State convention of the Democratic party 'for the nomination of State officers Baxter was the favorite for re-election as Governor, and probably would have been the choice, had not the more astute politicians put the United States senatorial "bee in his bonnet," which induced a letter, fervid and patriotic, declining the nomination. Baxter was confiding and honest, but not an adept in the wily ways of the politician. Augustus H. Garland was elected Governor, and in the United States senatorial race Baxter was "left at the stand." It was then, as it oft happens, that—

"God and the soldier all men adore,
    In time of war, and not before.
    When the war is over and all things
        righted,
    God is forgot, and the soldier slighted."

Augustus H. Garland was a Senator in the Confederate Congress in 1861, succeeding Baxter as Governor, then United States Senator from Arkansas, and subsequently a member of President Cleve-

HON. AUGUSTUS H. GARLAND

A learned jurist, broad and humane. A member of the Confederate Congress — Governor of and United States Senator for
Arkansas—A member of President Cleveland's Cabinet—Evidencing
in every position, that it was a selection "fit to be made."

land's Cabinet, evidencing in every position that it was a selection "fit to be made" not only for his ability and attainments as a statesman, but for rugged honesty of purpose and broad humanity as a man. Taking the reins of government at the zenith of a successful revolution, when violence sought gratification, desire rampant for prosecution and persecution, Governor Garland, by a conservative policy, soothed the one and discouraged the other—a policy early announced in his first proclamation, an extract of which is as follows: "Should there be any indictments in the courts for past political offences, I would suggest and advise their dismissal. Let people of all parties, races and colors come and be welcomed to our State and encouraged to bring her up to a position of true greatness." His friendship I highly esteemed, and, learning of his demise, could not but submit the following token:

"Tamatave, Madagascar,
"April 17, 1899.

"Editor Little Rock Gazette:

"Sitting in the Consulate, way down on the banks of the Indian Ocean, the Gazette comes to me laden with expressions of sorrow on the passing of my friend, ex-United States Attorney General A. H. Garland. Truly, 'a great man has fallen.' In him the nation has lost an eminent statesman and Arkansas a most distinguished citizen, celebrated for his intellectuality

and valued services to the Commonwealth.
I said 'my friend,' and I reiterate, in no
platform sense of that term. Twenty-five
year ago I was municipal judge of the
city, at the time when the conflict for party
ascendancy was most intense. When passion struggled for the mastery, as Governor, he was in reality to me a friend.
During his residence at the capital I have
never visited Washington without seeking
and as promptly receiving his kindly greeting. On several occasions his services,
eagerly given, were most helpful. He was
not only mentally eminent, but morally
great.

"Ever approachable, he was a manly
man, with courage of conviction, and, while
urging them with a zeal born of honest belief, had the inestimable faculty of winning adherents by strength of presentation,
blended with suavity of manner. He was
conspicuous in this, that his broad soul ex-
panded with tender and affectionate regard for the poor and humble. Reserved
in manner, magnanimous and catholic in
a spirit that embraced the 'world as his
country, and all mankind as his countrymen.' So in the archives of memory I make
haste to lay this small tribute to a departed
friend, who still seems as 'one long loved
and but for a season gone.' "

I was present, but not a delegate, at the
convention that nominated General Grant
for a second term, at the Academy of Music, in Philadelphia, in 1872.

The proceedings, reported and published, of a National Convention are always interesting, but lose much of the impression and force of actuality with which an auditor and spectator is affected. The gayety and magnetism of numbers, the scintillations of brain in special advocacy, followed by tumultuous accord. The intensity, the anxiety depicted, while results far-reaching and momentous are pending, furnish a scene vivid and striking that cannot be pictured. Here is being formed the policy of a party which is to be subjected to the winnowing fan of acute and honest criticism, and by denunciation by opposite parties, striving to obtain the administration of the Government, the fiat of which and the selection of the standard-bearer constitute the claim for the suffrage of the people. They are the preparatory cornerstones of self-government, fashioned and waiting for the verdict of the nation.

Committees on platform and resolutions are generally composed of the radical and conservative elements of a party, so that, while the canvass is up and on, it shall have steered between "the rocks of too much danger and pale fear" and reached the port of victory. Experience during the period since last it met may have had much to do with silence or brief mention of the heretofore darling shibboleth with which they were wont to inspire the faithful, rally the laggards, or capture converts. "Consistency, thou art a jewel" that daz-

(11)

zles, confuses, but doth not bewilder the
ordinary politician, who can allow a former policy noiseless and forsaken to sink
into the maelstrom of neglected and unrequited love. Prolific in schemes is the
procedure of a minority party, not the
least is the selection of a standard-bearer,
who has been the most sparse and reticent
in utterance, hence a record the least as-
sailable, that extracts from his opponents
the exclamation of one in Holy Writ, "Oh,
that mine enemy had written a book."

Among the men who made mark at the
convention above referred to was Oliver P.
Morton, of Indiana, styled the "War Governor," for the patriotism and alacrity
which he summoned his State in response
to the national call, caught up and followed by every loyal State during the Civil
War. A confirmed invalid, with lower
limbs paralyzed, with massive head and
inspired brain, assisted by two servants to
a chair to the front of the platform, he
made the speech of the convention. Another novel incident was the occupation
of the platform of a National Convention
by Afro-Americans. The Late Hon. William H. Gray, the faithful and eloquent
leader of the colored Republicans of Arkansas, and the late Hon. R. B. Elliott,
Congressman from South Carolina, were
invited to speak.

A few of their well-chosen words in exordium were as follows:

Mr. Gray said : "Gentlemen of the Convention: For the first time, perhaps, in the history of the American people, there stands before you in a National Convention assembled, a representative of that oppressed race that has lived among you for two hundred and fifty years; who, by the magnanimity of this great nation, lifted by the power of God and the hands of man from the degradation of slavery to the proud position of an American citizen."

Mr. Elliott said: "Gentlemen of the Convention: It is with great appreciation of the compliment paid my State that I rise to respond to your invitation to address you. I stand here, gentlemen of the convention, together with my colleagues from the several States, as an illustration of an accomplished fact of American emancipation, not only as an illustration of the management of the American people, but as a living example of the justice of the American people."

The speeches of which the foregoing are but a part of their introduction, expressive of gratitude and fidelity, a conception of the needs of the hour, delivered with an eloquence that charmed, elicited hearty response, the Academy echoing and re-echoing with the plaudits of the vast assembly. At each National Convention of the Republican party representatives of the race have shown not alone oratorical power, but an intelligent grasp of the political situation. At this period of General Grant's nomination, the nation's heart still jubilant with the success of the Federal arms; its conscience awakened by the dread penalty paid by contributions from every loyal hearthstone for the subjugation of slavery, was now eager and active in providing that the Negro who had been faithful in peace and heroic in war, should enjoy the rights of an American citizen. It was history repeating itself, for in England's history we read that it was Henry at Ajincourt who said: "Who this day sheds his blood with me today shall be my brother; were he ne'er so vile, today shall gentle his condition." For the Civil War, as' it matured, became no ordinary case of political contention; the soul of its suppression sprang from the most sacred impulses in the mind of man. It was response to the self-retort of Cain that came echoing down the ages. "Am I my brother's keeper?" Answer came in shot and shell.

But as time receded from these historic epochs, engrossed more and more in national development, mercantile aspirations, internal improvements, rivalry of parties, self-aggrandizement—in short, all the agencies and factors inseparable from human nature that influence on material lines, have effaced much of the general solicitude that formerly existed. This decadence of purpose is not unnatural; a wardship is a duty, and should not be a continuous necessity, its greatest blessing a consciousness that its ideals and purposes have been assimilated by its wards, and lifted higher in humanity's scale. Too much dependence is as hurtful as entire neglect. The more persistent the call for the forces within the greater the response from the assistants without. The lethargy or neglect to give the Negro protection in the exercise of his constitutional rights is developing a spirit of self-help and intensity of purpose, to find and adopt a course and measures remedial that may be practical and efficient; to ignore the sentimentality of politics and subordinate them to conditions irrespective of party. He has found that "the mills of the gods grind slowly;" that the political lever needs for its fulcrum a foundation as solidly mate rial as equitably sentimental.

Proclaim brotherhood, justice, and equal rights ever so much, men will nod acquiescence with a mental reservation of "but," significant of "Who are you? What can you do, or what have you done?" It is your current life's answer to these interrogatives that most interest people in this material world in your behalf. Only as we increase in commercial pursuits, ownership of property, and the higher elements of production through skilled labor will our political barometer rise. Upon these we should anchor our hopes, assured that higher education, with its "classic graces, will follow in their proper places."

Of the latter a humorous writer, in answer to the question from the president of an Eastern college, "Is there any good reason why our sons should not study the dead languages?" said: "While our sons are not on speaking terms with many live languages, it ill becomes them to go fooling around the dead and dying. I do not think it necessary that our sons should study these defunct tongues. A language that did not have strength enough to pull through and crawled off somewhere and died, doesn't seem worth studying. I will go further, and say I do not see why our sons should spend valuable time over invalid languages that aren't feeling very well. Let us not, professor, either one of us, send our sons into the hospital to lug out languages on a stretcher just to study them. No; let us bring up our sons to shun all diseased and disabled languages, even if it can't be proved that a language comes under either of those heads; if it has been missing since the last engagement, it is just as well not to have our sons chasing around after it with a detective, trying to catch and pore over it.

You may look at it differently, professor. Our paths in the great realm of education of youth may lie far apart; but it is my heartfelt wish that I may never live to see a son of mine ride right past healthy athletic languages and then stand up in the stirrups and begin to whoop and try to lariat some poor old language going around on a crutch, carrying half

of its alphabet in a sling. If two-
thirds of the words of a language are flat
on their back, taking quinine, trying to
get up an appetite, let us teach our sons
that they cannot hope to derive benefit
from its study."

But Lord Rosebery, ex-Premier of England, in a late address before the University of Glasgow on "Questions of Empire,"
in the following, on action and learning,
takes a serious view:

"There was a time, long years ago, when
the spheres of action and learning were
separate and distinct; when laymen dealt
hard blows and left letters to the priest-
hood. That was to some extent the case
when our oldest universities were founded.
But the separation daily narrows. It has
been said that the true university of our
days is a collection of books. What if a
future pholosopher shall say that the best
university is a workshop? And yet the
latter definition bids fair to be the sounder
of the two. The training of our schools and
colleges must daily become more and more
the training for action, for practical purpose. The question will be asked of the
product of our educational system: Here is
a young fellow of twenty; he has passed
the best years of acquisition and impression; he has cost so much; what is his
value? For what, in all the manifold activities of the world, is he fit? And if the
answer be not satisfactory, if the product
be only a sort of learned mummy, the sys-

tem will be condemned. Are there not thousands of lads today plodding away at the ancient classics, and who, at the first possible moment, will cast them into space, never to reopen them? Think of the wasted time that that implies; not all wasted, perhaps, for something may be gained in power of application; but entirely wasted so far as available knowledge is concerned."

And in keeping with this line of thought, the "Washington Post," of Washington, D. C., in a recent issue, makes the following pertinent and truthful mention:

"Almost without exception, the colleges and universities are beginning another year with unusually large classes. Many of these institutions report the largest number of matriculates in their history. The aggregate attendance is unquestionably greater by thousands than that of any previous year. This is due in part to the prevalence of business prosperity and in part to the steadily increasing approbation of higher education for women, while the natural increase of population is also something of a factor. The 'Cleveland Leader,' speaking of the reports of large classes of freshmen all over the country, says:

" 'That appears to be the best and most conclusive reply which the American people can make to those gentlemen of wealth and prominence who, like Mr. Schwab, of the Steel Trust, discourage higher education as preparation for the life of the business world. It is the solidest kind of evidence that the old love of knowledge for its own sake and the old faith in the beneficial effects of college training upon the youth of a country having such a government and social organization as this Republic has developed remain as strong as ever.' "

To which the Post replies :

"That is somewhat hasty and a probably erroneous conclusion. The "higher education" which Mr. Schwab discourages, the old-time classical course, has not grown in popular favor. The reverse is true. The demand for a more practical education in this utilitarian age has compelled the colleges and universities to make radical changes in their curriculum. The number of students who elect to take the old-time course is smaller in proportion to the population and wealth of this country than it ever was. Science, both pure and applied, takes a far more prominent place in collegiate studies than it formerly occupied. Many of the leading institutions of learning have introduced a commercial department. Everywhere the practical, the business idea is becoming dominant.

"While no intelligent man questions the value of classical studies or disputes the proposition that a knowledge of the classics is indispensable to a thorough understanding of our own language, the area of practical study has become so vast, by reason of new discoveries in science and the arts, that a choice between the two is compulsory to young persons who have their own fortunes to make. The old-time course of mathematics and classics furnishes splendid mental discipline, with much knowledge that may or may not put its possessor on the road to success in business. But the time required for that course, if followed by a three or four years' term of practical study, sets a young man so far along in life that he has a hopeless race with younger men who dispensed with the classical and went in zealously for the practical.

"The change from the old to the new lines of education is even more marked in the common schools than in the colleges and universities. The practical begins in the free kindergarten and runs with more or less directness through all the grades. Millions are expended upon industrial training. The business high schools are a great feature of the free school system. All this is comparatively new. It has come because of the necessities of an industrial age.

" 'Knowledge for its own sake' is becoming more and more a luxury, in which the sons and daughters of the rich indulge, while the representatives of families that are merely well to do feel that they must acquire knowledge for practical uses. And this tendency is likely to continue, for, as we have said, the field of the practical is expanding. Take, for example, elecricity and its uses. All that was known of this subject in the time of our grandfathers could be learned in a few days or weeks. To be an up-to-date electrical scientist and practical electrician in 1901 means that years have been devoted to hard work."

The crude notion held by some, that in far-off climes, to the American Negro unknown, who, with small capital and limited education; with an inherited mental inertia that is being dispelled and can only be eradicated by contact with superior environment, that there awaits him peace, plenty, and equality, is an ignus fatuus the most delusive. Peace is the exhaustion of strife, and is only secure in her triumphs in being in instant readiness for war; equality a myth, and plenty the accumulation of weary toil.

With travel somewhat extensive and diversified; residence in tropical latitudes of Negro origin, I have a decided conviction, despite the crucial test to which he has been subjected in the past and the present disadvantages under which he labors, nowhere is the promise along all the lines of opportunity brighter for the American Negro than here in the land of his nativity. For he needs the inspiriting dash, push, and invincible determination of the Anglo-Saxon (having sufficient of his deviltry) to make him a factor acknowledged and respected. But the fruit of advantage will not drop as ripe fruit from

the tree; it can be gotten only by watch-
ful, patient tillage, and frugal garnering.
Ignorance and wastefulness among the industrious but uneducated poor render
them incapable to cope with the shrewd
and unprincipled. The rivalry to excel in
outward appearance and social amenities
beyond the usual moderate means on the
part of the educated is a drawback to any
people, but one disastrous to the Negro
in his march through arduous toil and re-
stricted conditions to financial independence.

REV. JOSEPH A. BOOKER,

President of Arkansas Baptist College, and Editor of the "Vanguard."
Born 1859, at Portland, Arkansas—Studied at Branch Normal College—Graduated
At Roger Williams' University, Tennessee, Mainly by His Efforts this
College Only on Paper in 1887, has now Grounds and Buildings
Worth over $50,000 and Several Hundred Students.

CHAPTER XV.

At the Arkansas State election in 1876 I was selected as Presidential elector, receiving the highest vote on the Republican ticket. The national election of that year was followed by the memorable canvass of the contested vote for Rutherford B. Hayes, which was ultimately settled by a commission appointed under the Compromise Bill, which was passed by Congress in January, 1877, Florida, Louisiana, and South Carolina declaring for Hayes. That the compromise was the result of an agreement that the United States troops should by withdrawn from Southern soil cannot be doubted, and for so doing he was bitterly criticised and denounced by many of his party, resulting, as it did, in the transfer of those States in the South from Republican, by continuous and unblushing disfranchisement, to Democratic rule.

President Hayes, not unlike many of historic fame, may have been "born before his time;" that his action in removing U. S. troops was immature, a continuation and increase of intimidation and violence abundantly proved. At what period of their remaining on Southern soil would have been a fitting time for removal, is an

enigma hard to elucidate. Their retention
ultimately rested with the sentiment and
judgment of the nation. In the South the
menace of their presence was galling and
increasing in intensity. The North was
daily growing averse to the bivouac of
troops over a people who swore that they
were on terms of "peace with all the world
and the rest of mankind." Would compulsion soften animosity? Hayes was undoubtedly honest and sincere, but not of
that class of epoch-making men who anchor
on the right, await and buffet the advancing storm. Conciliation coyed as gently
as loving dove his mate, while within easy
reach glistened the jewel "President" of a
fraternized Republic.

There are possibly men who would
have spurned the enchantress. But an
array of figures and ability to enu-
merate would not be sorely taxed in
finding the number. I was among those
at that period who saw the inutility of
depending on physical force to extract justice and lawful methods from an unwilling constituency; that the reaction from a
forced compulsion in the moral world was
as evident and unfailing under the conditions as from compression in the physical.
I was hopeful of good results, and so expressed myself in an interview with the
President. He replied that he was "sincere in his policy, and should adhere to it
unless it seemed impracticable that the
policy of force and musket had been tried

PROF. I. G. ISH.

Principal of High School, Little Rock, Arkansas.
An Erudite Scholar and Zealous Tutor.

in the South and had failed and public
sentiment now demanded a change." We
had and have the change, and it would
have been a bright jewel in the autonomy
of many of the Southern States had it been
more liberal and righteous.

History, as a record of the lower to a
higher status of civilization increases in
intensity and value as it records superior
conditions, and the degree of unrest and
earnestness of appeal for the abrogation of
oppression is indicative of the appreciation
and fitness for the rights of citizenship.

It should be remembered that as it became men dowered with the proud title
of American Citizen, the Negro has not
been remiss in stating his grievances and
appealing for justice. To have done less
would have banished sympathy and invited
contempt. In Arkansas and some other
Southern States there is a growing demand for the forms of law and the maintenance of order, and, while not attaining
the zenith of accomplishment, it will be
observable when contrasted with the lawlessness depicted in the following resolutions of a convention of colored men held
in Little Rock August 29, 1883. They contain views and convictions I there presented, the equity of which 'tis fondly
hoped have not been lost by lapse of time:

"Be it resolved, That this convention of
colored men of the State of Arkansas have
still to complain that violence and injustice to their race still exists to an alarm-

ing extent. In most cases the perpetrators
go unwhipped of justice. That when they
are arraigned the law is administered with
such laxity and partiality that the escape
of the criminal is both easy and possible.
In no instance is the penalty of the law enforced against a white man for the murder
of a Negro, however palpable the case may
be; whilst in most instances the bare accusation of a Negro committing a homicide upon a white man is sufficient for law,
with all its forms, to be ruthlessly set aside
and the doctrine of lynch, swift and certain to be enforced.

Case after case is chronicled by the
press of Negroes hung by infuriated
mobs without trial to determine their
guilt or innocence. The farcical proceedings at law in their inefficiency of
prosecution, the selection and manipula-
tion of jurors, and the character of public
sentiment have had painful illustration in
several cases, and but recently of Johnson,
the colored man murdered in this, the capital county of the State. The homicide of
this man, a servant at a picnic, of a Chris-
tion society of white people, and in their
presence, without provocation, was uni-
versally admitted. Notwithstanding, a
jury of twelve men, with almost indecent
haste, finds the murderer not guilty. A
verdict fit to shock the sense of every
friend of right and justice. Robinson, a
white man, for killing a colored man because his victim asked for the return of

money loaned, received but two years in
the penitentiary. Burril Lindsey, a colored farmer, who had homesteaded land
in Van Buren County and had commenced
cultivation, was waited upon and told he
must leave; that they would have no "nig-
gers" in the settlement. They came back
at midnight and broke down his door. One
of the mob, lying dead on the threshold
was Burril Lindsey's response. The press
of our city—to their honor be it noted—
said he did the proper thing. Respectable
men in the neighborhood who knew Lindsey said the same. But yet, after being
harrassed by threats and legal persecution
for months, a jury found him guilty of an
assault with intent to kill, and six years in
the penitentiary at hard labor is the penalty for defending his home.

Homicide has no local habitation; it is
the accident of every community, in every
nation, and the justice and impartiality
with which the law is administered is the
measure of their humanity and civilization. But here we have the spectacle of
the press, pulpit, and rostrum of the State,
with exceptions scarcely to be noted, either
entirely dumb or a mere passing allusion,
more often in commendation than censure.
We are positive in our confidence that
those, and only those who expose and denounce and lay bare this conduct, and
thereby create a sentiment that will lessen
this evil, are the only true friends to the
State's moral as well as its material prog-

(12)

ress. That the attempt to deny and evade responsibility does not meet the issue in the minds of thoughtful men, who believe that no life is safe where the humblest is unprotected.

"We insist that value of the colored brother as a tiller of the soil, the increasing thrift and economy conceded in securing homes and taxable property, their favorable comparison (by fair judgment) with any other classes as to their moral and law-abiding character, should at least merit justice in the courts, and we ask for him consideration and fair settlement for labor. For where could superiority and nobility of character be better displayed than by generous treatment to the former bondsmen. That the better element of the Democratic party do not favor this lawlessness we are continually assured. But the ugly fact stands out in bold relief that they are unable or unwilling, with forces of wealth and intelligence, to create a healthier sentiment. To them, and just men everywhere, we appeal to assist in bringing the moral power of denunciation against this great wrong, that impartial justice shall be the law for every citizen of the Commonwealth; and that the president and secretary be empowered to sign a petition in behalf and as the earnest request of this convention for presentation to his Excellency the Governor, asking executive clemency in the pardon of Burril Lindsey, now incarcerated in the penitentiary, under a sentence of six years."

The Governor was graciously pleased to
pardon him, but for personal safety he was
compelled to abandon his homestead and
leave the State.

For some time a general unrest among
the colored people on account of violence
had permeated the South, and thousands
of the most substantial planters had already settled in Kansas, Indiana, and
other Western States to enjoy legal protection hitherto denied them. Upon the
question of Negro emigration the white
South were divided. The planters and
leading politicians were adverse. The
planter for the reason that he could not
supplant him by more efficient and tractable labor; the politician for fear of reduc-
ing Congressional representation, each regardless of the conditions creating his discontent. A minority respectable in numbers and prominent for standing, approved
of his removal, alleging that the movement would be mutually beneficial, that
it would induce white immigration, relieve the congested overproduction of the
staples of the Southern States, introduce a
higher class of industries, and simplify the
so-called problem by removing the bugbear
of Negro domination by means unobjec-
tionable.

Of this class of opinion the "Nashville
American," of the State of Tennessee,
was a fair exponent. In its issue
of May 9, 1879, it had this to say: "We
rather rejoiced at a movement which will

bring about a better understanding and teach both races a lesson they ought to learn. To the Negro it is simply a question as to whether he will be better off there or here. If there, he ought to go; if here, he ought to stay; and this simple economic proposition will settle it."

This, the sentiment of the best Southern thought, encountered an adverse which, while unwilling to grant the Negro the right of an American citizen, maltreated and imprisoned immigrant agents; desiring his retention in a specious of serfdom. Such being the conditions existing at the time of the meeting of the Nashville Conference in 1879, induced it by resolution to request Senator Windom, Chairman of the National Executive Committee, to appoint a committee to visit the Western States to ascertain what inducement they offered for immigration.

In pursuance whereof I received the following, containing words of wisdom warranting their insertion here:

"United States Senate,
"Washington, D. C., Jan. 10, 1879.

"My Dear Sir: In compliance with the resolution of the Nashville Convention requesting me, as Chairman of the National Executive Committee, to appoint a committee of three to visit Western States and Territories and report, not later than the 1st of November, upon the health, climate, and productions of said States and Terri-

tories, I have the honor to designate you
as one of the number of said committee.
In doing so I may add that the
duty involves great labor and responsibility on your part and requires
the exercise of that sound discretion for which you are noted among
your friends. The exodus of the colored
people involves the greatest consequences
to themselves and should only be under-
taken after the most careful inquiry and
preparation. If judiciously guided and
regulated, I am thoroughly convinced that
it will result in great good. If not so
regulated, it may cause incalculable suffering to the colored race, and work great
injury to the industrial interest of the
South. If the Negro can have fair treatment as a citizen and a man in his present
home, he will probably not care to remove.
If he cannot obtain such treatment there,
it is his right and duty to secure it by every
means in his power, and no one has the
right to say he may not change his residence at his own will and pleasure.

"Your proposed inquiry will contribute
much to inform and control the action of
those who may desire to emigrate and your
discretion gives the best assurance that no
rash action will be advisable. I regret the
committee has no funds at command to
pay your necessary traveling expenses.

"Hon James P. Rapier, Member of Congress, of Montgomery, Alabama, I have
also designated as a member of said com-

mittee, but I am not sufficiently advised to
name the third member.

"Very respectfully yours,

(Signed.)   "WM. WINDOM,

"Chairman.

"Mifflin W. Gibbs, Little Rock, Ark."

It often happens that distance lends enchantment to the view; that while contend-
ing with hardship, disappointment, and
earnest toil, we are apt to imagine that at
some far locality, amid new surroundings,
there abides a reign of contentment and
happiness, where labor has its highest rewards and where there is a minimum of
those trials inseparable from human existence. The gratification of this migratory
impulse has in many instances proved disastrous, the yielding to which should be
only indulged after every possible effort
has been made to remove local obstacles
by uprightness, softening animosities, and
by industry accumulate wealth. But emigrants have been illustrious as nation
builders, their indomitable spirit blessing
mankind and leaving impress on the scroll
of time. The bump on the head of the Negro that the phrenologists call "inhabitive-
ness" is very prominent; he is not naturally migratory—"content to bear the ills
he has, than fly to those he knows not of."
Hence there appeared reason, if not entire
"method in his madness."

In all movements of like character there
are always conflicting rumors and re-

HON. JOHN P. GREEN.
United States Stamp Agent.

Educated at Cleveland, Ohio—A Leading Member of the Bar—Twice Elected to
the Senate of the Ohio Legislature.

ports as to success or failure of the benefit or loss of the venture, and this was no exception. Colored immigrants to the number of 10,000 had left the South during a brief period, and the wildest rumors circulated as to reception and success of these forerunners, and, as bad news is ever alert, much was heard that was discouraging and demanded investigation; hence the action of the Nashville Conference referred to. In pursuance of our appointment, J. T. Rapier and myself, in August, 1879, went to Topeka, Kan., and from there, chiefly by wagon travel, visited different colonies of the immigrants. Kansas had received seven or eight thousand. At Topeka we found nearly 100 at immigrant camp receiving rations, some sick, others looking for work; the balance had settled on lands or had found work as laborers. At Dunlop we found a colony of 300 families settled upon 20,000 acres of land. In Wabunsee County 230 families had settled on their land, while in Lawrence and other counties hundreds had found work. Mechanics receiving $2 to $2.25 per day and farm hands $13 to $15 per month and board. We found women in great demand for house servants from $6 to $8 per month.

In our interviews with the colonists we found the list and nature of their grievances were the same as have impelled men in all ages to endeavor to better their condition, and should five or ten thousand, for

a period, annually leave the South and settle in Western States and Territories, the
effect would be mutually beneficial to
whites and blacks alike. In Emporia we
found the colony in a very prosperous
state. Out of 120 families one-half owned
their houses and land on which they lived.
We remained twenty days in Kansas and
had not opportunity to visit Indiana and
other States that had received immigrants.
But the information we received, with few
exceptions, was similar to that of those
visited. There had been suffering and des-
titution in some localities during the past
winter; that was to be expected, as many
had come wholly unprepared and without
that push and ready adaptation to the
status of a new country.

We made an extended report to Senator Windom, which contained data as to
the success and prosperity of the many
and advice to the moneyless to avoid the
suffering which might lie in wait.

CHAPTER XVI.

In 1877 I was appointed by the President Register of the United States Land Office for the Little Rock District of Arkansas. The State was blessed with a valuable patrimony, by having at the time of its admission into the Union an extensive area of agricultural, besides thousands of acres of swamp, school and other lands, under State control and disposition. The United States Government had reserved many millions of acres, which under its homestead law became available for applicants for 40, 80, or 160 acres. No economy of the Government has been more fruitful in substantial blessing upon the industrious poor than throwing open these lands for entrance and ownership of homes by the payment of a nominal fee for recording and proof of actual settlement thereon.

The renowned and lamented Robert J. Ingersoll, once, while extolling the benignity and patriotic effect of the homestead law, said: "Who do you suppose would take up arms to defend a boarding house?" The opportunity to enjoy the ownership of a home strongly appeals, not alone to our avarice, but to the instincts of our nature. For

here is located the citadel of our hopes and
fears, our joys and griefs; here congregated
are ties the most sacred, and a love devoted. It is the ever-burning light, the
steady heat-giving impulse, and inspiration
to deeds of domestic utility or of noble daring. For its protection the heart leaps and
the arm strikes. Hence, for domestic felic-
ity, or national autonomy, the home is an
experience, and for liberty a conservator.
Having these convictions during my 12
years' service in the Land Office as Register and afterwards as Receiver of Public
Moneys, I was earnest in my endeavor to
have the poor of all classes enter these
lands. On the political stump at every
election, while having as my mission the
political ascendancy of my party, I always
felt it a duty to dwell impressively upon
that theme. Upon asking all those living
on their own lands to hold up their hands,
the gleam of pride on the countenances of
many of my colored auditors as, standing
tip-toe, with hands at arms' length, was
shared by me, and a stimulus to the luke-
warm, for on subsequent visits I would find
an increase of holdings.

For the Negro ownership of land and
home is not only an important factor, in
his domestic life, for as taxpayer, there is
a mutuality of interest between himself
and other members of the body politic, business and trade seek him, it impels reverence for the law, and protection of the public peace. His own liability to outrage be-

comes small. His character for credit increases in the ratio of his holdings, and
while manhood suffrage is the professed
but often disavowed legacy for all born beneath the flag, his rights of citizenship are
more often accorded.

While in the Land Service of the United
States there were many examples of heroic
conduct by colored settlers worthy of the
highest praise. Many of them, emigrants
from other Southern States, seeking better
conditions, and arriving with barely sufficient to pay entrance fee, and nothing to
sustain them in their fight with nature to
clear their heavily-wooded land and fit it
for cultivation. Hiring to others for brief
spells, as necessity compelled them, to obtain small stocks of food and tools, five
years after entrance, when they proved up
their holdings and got their deeds, found
them in comfortable log or frame houses
of two or more rooms; sheds, with a cow,
calves, swine, and poultry, and ten or more
acres under cultivation, according to the
number and availability of labor in their
families. And, best of all, better than the
mere knowledge of success, themselves
crowned with that pride of great achievement ever and only the result of rigid self-
denial and incessant toil.

In the National Republican Convention
held at Chicago, June, 1880, was a contest
that will be ever memorable as pertaining
to a third term for the Presidency.

Landing at San Francisco, September,
1879, from his tour of two years around

the world, and the honored guest of the crowned heads of Europe, General Grant's travel through the States was a continued ovation. On his arrival at Little Rock, Ark., citizens from all over the State hastened to do him honor, culminating with a banquet at the Capitol Hotel. The gathering was democratic in the best sense of that word, political lines were erased, Republicans and Democrats vieing with each other in giving the distinguished man a fitting reception. Nor were social lines adhered to, the writer being a guest and responding to the toast "The Possibilities of American Citizenship."

At the Arkansas Republican State Convention in 1880 I was elected a delegate to the National Convention of June 2 of that year. As a memento I highly prize my bronze medal proclaiming me as one of the historic "306" that never surrendered— compact and erect, "with every gun shotted and every banner flying," went down with General Grant in an unsuccessful effort to nominate him for a third term. It was there that Roscoe Conkling made the nominating speech in behalf of the General that will live in history, stirring the hearts of the immense audience to a climax of patriotic fervor. When he said, "Should you ask from whence he comes, the answer it shall be, He comes from Appomattox and the famous apple tree."

The fiat of the Convention was an illustration of the ephemeral character of co-

temporary popular acclaim. Ambitious
rivalry, the anticipations of envy, the bitterness of disappointed office seekers during two former Administrations, the honest belief of the timid that a third term
for one soever trustworthy presaged and
paved the way to an imperial monarchy;
the mistakes unavoidable from misplaced
confidence, happening in the career of all
men and inseparable in the administration
of government—all these elements, although incongruous in their nature and
make-up, when they conspire are a formid-
able factor, and as such accomplished his
defeat. Though dead, Ulysses Grant still
lives on; the attributes of his personal nobility as a man, his patriotism as a citizen
of the Republic, his ability and clear per-
spective as a statesman, his genius as a
warrior, his magnanimity and kindness to
a chivalrous, heroic but fallen foe, will ever
typify his greatness in civic virtues and
valiant deeds.

The manner of General Grant's defeat
was peculiar. The name of James A. Garfield, the successful nominee, and in political parlance the "dark horse" (undoubtedly foreplanned but kept in the shade),
was suddenly sprung upon the Convention
and amid a whirlwind of excitement quickly received adherents from the opposition
which increased in volume at each successive balloting, until the climax was reached
that gave General Garfield the coveted
prize. For some time there was much bit-

terness, and interchange of compliments
more emphatic than polïte. Within the
party charges of infidelity to promises were
rife. But the second sober thought of a
wise conservatism, which is ever evidence
and measure of a people's civilization, tem-
pered strife and assuaged the pangs of disappointment. He was handsomely supported and elected, and on the 4th of
March, 1881, was inaugurated as President,
amid acclaim, with promise of a successful
Administration. But upon what a slender
thread do human plans rely! Scarcely had
five months elapsed when President Garfield was assassinated by Charles Guiteau,
a man of no repute, and emblems of sorrow
drooped throughout the nation. This national calamity necessitated the second
inauguration of a President during the
year 1881. The then Vice-President, Chester A. Arthur, was duly installed September 30 of that year. His execution of the
duties of that high office, assumed under
conditions intricate and most trying, dis-
armed criticism by its wisdom and ability.

When a prospective candidate for re-
election in 1884 the press of New York,
having solicited expressions of fitness from
delegates to the last National Convention,
I was pleased with the opportunity to
make this small contribution.

Little Rock, Ark., Aug. 1, 1884.
Dear Sir:

I but voice the sentiment of the country
when I say that I consider the Adminis-

tration of President Arthur has been signalized by its justice, eminent statesmanship and wise discretion."

Such was the tenor of mention, but much more pronounced, by men of the party, and Mr. Arthur's nomination previous to the assembling of the next Presidential Convention seemed a foregone conclusion. Nothing I can write will fittingly describe the personnel of James G. Blaine, who was to be the prime feature of the Convention on nomination day. As a man in the field of statesmanship and in intensity of devotion, he was more idolized than any since his prototype, Henry Clay. With political erudition was blended an eloquence inspiring and fascinating; a nobility of character often displayed as the champion of the weak; a disputant adept in all the mazes of analysis, denunciation, or sarcasm, he had created antipathy as bitter as his affections were unyielding. While Speaker of the House, with his counterpart in eloquence, Roscoe Conkling, he had many tilts. One of the most noted and probably far-reaching in impeding his Presidential aspirations, was his defense of General Fry, whom Conkling sought to have impeached, but who was successfully vindicated and afterwards promoted by the War Department. During the struggle Conkling hurled a javelin of taunt and invective, incisive, but thought to be unjust, inducing a response said to have been terrific in its onslaught, confounding the speaker and raising excitement in the House to the highest pitch. I transcribe an epitome of the speech, which will be seen to have bristled with galling ridicule: "As to the gentleman's cruel sarcasm, I hope he will not be too severe. The contempt of that large-minded gentleman is so wilting, his haughty disdain, his grandiloquent swell, his majestic supereminent, overpowering turkey-gobbler strut, has been so crushing to myself and all the members of this House that I know it was an act of the greatest temerity for me to enter upon a controversy with him." Then, quoting ironically a newspaper comparison of Mr. Conkling and Henry Winter Davis, ascribing qualities held by them in common, he proceeded: "The resemblance is great, and it has given his strut additional pomposity. The resemblance is great, it is striking— Hyperion to a satyr; Thersites to Hercules; mud to marble; dunghill to diamond; a singed cat to a Bengal tiger; a whining puppy to a roaring lion. Shade of the mighty Davis, forgive the almost profanation of that jocose satire!"

But James G. Blaine, that master of diplomacy and magnetic fame, with an astute following inspired and wild with gilded promises; the nominating speech of Robert J. Ingersoll, prince of orators, lauding the nominee as "like a mailed warrior, like a plumed knight"—all these forces contributed to turn the tide from Arthur and give him the nomination. I was one of a lonely three of the Arkansas delegation that sood by the State's instructions and voted for Arthur, nine of the delegation voting for Blaine. For obeying the State and not the after conclusion of the delegation, in my next race for a delegate I was "left at the stand."

My failure reminded me of the boy—a humble imitator of the great George Washington—who hacked to death a choice tree. When asked who did it, jolly, gushing and truthful, said, "I did it, pap." The old man seized and gathered him, stopping the whipping occasionally to get breath and wipe off the perspiration, would remark: "And had der imperdence to confess it." The boy, when finally released, between sobs sought solace by saying, "I will never tell the truth again as long as I live." I did not conclude that one should be false to an implied promise with instructions received, but I was impressed with the conviction that it is unwise to trammel a delegation with decisive instructions. A general expression of the feeling or bias of the State Convention is proper, but so much can happen during the interim to change conditions that ultimate action should be largely left to the judgment and integrity of the delegation.

The manner of choosing a President is entirely different from that designed by the founders of the republic. The selection of candidates by an organized party was not anticipated. It was intended that men

(13)

of high character should be chosen by the
citizens of each State as electors, and they
should select the men they deemed most fit
to be President, and the selection thereafter ratified by the vote of the people.   An
elector now is but the mouthpiece of his
party; no matter what may be his individual judgment, he dare not disregard its fiat.
The result of the national election was the
defeat of Mr. Blaine and the election of the
Democratic candidate, Grover Cleveland.
Mr. Cleveland had an independent person-
ality and the courage of his convictions.
Affable and cordial in his intercourse with
Afro-Americans, and to those of his political household was prodigal in the bestowal of appointments.   The effect of this
was that many colored men, leaders of
thought and race action, not seeing an increase of oppression, so freely predicted in
the event of a Democratic President, advocated a division of the colored vote, with
a view of harmonizing feeling and mutual
benefit.   A welcoming of that approach in
the South may be deferred, but will yet be
solicited, despite its present disloyalty to
the fourteenth and fifteenth amendments
to the Constitution.

CHAPTER XVII.

The closing decade of the past century was conspicuous for exhibitions of products of nature and skill intended to stimulate a country's consumption, but mainly to increase exportation; for a nation, not unlike an individual, that buys more than its resources warrant, bankruptcy is inevitable. Hence the industrial struggle of all progressive nations to produce more than they consume, export the residue and thereby add to the national wealth.

The United States not only excels in the magnitude of natural productions, but in skill in manufacturing articles. The vast stretch of agricultural lands for natural products, superiority of mechanical appliance, and the expertness of American workmen herald the supremacy of the United States for quantity, quality and celerity. For Yankee ingenuiy has not only invented a needed article, but has invented a "thing to make the thing."

National and State expositions for the extension of American commerce and development of State undertakings have been marked features of American enterprise, creating a national fraternity, and stimu-

lating domestic industries. While the
financial motive is ever in the forefront
and the impetus that gives it "a habitation
and a name," the moral effect is the reflex
influence of contact, the interchange of
fraternal amenities that ripen and become
helpful for the world's peace, progress and
civilization. At the present time Consuls
of our Government inform the State Department that agents of American manu-
facturers of steel, electric apparatus, city
railroads and improvements in machinery
are in evidence in Europe to an extent hitherto unknown. The directors of the World's
Exposition held at New Orleans, La., in
1884, gave a pressing invitation to Afro-
Americans to furnish exhibits of their production from farm, shop and home. The
late B. K. Bruce, having been created Chief
Director, appointed commissioners for the
various States to solicit and obtain the
best specimens of handicraft in their respective localities for "The Department of
Colored Exhibits," and to which the following refers:

Washington, D. C., Aug. 13, 1884.
Hon. M. W. Gibbs,
Little Rock, Ark.
Dear Sir:
By virtue of authority vested in me as
Chief Director of the Department of Col-
ored Exhibits of the World's Exposition, I
have nominated you for Honorary Commis-
sioner for the State of Arkansas. It is un-
necessary for me at this time to make any

suggestions relative to the importance of managing this business in a manner that will reflect credit on all immediately concerned and our people in general futher than to say that my heart is thoroughly in the work. I will communicate with you from time to time, after being advised of your acceptance, giving necessary information and instructions.

Hoping that you will undertake the fulfillment of the trust, I am,

Very respectfully and truly yours,

D. K. BRUCE,

Chief Director.

I therefore accepted, and proceeded to canvass my State urging the great opportunity offered to show our progress in industry and culture, on the fields of nature or within the realms of art. The movement was a novel one, and the leading colored men and women in the different sections of the State had much to do to awaken the interest that resulted in a very commendable showing.

One of the specialties of these expositions was what was designated as "Emancipation Day," or colored people's day, for the twofold purpose of directing the attention of the general public to race advancement, and inducing a larger attendance of the class directly concerned, and thereby stimulate race pride for greater achievements. With some of our brethren this appointment of a particular day seemed derogatory to their claim of recognition and equality of citizenship, and evoked considerable discussion. In this I thought some of us were unduly sensitive. Where intention can be ascertained it should largely govern our estimate of human action. This exposition was not only open each and every day to our people, but we were constantly invited, and the few who attended were most cordially treated and our exhibits were properly placed without distinction.

The directors of the exposition were gentlemen known to be most liberal in their dealings with us, and regretted the small attendance, remarking that aside from our patronage, the exhibits would be benefical as object lessons, educating and inspiring, and proposed a day—"Colored- People's Day." It was not unlike in design and effect "Emancipation Day" at the Minneapolis Exposition, where noted colored leaders from various States attended and spoke, and were not impressed that it was derogatory to the race.

We have a deal of "gush" about recognition. A demand for recognition presupposes a rightful claim based upon an inherent interest—deportment, special fitness, or legal right. In politics we rightfully claim recognition in the ratio of our numerical contribution to the body politic, and from public carriers, for the reason of performance of our part of the contract.

In our demand for a more extended rec-

PAUL LAWRENCE DUNBAR.

Born in 1872 at Dayton, Ohio—Author and Poet—The Foremost of his Race for
Versatility in the Field of Literature—His Poetry and Prose are Read
in Every Clime Where Men Love Truth and Nature the More
For Being Clothed in Beauty of Diction, or Quaint-
ness of Dialect — He has Published a
Number of Books.

ognition on these material lines, we should first remember that our contributions are generally meager, and that these exhibitions are quite the product of the business ventures and expenditure of our "brother in white," and then brace up and thank Providence that excessive modesty will never "strike in" and kill the Negro. We have the men, the money and the ability to do much, very much more, on many business lines that are now almost exclusively followed by our more prosperous fellow-citizens. No man in our country need beg for recognition; he can compel it if he labors assiduously and takes advantage of opportunity. It can be truly said of Little Rock that the press and leading citizens have been more just and liberal to her colored citizens than any other Southern city. I well remember when her institutions relating to commerce, literature, professions, Board of Trade, Real Estate Exchange, bar and lyceum were open to us, whilst two-thirds of their members were our political opponents. These required but a moderate yearly outlay, repaying, largely, in the amount of information received. Scarcely any availed themselves of these opportunities. If for any reason we do not wish to profit by these overtures, when these trees bear let us not insist upon receiving the choicest of the fruit.

At an indignation mass meeting some time ago a good brother reached the climax of the grievance and then exclaimed:

"How long, O Lord, are we to bear these discriminations?"

"For some time longer," I answered, and then said: "All things considered, we are making progress, and will continue in the ratio we obtain education and wealth, and come forward in the incipiency of public enterprises with our money and practical knowledge from the best possible sources; and, although race identity still exists, the antagonisms and much of the prejudice of which we now complain will be buried under higher activities and greater enterprises—when we have more bank and railroad stock, fewer high-sounding societies, such as "The Seventeen Stars of the Consolidation," "The Rising, Persevering Free Sons of Joshua"; "more landlords and fewer tenants, more owners of plantations and fewer share-workers, more merchants and fewer dudes, more piety and less religion, more economy and less wastefulness, more confidence and less envy. I simply rise to submit these as irresistible claims to a higher recognition." I succeeded in making my escape, for which I was thankful.

CHAPTER XVIII.

Previous to the exposition at New Orleans in 1885, Mr. Henry Brown, of Oberlin, Ohio, visited the Southern States to obtain information as to the views and desire of leading colored men regarding the establishment of "Schools of Trade" in the South where the race could become proficient in all the mechanical arts. He came at the suggestion of philanthropic men of capital in Northern States, who thought by such special means colored men and women could have an opportunity to equip themselves with handicraft, denied them by the trades unions and other influences in the country.

On his presentation of the project in Little Rock, it being so completely in line with my view of a factor so important for the uplifting of the race to a higher manhood and financial standing, I eagerly co-operated. It was determined to take advantage of the attraction of the exposition at New Orleans, issue a call for a conference at that point, and thereby have a representative gathering to obtain their views. I therefore proposed, had printed and issued the following:

CALL FOR A CONFERENCE ON "SCHOOLS OF TRADE."

"Emancipated, turned loose, poor, ignorant and houseless, continually surrounded by difficulties and embarrassments sufficient to appall and retard, by commendable effort on their part, sustained by the generous aid of philanthropists friendly to education, our race in the South has made gratifying advance, mentally and morally. But with this progress of mind and morals, we are confronted with the need of opportunity to qualify ourselves for those activities and industries necessary to make a people prosperous and happy. Our great want now is 'cunning hands' to accompany cultured brains. After obtaining the benefit of our public schools our boys should be fitted for some useful and profitable means of livelihood. The restrictions engendered by trades unions, and the obstacles of race prejudice concur to make it impossible for them to obtain trades in the workshops of the country. Therefore, we need industrial schools where our youth can qualify in the various mechanical pursuits and thereby ennoble themselves, and add value to the State. For the establishment of these "schools of trade" we require a united effort and should make earnest appeal to the philanthropy of the nation.

"In view of this vital necessity the undersigned do hereby call a conference, without distinction, of delegates appointed by mass meetings in cities and counties; presiding officers of colleges, principals of schools, bishops, and leading ministers; editors and publishers friendly to the movement are also invited 'to meet at New Orleans, La., January 15, 1885, for expression on this subject. Signed,

"M. W. Gibbs, Little Rock, Ark.; Hon. J. C. Napier, Nashville, Tenn.; A. De Pose, New Orleans, La.; Hon. J. C. Clousen, Charleston, S. C.; Rev. B. F. Tanner, Philadelphia, Pa.; Joseph Carey, Galveston, Tex.; H. C. Smith, Cleveland, Ohio; W. G. Simmons, Louisville, Ky.; Peter H. Clark, Cincinnati, Ohio; Hon. B. K. Bruce, Washington, D. C.; P. A. Bell, San Francisco, Cal.; J. W. Cromwell, Washington, D. C.; J. Henri Herbert, Trenton, N. J.; Hon. Henry Demas, New Orleans, La.; Rev. E. Lee, Jacksonville, Fla.; W. H. Russell, Indianapolis, Ind.; F. L. Barnett, Chicago, Ill.; A. H. Grimke, Boston, Mass.; E. N. Overall, Omaha, Neb.; H. M. Turner, Atlanta, Ga.; Hon. James Lewis, New Orleans, La.; John S. Leary, Fayettville, N. C.; Hon. Fred Douglass, Washington, D. C.; T. Thomas Fortune, New York; Rev. M. Van Horn, Newport, R. I.; Lloyd G. Wheeler, Chicago, Ill.; J. W. Birney, La Crosse, Wis.;˙ M. M. McLeod, Jackson, Miss.; George T. Downing, Newport, R. I.; D. Augustus Straker, Columbia, S. C.; Hon. P. B. S. Pinchback, New Orleans, La; Peter Joseph, Mobile, Ala.; H. O.

Wagner, Denver, Colo.; Hon. W. A. Pledger, Atlanta, Ga.; H. Fitzbutler, Louisville, Ky.; J. L. Walker, Atchison, Kan.; E. P. Wade, St. Paul, Minn.; F. G. Barbadoes, Washington, D. C."

As a duty, mingled with pleasure, by this humble means I reproduce a record of the names of men who in the last century were intent upon every occasion to promote the welfare of the race, many of whom were conspicuous in their battle for justice and the betterment of their fellow man, thus fitting themselves for harmonies of a higher clime, have now "quiet sleep within the grave," while with the residue "life's shadows are meeting" and will ere long "be lost to sight," with, let us hope, their memory only dimmed by greater activity and deeper consecration by their successors for the ideals they cherished. Ever loyal, we should not—

"Rob the dead of their sweet heritage,
   Their myrrh, their wine, their sheet of
      lead and trophies buried"—
but—
"Go get them where they got them, when
      alive,
   And as resolutely dig or dive."

With the departed was Hon. B. K. Bruce, who, living to manhood under the blighting influences of slavery, by honesty, native ability and persevering study, placed his

BLANCHE K. BRUCE,
Late United States Senator, Register of the United States Treasury.

Born a Slave in 1841 in Virginia—Studied at Oberlin—Sergeant-at-Arms of the Senate of Mississippi—Elected United States Senator in 1874—President Garfield Appointed Him Register of the Treasury May, 1881—A Record Honorable and Inspiring.

name in the forefront, leaving his career
as a model. With an astuteness of perception for the retention of friends, he had
suavity of manner for the palliation of
foes; with diligence and faithfulness winning a constituency that honored him with
a seat in the United States Senate.

The conference called at New Orleans,
La., to promote industrial education, above
referred to, failed to be fruitful. Members
of different religious organizations, without suggestion that their particular sect
would furnish a modicum of the large expenditure necessary to the establishment
of such "schools of trade," strove to have
the movement inaugurated, and launched
under some particular denominational control.

Mr. Brown, whose only object in desiring
to have a conference, was to elicit an expression from leading colored men, an earnest desire for such "schools of trade," and
helpful suggestions, looked on the needless strife with amazement and regret, and
finally determined, as unity of purpose and
a proper concepion of what was needed
were so sadly lacking, to abandon such an
instrumentality to favor his purpose.

It can be properly noted here that among
the many helpful signs of race advancement not the least is a broader fraternal-
ization of our religious bodies, an increasing tolerance, indicative of greater intelligence, the product of a more widely dis-
criminated educated ministry. Our

churches, being our largest organizations numerically (and greatest of moral educators), having the ear of the masses, their opportunity and growing disposition to unite for the material as well as the spiritual progress of our people, cannot be too highly commended.

Industrial fairs, promulgated and held by the colored people in different Southern States, have been exceedingly beneficial and cannot be too often repeated. Several have occurred at Pine Bluff, Ark., on the extensive race and fair grounds owned by Mr. Wiley Jones, who, with Dr. J. H. Smith, Ferdinand Havis and other prominent colored men of the State, by executive ability, tact and judgment made them a success.

The following notice is from a correspondent of the Arkansas Gazette:

"Pine Bluff, Ark., Oct. 21, 1886.

"This, the third day, of the fair was sunny and bright, and the hearts of the management were correspondingly light. Even before the gates were open a long array of teams were seeking admission. The executive officers were early at their posts and no time was lost in beginning the exercises of the day. President J. H. Smith won golden opinions by the pleasant yet firm manner he performed his duties. This morning the Capital Guards were formally received by the Colored Industrial Association.

"Judge Gibbs, of Little Rock, delivered the welcome address, which was a very eloquent and scholarly effort.

"He first praised the directors of the fair for their wonderful success, and said it argues well for the future of the colored people in that they have had extended such cordial support; that nations were influential in the ratio of their agricultural and mechanical development, and that the array of production here made proclaimed in hopeful tones that 'we are coming.'

"He recognized in the formation of the Capital Guards a hopeful omen. Drill develops precision and accuracy, aside from physical development; discipline is invaluable in inculcating the idea of subordination, without which no constitutional government can long exist. Even if they never come within the reach of fiery shot and shell, they would be benefited, and if war's stern summons swept over the land, he felt confident that no more ready response would be made by any class than by the Negro."

Captain Thompson responded in behalf of his company, and alluded to the whole-souled hospitality that had been bestowed upon them by the authorities of the fair and the citizens generally. The Press Association had by their speeches proclaimed that the "pen was mightier than the sword," which he denied; that the independence of this country from the thraldom of England was won by Washington's sword, and that Lincoln's pen only became effective after the sword had paved the way. It was a recognized arbiter in the disputes of nations, although the pen could render secure what the sword had won." The Captain put his company through several evolutions that were very creditably performed.

In affairs of this character the comingling of the substantial and best element of the white race, their liberal subscriptions and fraternal endeavor, give impetus and valuable assistance, emphasizing the fact along the lines of a higher industrial advancement that they are in hearty sympathy. We cannot too often have these object evidences of our progress. They speak loud and convincing far beyond oral announcement the most eloquent. It stimulates the farmer to extra exertion and more careful measures for increase of quality and quantity of his crop; it inspires the artisan and mechanic for his best handiwork, and welcomes articles the product of our cultured and refined women from the realms of the home. We need this continued stimulus, shut out as we are from most of the higher industries, the incentive born of contact, and which promotes rivalry, to us is denied; hence our inspiration must be inborn and unceasing.

In the economy of God and nature, His handiwork, prominent is "the survival of the fittest." The fittest survive because they excel. Whether within the student's study or the mechanic's bench, it is excellence that counts and heralds its own superiority. If we desire not only the best personal success, but to be helpful to the race, it is not enough for one to be known as doctor, lawyer, mechanic, or planter; but it is upon what round of the ladder of science mechanics or agriculture he stands. Is he above mediocrity; does he excel? The affirmative answer to this is the heroic offspring of self-denial and unceasing mental toil.

A feature of attraction at these fairs has been the drill and martial bearing of our military companies, for while jubilant in the "pride and pomp and circumstance of glorious war," the measure of praise for precision of manouver of the soldier is only excelled by commendation for his bravery in action. The colored citizen took quiet pride and much interest in these companies and were saddened when many were commanded by the State authorities to disband. The motives which conspired and demanded their dissolution were not commendable, but ungrateful, for the Negro soldier in every war of the Republic has been valorous, loyal, and self-denying, and has abundantly earned a reputation for discipline and obedience to every military requirement.

The organization of these companies, furnished with State arms, authorized and under the patronage of the government of many of the Southern States, created an

(14)

"esprit d'corps," a fellowship and worthy ambition conducive to harmony and the general welfare.

Political friction, no doubt, had much to do with their displacement. But now the Democracy, so long in power, with majorities in many of these States almost cumbersome, could well afford to allow and patronize these conservators for peace and efficient protectors in war, who are ever ready to say, as Jehu to Jonahab, "Is thy heart right, as my heart is with thine heart? If it be, give me thine hand."

Previous to a Presidential campaign I attended a meeting of leading colored Republicans at New Orleans, La. It was not called as a strictly political conference in the interest of any particular candidate, but to exchange views and hear suggestions relating to pending legislation in Mississippi and South Carolina for curtailing, if not abolishing Negro suffrage in those States. Although the political condition of the Negro was then and continues to be of such moment that at no intelligent gathering will it fail to "bob up" and demand a hearing, and this was no exception. While the claims of Reed, Morton, Allison, Harrison, and McKinley were freely discussed, the suffrage was the leading topic.

Prominent among the attendants were T. T. Fortune, of New York; N W. Cuney and E. J. Scott, of Texas; W. A. Pledger and H. E. Johnson, of Georgia; P. B. S. Pinchback, James Lewis, and J. Madison

TIMOTHY T FORTUNE.
Editor and Publisher of "New York Age."

Born in Jackson County, Florida, October 6, 1856—Polished and Able—On the Staff of the White Press at Metropolitan Centers—The Most Aggressive and Trenchant Writer of the Negro Press.

Vance, of Louisiana; Stevens, of Alabama; Stevens, of Louisville, Ky., E. Fortune, of Florida; C. W. Anderson, of New York, and others.

The late N. W. Cuncy, of Texas, was a man of commanding presence, forceful and emphatic as a speaker; honest, tireless and self-sacrificing. His sterling qualities as a leader of men grows brighter as time recedes from his demise.

Fearless in enunciation, the timid thought him impractical. But there is ever this concerning unpopular truth: When it induces honest thought that burns to be spoken, you can depend it is not confined to a single possessor; it has habitation in many hearts. But he alone is the "leader of leaders," who, with Eolion harp or trumpet call summons its worshipers. Among matters discussed was the charge that Negro delegations were a marketable commodity, with no convictions as to national policy, no regard for manly probity, and were ever at the beck of the highest purchaser in the political market. Such a sweeping charge is most unjust; but, if granted, the admission cuts deeply in the opposite direction, requiring no analysis to discover the preponderance of venality. It may happen between the receiver of stolen goods and the thief that impulse to steal is sometimes weakened by uncertainty of market. The Negro delegate has no market to seek; the market is jammed under his nose at every turn by immaculate white

men, often entrusted with large sums to
be placed "where it will do the most good,"
report to those interested the purchase of
Negro votes, when such was not the fact.
Satisfied they had placed it where it would
do them the most good, by allowing it to
rest in their pockets, this was not only hard
on the Negro, but mean to charge him up
with it, then not let him have it. To say
there were no colored men susceptible to
such advances would be as idle as to say
there were no white men thereby influenced; but in either case let us hope it was
the exception and not the rule.

Conferences for statement and appeal
for removing harsh conditions are historic,
antedating and creating constitutional government; for, implanted in the hearts is a
consciousness of right, however much selfish hate may shut out recognition, or avarice stifle its egress, and the measure of accord granted just claims of the petitioner
is the moral and Christian status of a commonwealth.

It may be noted here that the character
of accord given the Negro in his now severe
battle for justice and equality before the
law by the Christian churches and other organizations is of a peculiar kind. While
the benefactions for moral and Christian
education is to him indispensable, it is not
the kind most prominent and effectually
practiced by the Divine Master to dissipate
wrong. He forbids the cry of peace when
there is no peace. He was aggressive and

distinct. The peculiarity of accord can be accounted for in this, that it is so much easier for the well-to-do Christian to donate to the Negro than by word or pen to denounce the wrongs to which he is subject. Wrong smiles complacently at any mode save direct attack. It is not in silent acquiescence, but on the forum of agitation and denouncement, that reform finds lodgment, so sadly needed in many of the States where he is the victim of lawlessness and murder, his ballot suppressed, and denied representation. The partiality and indecent haste with which he is tried and almost invariably sent to the penitentiary, where as convict he receives the most barbarous treatment. As a people no one denies that they are law-abiding; as laborers in all the avenues of industry in which they are capable they are faithful and honest: as patriots at the incipiency and duration of the Government they have been faithful and brave. If, then, in the roll of patriots, citizens and producers, they have maintained character for fidelity, deportment. and industry, surely they can rightly claim and demand as citizens of the Republic protection from outrage, justice in the courts and in every way equality before the law. They ask for nothing more, and would be unworthy to be content with any less.

The cry of "Negro domination," like the "baseless fabric of a vision," has as little foundation. The problem to be solved is not what is or shall be the status of the colored man born beneath the flag, but whether the forces of Christian civilization, the genius and spirit of our Government, impartiality in the execution of law, without let or hindrance, are equal to the performance of their missions, or are only "sounding brass and tinkling cymbols." That is the problem for our white fellow-citizens to solve. That which most troubles the Negro is has the nation sufficient Christianity and regard for justice to allow these forces to prevail? The assumption that citizens of a common country cannot live together in amity is false, denying as it does that lawful citizenship is the panoply and bulwark of him who attains it, that should vindicate and shield him, whether he be high or low, at home or abroad, whenever or wherever his civil rights are invaded.

CHAPTER XIX.

Never in the history of conventions was there recorded such evidence of unswerving fidelity by an equal number to the nominee of their choice as that shown at the National Convention in 1880, when General Grant's name was before the assembly. Ordinarily when a leader is nominated for ballot his supporters are faithful as long as his prospects are inviting, but at the first evidence of decadence no flock of partridges scamper more readily to find cover. For years his birthday has been celebrated by a reunion of the 306 who, from the first to the last of sounding of the 36th ballot, stood with ranks solidly closed and courage undaunted. At such a reunion at Philadelphia, in 1893, eighty were present, and with speech, reminiscence and good cheer "a feast of reason and a flow of soul," time sped "till the wee sma' hours." Of the colored delegates, Mr. Ferdinan Havis and the writer were present.

Mr. Havis, of Arkansas, "to the manor born," deserves more than mere mention as the representative of a class in the South.

He is a gentleman of fine qualities of head and heart. As a member of the Ar-

kansas Legislature in 1873 and Clerk of
Jefferson County for many years, he has
by honesty as an official and courtesy of
manner made an unimpeachable record,
and was only dethroned "by fraud and
force and iron will." During his leadership
of Jefferson County,where three-quartersof
all voters are colored, he was ever conservative and regardful of the views and business interests of the numerically weak but
financially strong minority of Democrats,
and by supporting a compromise ticket
that gave most prominence to the minority
sought to preserve harmony. But the efforts of such men have proved unavailing
to stem the tide of political usurpation,
now rampant at many places in the South.

The greatest menace to representative
government is not solely the disfranchisement of the Negro, for according with the
eternal verities there cannot be a continued
disregard for the ballot in his hand and
protection for his life, and respect for them
in the person of the white man. Under the
genius of our Government the rights of
claim and exercise are linked and interlinked.

This truth stands out in bold relief on
historic page, and should the future historian record the dismemberment of the
Republic, he will indite its decay from the
commencement of the violation of this
basic principle of civil government, his being but another link in the evidence that
rapidity of material, without equality of

moral, advancement is ever attended with national decline.

Meanwhile, it is the duty (which is ever the highest policy) of the Negro to be patriotic in his devotion to his country, manly in his appeals for justice, and wise by discarding, by word or action, the fomenting of strife; ever on the alert to close the breach by increase of intelligence, moral worth and financial progress, and thus in great measure dissipate ignorance, vice and poverty, the abolition of which can be assisted, but not dispelled, save by a spirit of self-sacrifice on his part, subjecting his lower nature to the control of the higher. With such effort, united to a faith in God and the American conscience, he will yet soften ascerbities, dispel hindrance, and stem the tide.

Philanthropy may assist a man to his feet, but cannot keep him there unaided by self-effort and an unconquerable will power to stand; while relinquishing no part of his claim upon his white brother as recompense for more than a century of unrequited labor, if with an equal chance for work, education and legal protection, he cannot not only stand, but advance, exertion in his behalf is "love's labor lost," he having no rights worthy of respect.

But in no fair mind can there exist doubt as to his advancement. A people nine-tenths of whom 40 years ago did not legally own themselves or property, now having 140,000 farms, homes and industries worth $800,000,000; a people who, for a century previous to emancipation, were by law forbidden to learn to read or write, now have 3,000,000 children in 27,000 schools, and have reduced their illiteracy 45 per cent., have school and church property to the amount of $50,000,000, contributing themselves thereto $20,000,000; have written 300 books; have over 250 newspapers issued each week. His comparative success as merchant, mechanic or other line of industry which he is permitted to enter, speaks for itself, and finally, with per capita valuation of $75. Yet, in face of such statistical evidence, there are not wanting the Tillmans, Morgans, Burke Cockrans and other seers of a Montgomery convention, who, because the Negro, trammeled, as he is, does not keep step with the immense strides of the dominant class in their wondrous achievement, the product of a thousand years of struggle and culture, unblushingly allege that he is relapsing into barbarism, and with an ingratitude akin to crime, are oblivious to the fact that a large measure of the intellectual and material status of the nation and the cultured ability they so balefully use to retard him, are the product of a century of his unrequited labor.

The feeling that the results of the civil war have been beneficent, harmonizing theory and practice in the autonomy of the nation is manifest and conceded. The growing unity of the people of our country who 40 years ago were engaged in fraternal strife, should be a source of pleasure and welcomed by every patriotic heart; for, while bitterness can be assuaged, and laudable effort made to conform to new conditions, still convictions formed and baptized in the fiery ordeal of war, blood and material loss require fortitude, generosity and pariotism to soften their asperity, and much kindly intercourse to promote the general welfare. The increased desire in this direction is evidenced at each recurring "Decoration Day," when the Blue and the Gray harmoniously intermingle, recalling memories and incidents of the internal strife. The soldiers of each vieing in reciprocity, as with "a union of hearts and a union of hands" with fragrant flowers they bedeck historic sod.

But will the nation remember that after all that can be said or written, of heroic circumstance of war, or in praise of its participants, all these bereft of humanity and justice to the weak, fail to constitute an enduring State, for eternal and immutable is the decree that "righteousness exalteth a nation." Relative to this intermingling of former foes, whatever our estimate of the results of human action may be, we cannot unerringly divine impurity of motive; hence respect for honest conviction must be the prelude to that unity of patriotism which is ever the safeguard to the integrity of a nation.

The spirit that impelled contributions for the erection of the Confederate monuments in different sections of our country from donors, irrespective of former affiliation, has been benign in its influence. In 1897 the Hon J. N. Smithea instituted a movement for such a memorial in Little Rock, Ark., stipulating that responses should be limited to one dollar. Impressed that our race should not be indifferent to such an appeal, I transmitted the following:

J. N. Smithea, Editor "Gazette,"

Little Rock, Ark.:

I notice your effort to erect a monument to the Confederate dead. A third of a century has elapsed since the civil war. Conviction in the minds of the participants on either side as to who was right and who was wrong is as firmly fixed as the eternal hills. Given, that a view of events leading up to that fraternal strife, the bravery of the one or heroic conduct of the other from standpoints necessarily different will never find mutual ground for justification, it seems the mission of patriotism and national unity to give the hand of welcome to every effort that will unite us in all that will promote the common glory of the Republic. As one of the representatives of a race, especially in this southland, I cheerfully subscribe my dollar to the fund, feeling that the Negro should joyfully hail every effort to soften animosities which are the outgrowth of a struggle in which, unwittingly, he was so important a factor.

WILLIAM A. PLEDGER,
Chairman Republican State Central Committee of Georgia.

Born near Athens forty-five years ago—Has been a delegate to every National Republican
Convention for the last twenty-five years—A leader trusted and tried.

No one should be more anxious to cement
the friendly and good offices of our more
favored fellow-citizens, from whom we are
receiving the largest share of our educational and material assistance, so greatly
needed to bring us up to the full measure
of a noble citizenship. By the providence
of God we are here, and are here to stay.
We are producers of wealth and the conservators of peace. Therefore, encourage
us by the exercise of justice and magnanimity, that we can say to you, as Ruth to
Naomi in Holy Writ: "Entreat me not to
leave thee, or to return from following after thee, for whither thou goest I will go;
and where thou lodgest I will lodge; thy
people shall be my people, and thy God
my God; where thou diest will I die, and
there will I be buried; the Lord do so to me
and more also, if aught but death part thee
and me."

Very truly yours, etc.,

Monuments are the mute mile stones, the
connecting links between a finished effort,
and an inspiration for continued struggle.
But monuments are not created after the
death of those they commemorate, although they may seem to be; they are but
memorials of the structure already built,
the solidity of whose base and symmetry of
whose lines were projected and fashioned
by intensity of conviction and the unswerving courage of their prototypes in amelio-
rating conditions while they lived. Bereft

of this, "monuments themselves memorials need."

Having administered the office of Register of United States land by appointments from Presidents Hayes and Arthur, my last service in the Interior Department was under an appointment from President Harrison, who, in 1889, placed me as Receiver of Public Moneys at Little Rock, Ark., Land District. It was during this term that the Department ordered and appointed Special Commissioners to conduct the sale of unsold lots on the Hot Springs Reservation at auction. As one of the Commissioners and Receiver of Public Moneys, I was required and gave a qualified bond for $100,-000 for the faithful performance of the trust, and with Register Raleigh proceeded and discharged the duties thereto. Harrison's term ended a career of twelve years in the land office. If in retrospective moments amid the many beneficent things you might have done, but left undone, you catch here and there glimpses of unselfish ambition or benefit you have conferred, it does much to abate regret, for the recollection to me is a source of pleasure that during those terms by personal convass and unofficial publication I contributed in inducing thousands of immigrants and others to homestead the virgin soil of Arkansas, who have now good homes, comprising 40, 80 or 160 acres of land, besides assisting them in establishing schools for their children.

CHAPTER XX.

In October, 1897, by telegrams from my friends, Nathaniel McKay and Dr. Purvis, of Washington, D. C., I was informed that I had been appointed United States Consul for the island of Madagascar.

It was a surprise; for, while truth compels the admission that I was not averse to "being taken in and done for," Madagascar had not come within my purview; its distance had not "lent enchantment to the view." I gave it some thought, but could not perceive that I had been so annoyingly persistent to merit a response from the President, not unlike that given by Mr. Blaine to one Mr. Tite Barnacle, who was willing to compromise on a foreign appointment. "Certainly," was the reply; the "foreigner the better." I concluded, however, that the bard may have been right when he wrote "There is a destiny that shapes our ends," for it often happens that what a man desires is just what he ought not to have; and whether what he gets is to be beneficial depends largely upon its use.

I was summoned to Washington, and after a conference received my commission, returned to Little Rock to prepare for departure to my post, "10,000 miles away."

I received a warm greeting and a "jolly send-off" at a banquet given me on Christmas eve by many friends. To name a few of the devoted would be invidious to the many. It will suffice to say I felt grateful and touched by the many expressions, which added testimony to their valued appreciation. Arriving at New York I was met by Mr. W. H. Hunt, who had applied and been highly commended for the position of clerk to the consulate, and who, after a year's faithful service, in pursuance of my recommendation, was appointed Vice-Consul, and is now Consul.

This, my appointment as Consul to Tamatave, severs a decade's connection as "Secretary of the Republican State Central Committee," and especially with its Chairman, Mr. Henry Cooper, who, indefatigable as a worker, genial, but positive in his convictions, has managed the machinery of the party with but little friction. The remembrance of the partiality, honors and kindness of which I have been a recipient from members of the party, irrespective of "race or previous condition," will be ever bright and cheery.

On January, 1, 1898, we embarked on the French steamship Champagne, and arrived at Havre on the 9th, and took train for Paris. The cars either for comfort or retirement in no way equal ours, eight in a compartment, sitting omnibus fashion, face to face. We rolled on to the Capital, passing many fine villas, the product of French

architecture. Everywhere one is impressed
with the national peculiarities—the houses,
the streets, modes of conveyance and transportation. Compactness, neatness, order
and precision pervades their every under-
taking; but for celerity and despatch of
business they were painful to encounter or
behold, for it ill accords with the American
mode. A ride of fours hours and we reach
Paris. At the depot the baggage is placed
on long tables awaiting examination by
custom-house officers. Mine was passed
without. Took cab for "Hotel de Binda,"
exquisitely furnished and centrally located,
having easy access to places of note.

This being the most disagreeable time of
year, a fire in the rooms was necessary, for
outside everywhere was a damp, penetrat-
ing air, remaining here 15 days with the
sight of the sun but once.

The next day after my arrival I called on
the American Ambassador, Mr. Porter, in
relation to my exequator, to be issued by
the French Government. It is a recognition of status, and a formal permit from
one nation to another to allow their respective Consuls to exercise the duties ap-
pertaining thereto and a guarantee of protection in their performance. Had a very
cordial reception from Mr. J. R. Gowdy, our
Consul at Paris. Visited the Paris office
of the New York Herald, where many files
of American and European papers can be
perused. A visit to the "Louvre" is a joy
for the layman, as for the connoisseur, gal-

(15)

leries a mile or more in length hung with paintings grand in imagery and beauty of old masters, French and Italian, centuries old. Many showed the silent, slow and impressive steps of age. But "you may break, you may scatter the vase if you will, the scent of the roses will linger there still," for on shrunken canvas or from luster dimmed was imperial tone of materialized conception "not born to die."

Among the guests of the hotel were two gentlemen, one an American capitalist, the other a German merchant from Berlin, the latter speaking French like a native. We became pleasant companions, and concluded on Sunday evening to go to the "Follies Bergere"—in American parlance a variety theater.

Ten minutes' drive brought us to a very large building, lighted as if by sunlight, where a hundred finely-dressed men and women crowded for entrance. Outside of what we term pit and dress circle is a partition, three or four feet high, dividing them from a promenade ten or fifteen feet wide. You can stand or sit in this promenade, and see the performance. Our friends suggested this plan, as we could see and hear more of Parisian peculiarities. Here many very beautiful women promenaded. They had evidently been touched by artists, for their make-up was superb. But I could not but think of the refrain of a song we have all heard, "Oh, but what a difference in the morning." They had sweet, pretty sayings, clothed in all the softness of modulation and earnestness of gesture of the French people. My American friend, like myself, was Frenchless, and as a consequence invulnerable. The appearance of the occupants of the front row of seats very forcibly reminded me of a similar locality at the Capital Theater in the City of Roses, on similar occasions, where many of my old friends with gaze intent loved to congregate. The performance was spectacular and acrobatic, with usual evolutions, with more "abandon" and very artistic. Passing through the cafe, where hundreds of finely-dressed men and women were sitting at tables quietly talking, smoking and drinking wine or coffee, we passed to the street.

There is much to delight in a walk through the Tulleries and "Palace de la Concord." These public squares have an acreage of several hundred, and are adorned with flowing fountains and marvelous statuary. Passing through the Tulleries brings you to the "Dome de Invalids," in which is Napoleon's tomb. The building and dome is of the most exquisite architecture. Upon entry everywhere your gaze is confronted by stately columns of Italian marble arches, statuary, flags of many varieties, captured by Napoleon from his enemies on many battlefields, besides other trophies of war.

As you look down a circular pit twenty feet deep and forty feet wide, enclosed by a balustrade of Italian marble, you see the sarcophagus, in which is inclosed all that was mortal of the great Napoleon. The mosaic pavement at the bottom of the pit represents a wreath of laurels; on it rests the sarcophagus, consisting of a single block, highly polished, of reddish brown granite, fourteen feet high, thirteen long and seven wide, brought from Finland at a cost of $25,000. Above rises a lofty dome 160 feet high, divided into two sections, one of twelve compartments, each containing a figure of one of the twelve apostles; the other representing St. Louis offering to Christ the sword with which to vanquish his enemies.

While in Paris I visited Mrs. Mason, widow of James Mason, deceased. Mr. Mason was formerly a member of the Arkansas Senate and Sheriff of Chicot County. It will be remembered by old residents that the death of Mason's father, an old bachelor and rich planter, who died intestate, caused a suit at law of great interest and importance. It was an exciting trial, as many thousands of dollars were at stake in the issue. The fatherly care he had ever evinced for the education of his children (James having been educated in France and Martha at a Northern college); the solicitude and unfailing recognition, the many instances of which he had designated them as direct heirs, and other evidence, collateral and convincing, were availing. They received a jury award.

HON. JOHN C. DANCY,
Recorder of Deeds for District of Columbia.

Born at Torboro, S. C., May, 1857—Entered Howard University—Elected Recorder of Deeds of Edgecombe County, S. C., in 1880 and 1882—Late Collector of the Port at Willmington, S. C.—Christian and Progressive in the Church—Eminent and Eloquent in the State.

An appeal to the Supreme Court of the
United States was taken, which dragged
its weary way for a number of years, but
resulted in confirming the decision of the
lower court. Mrs. Mason was for many
years, through the patronage and kindness
of Senator Garland and other members of
Congress from Arkansas, a clerk in the
Land Office at Washington. I found Mrs.
Mason living in well-appointed apartments
with her daughter, an artistic painter of
some note, with studio adjoining, where I
was shown many beautiful productions of
her brush. I was conversant with many instances in the North where Southern planters had brought their colored families to be
educated, purchasing and giving them
property for settlement and sustenance, especially that their girls might escape the
environments which undoubtedly awaited
them at the South. These were in fine and
valuable contradistinction to many cases
similarly related, where they were sold on
the auction block to the highest bidder.
But in all candor it cannot but be supposed
that in many instances the sale of the
planter's own flesh and blood was involun-
tary. High living, neglect of the comparative relation of resource and expenditure,
gambling for big stakes on steamboat and
at Northern watering places, brought the
evil day with attending results to the
"chattel" subject to the baneful caprice of
unrestrained liberty.

On the 23d of January, 1898, I was taking my leave of Paris to meet my steamer

at Marseilles for a 20-day voyage for Madagascar. My stay at the hotel had been pleasant, and I supposed had received all necessary attention from the servants that occasion demanded; but in character it had been individual. Now it was united, for in doorway and on staircase they were (like Tennyson's cannon) servants "to the right of me and servants to the left of me," smiling and gracious. One, of whom I had no recollection of having previously seen, approached me with an obeisance decidedly French to remind me that he was the "baggage man" and attended to it when I arrived. I replied, "You are not the man who took up my baggage." "No," he said; "I am the man who looked after the man who watched the man who did take it up." "Oh!" I said; and then remembering that he and I had much in common, his English and my French being twins, I conceded his claim, "tipped" others that impeded my exit, and made hasty retreat.

Leaving Paris at 2:30 P. M., at 2 in the morning we reached Lyons, stopping 25 minutes for coffee and refreshments, which reached a long-felt want, arriving at Hotel de Louvre et de la Paix, at Marseilles, three hours later. Paris is prolific in names of its hotels, but this was commensurate in luxury and first class in every particular, very large, the finest in Marseilles and said to be unsurpassed in France. It is approached by a hall-way fifty feet long from Rue Canebrian (the street), which leads you into an oval-shaped court 100 by 200 feet. Around this court in niches are finely-sculptured statuary, paintings and choice flowers in porcelain vases. Out of this court you are conducted into the hotel proper. Spacious stairways of Italian marble, the tread of which covered with Turkish carpets, leads you to the interior. The court in the inner center of the hotel rises to a height of five or six stories, and is covered by parti-colored glass, which emits a soft and pleasing tint on all below. The dining room was "a thing of beauty," and the menu "a joy forever." The adornments of the room would well befit a palace. Oh, that I had the tongue of an orator or the pen of a ready writer, to fitly describe! Took breakfast and then a stroll along the principal streets of the city and the wharves of the Mediterranean. The city resembled a bee hive; the houses and streets are literally crowded with men and women of all nationalities and costumes.

Wending our way to "Notre Dame," a magnificent church on a hill, one thousand feet above the level of the city, entirely overlooking it, while the Mediterranean lies sparkling in the distance directly below. On the top of the dome of this edifice is a figure encased in gold, representing "Holy Mary" with the Christ in her arms. A gallery surrounds the church, from which the view is grand and imposing. Ascent and descent can be made by an elevator.

On the 25th of January we embarked on
board our ship, the "Pie Ho," and found
state room comfortable for the longest voyage of our travel. The view as we pass out
of the harbor of Marseilles is quite picturesque, with its quaint old buildings, mountainous surroundings, its medley of ships,
soldiers and sailors of every nation, differing in uniform and costume. Here, as I
suppose it is everywhere where love and
friendship dwell, hundreds had assembled
at docks and quays and other points of vantage to waive hands and handkerchiefs of
a loving farewell. I thought of my dear
daughter on the wharf at New York and
her anxious gaze until we were lost in the
distance. This ship, the "Pie Ho," of a
French line, is said to be old, but staunch,
comfortable and giving good service; but a
failure in that particular the want of which
retards the success of many people of whom
it could be truthfully said by Christian and
moralist that they were good and reliable.
The "Pie Ho" is not swift, but if she retains
the commendation that oft accompanies
slowness, that of being sure, we should be
content. But age has its limits, and happy
should all be who safely and honorably
round up the voyage of life.

We are now in full view of Mount Strom-
bol in the Mediterranean, a volcano in full
blast, emitting fire and clouds of smoke.
Yesterday we entered the Ionian Sea; today we have land on either side, Sicily on
our right and Italy on our left, with a good

view of its coast lines; cities, towns, cultivated fields and trains in motion. At 2
P. M. January 30 we see Dermot Light-
house, and at 3 reach Port Said. The Khe-
dive's dominion, a Government and business point, with many consular residences.
It was the first sight of the "old flag" since
leaving Marseilles. It is a new baptism of
patriotism for one to see the national banner so far from home, and impromptu he
sings, "long may it wave," for "with all thy
faults I love thee still."

We anchored out in the bay, and with
small boats went ashore. Port Said is quite
cosmopolitan both in its business and residence features. Nearly every nationality
has its representative in trade, but numerically the unspeakable Turk is very much
in evidence. On landing one of the guards,
numerous and whose charges are fixed by
law, took us in charge to show us the city.
The streets generally were unimproved and
irregular, both in architecture and location.
Through several dingy and untidy streets
he led us to the public park, which made
considerable pretension to order and neatness. The turban, the wrap, the sandals
and other Oriental costumes, which made
up the dress, were not more varied than
the complexion of the people, but their
features were generally fine-cut. A marble
bust of De Lesseps, the contractor of the
Suez Canal, which we shall soon enter, has
a prominent place.

Through several streets, monotonous for
disorder and uncleanliness, we reached the

"Mosque," the Mahomedan place of worship. In the minaret high up on the tower stood an officer awaiting the hour to lower the flag as a signal to all Musselmen that they could eat, the day being one of their fast days. In all the streets through which we passed could be seen groups of the faithful with anxious look toward the minaret to catch the first downward movement of the flag. It came at last, and with it the shouting and running of the crowds to booths and stands for eating purposes that lined the sidewalks. We approached the "Mosque" with all the solemnity possible for hypocritical heretics to assume, and were met at the door by a grave and reverent sire, who interviewed the guide.

We had been told that we would have to take off our shoes (just here we noted the same pliancy observable in many of our own denomination when there is prospect of getting the almighty dollar). In some way the matter was compromised by putting on over our shoes large sandals made of straw. After paying 50 centimes each (equal to 10 cents in our currency), we entered a large room without furniture or other adornment, with stone floor, some matting, upon which a number of worshipers were kneeling and supplicating "Allah," their supreme being. There was an earnestness that bespoke sincerity, and an all-abiding faith. I could but think how few of us who would criticise are true to the creed we profess.

In a kind of lavatory adjoining could be seen men washing their feet and doing oddities unmentionable preparatory to worship.

After wandering about the building for some time I was accosted by one of the attendants, and was made to understand that one of my feet was uncovered. I had lost one of my sandals. I was rather uneasy for a while, not knowing what they might do with that unholy foot that had desecrated the temple. The guide found it, however, and "Richard was himself again." After leaving the "Mosque" the guide escorted us shipward through the business portion of the city, neat and cleanly, with hotels and stores creditable to a metropolis. But for beggars of unrivaled persistency I commend you to Port Said, for with a pitiableness, sincere or assumed, they dog your every footstep.

At the southern part of the city is a large cemetery, having stones with many hieroglyphics and inscriptions denoting the former locality, character and virtues of the dead. With the scholar are interred copies of his literary productions; with the soldier, his sword; with the statesman, a roll of his achievements for the good of the state, for presentation to "Allah."

CHAPTER XXI.

The passage through the Suez Canal was somewhat monotonous, but a continued reminder of bible history. On either side as far as the eye could reach the desert spread out its sandy atoms glistening in the sun.

Out of the canal we are in the Gulf of Suez, and in a few hours in the Red Sea, an interesting locality in ancient history. It is there we learn that Pharaoh and his hosts met their Waterloo (with the accent on the water) in the pursuit of the children of Israel. But here we find conflicting opinions. Some say that Pharaoh, arriving at the bank and seeing the impossibility of overtaking them, turned and retired; others, that there were shoal places in those far-away days where any one could cross; others, that they crossed on flats very like the ordinary modern mortal. But I do not accept this attempt to question the orthodox version, but will verify it as far as my observation will admit. The sea was likely red in those days, and has very properly retained its name on account of the locality being red-hot at times, or, perhaps, chameleon like, changes its color. This morning, however, it is a deep blue. As to Pharaoh and his hosts getting drowned, there cannot be doubt, if it was in its present condition and they attempted to cross on foot.

But this we do know, that the success of the "Children of Israel" in not being "overtaken" has been the prototype of father to son in every effort to do so from that day to the present. There is a serious view, however. Here the sea, sky and neighborhood of Jerusalem, pyramids, monuments and sacred traditions all conspire to have a solemn and awe-inspiring effect. Thousands of generations of men have lived and moved in the activities that engage modern humanity, but have passed like fleeting shadows, leaving only these sentinels as perpetual reminders. While the "Red Sea" sings in murmuring cadence that "men may come, and men may go, but I go on forever," doubly impressing us that

"So the multitude goes, like the flower or weed,
That wither away to let others succeed;
So the multitude comes, even those we behold,
To repeat every tale that has often been told."
But a truce to moralizing on the past.

The children of Israel seem to have made and kept their record as "passengers." I was interested in the passage of a child of Ham. I am somewhat deficient in Bible history, and am without knowledge of the whereabouts of Ham's children at that

time, or whether they had "crossing" to do;
but if they possessed the proverbial character imputed to some of their offspring,
antipathy to water, especially for lavatory
purposes, I am of the opinion they took no
desperate chances, "content to bear the ills
they had than fly to those they knew not
of."

Passing Hurich Island, a British possession, and having had a very pleasant passage on the Red Sea, we arrive at Djiboute,
Abyssinia, the terminus of King Menelik's
domain, the scenes of recent conflict between Italy and the King's forces, the "un-
pleasantness" resulting unprofitably to the
Italians. There were landed from the ship
many boxes of rifles and ammunition for
the King's governor, who resides here. During the few hours we remained there, we
were interested in and enjoyed the gathering of ten or fifteen native boys around the
ship diving for centimes or francs thrown
by the passengers, their dexterity as divers,
securing every penny, was as clever as gro-
tesque. They remained in the water six or
eight hours during the ship's stay. A few
hours brought us to Aden, a very strongly
fortified appendage to the British Empire
at the south end of the Red Sea. For armament and strategical locality it is the
Gibraltar of the southern seas.

The rivalry of native boatmen for passengers and luggage to take ashore was
appalling. When I say it surpassed a third
ward political meeting in "ye olden times"

in Little Rock I faintly describe it. Sunday morning; once more on the way; one more stop, and then to Tamatave, our destination.

Looking this beautiful morning on the foam-crest waves as they roll in sportive emulation, with a cloudless sky coming down on every side to kiss the horizon, shutting out human vision of all else beyond, one could not fail to be impressed with the greatness, the omnipotence of the Creator. This being but a speck of that vast whole, comprising the celestial and terrestrial aggregation, he, indeed, who regards this sublime workmanship as the product of chance and not that of a superhuman architect and law-giver, by Whom every atom of nature is controlled, is more to be pitied than condemned.

To conclude our voyage, we have six or seven days of "innocuous desuetude." That is what I believe President Cleveland designated a monotonous and unprofitable period. I am not certain, however, and one should be careful in quoting great authors.

We pass the Gulf of Aden and enter the Indian Ocean, Rem Huffien Island to the right, and now appears the eastern coast lines of the continent of Africa. On that continent, I learn, lies the ashes of my forefathers. Peace abide with them, and may peace crowned with justice come to such of their descendants as are still the victims of dishonesty and inhumanity by enlightened and professedly Christian nations.

Travel by sea loses in interest as you re-
cede or are midway between distant points.
You somehow feel yourself located in the
neighborhood of "Mahomet's coffin," and
have a sort of a "don't-care-a-continental"
atmosphere surrounding you, with nothing
to arrest attention save the usual incidents
of ocean voyage, with no land in sight. The
constitutional promenade on deck before
and after meals, with the French etiquette
of raising your hat or cap as you pass;
reading or lounging on sofas or reclining
chairs; relating individual experiences of
life or travel; criticising the conduct of others than yourselves; the welcome sound of
the bell that calls you to meals; the last
view of the sun as it bids you "good-bye,"
with its ineffectual rays, and gently sinks
beneath the horizon; the rising of the
moon, shedding its sheen of sparkling light on the dancing waves; retirement to your couch to listen awhile to
the heavy breathing, and feel the pulse-
beat of the iron monitor as it speeds you
onward; finally to sleep, to dream of loved
ones at home.

The suavity of the French is in notable
contrast with the more taciturn deportment of the English; amiable contact has
much to do with softening the asperities
of life.

We are now crossing the heretofore
much-dreaded equator—weather splendid,
light, cloth suit not uncomfortable, but we
are at sea and not on land. The forward

deck is today given up to the sports of the
sailors (the custom when crossing the line),
and is now the center of attraction—running "obstacle races," the two competitors
getting under, and from under a canvas-
sheet held to the deck by a number of their
fellows, and then running for the goal,
picking up potatoes as they ran. Afterwards, with bucket of paste and paint-
brush, lathering head and face, shaving
with a large wooden razor the unlucky
competitor—were a part of the amusements they imposed on "Old Father Time."

Arrived at Diego Suarez, on the northern port of Madagascar, a French naval
station, having a land-locked harbor, providing good shelter and anchorage. The
town is located on a plateau overlooking
the bay. Many officers disembarked and
a large amount of freight discharged. The
resident population consisted of a medley
from all eastern nations. Anchored a mile
off and in small boats, and after 20 minutes' rowing we were landed. A dozen
stores, barracks and the hospital on the opposite side of the bay were the only objects
of interest. The large amount of freight
discharged indicated it to be a prominent
distributing point for the interior. Leaving Diego and running down the eastern
coast with land in view, mountainous and
apparently sterile, we reach Tamatave and
anchor in the bay.

(16)

The ship was soon boarded by a messenger from Mr. Wetter, the outgoing American Consul at Madagascar, and I was piloted ashore. The view of Tamatave from the ship was not prepossessing, and my walk through the city to the hotel was not inspiring. The attempt to dignify the six or eight feet wide alleys (which were the main arteries for travel) as avenues or streets, semed ludicrous, and the filthy condition, the absence of all sanitary regulations in a province pretending a civilized administration, was to me a revelation. The natural sequence of such neglect was the visitation of the "Bubonic plague" a few months after my arrival and an immense death-rate. The alarm proved a conservator for the living, for the burning of the effected districts, widening the streets and enforcement of sanitary rules have tended to lessen its virulence, although it has been yearly in its visitations; for while foul surroundings are recognized as hot-beds for the propagation of the germs of this pest, recent experience has demonstrated that while cleanliness and rigid sanitary measures are less inviting, they are not positive barriers to its approach and dire effect. The "terror" originally supposed to be indigenous only to India, Egypt, and China, and so domestic in its habits as to confine its ravages to few precincts, now stalks forth as on a world mission—to Mauritius in Indian Ocean, to Japan, Brazil, Australia, Honolulu, and last and not least, interesting from an American point of view, are the stealthy footsteps of the unwelcome guest in the city of San Francisco, Cal. "While medical information relating to the plague is still less definite and extensive than it should be," says an eminent physician, "it is now well demonstrated that the disease depends upon a specific microbe."

It may be communicated from one person to another through expectoration, oozings from the mouth of dying persons, or through the excretions of the body. "The fears it inspires are well grounded, for the recoveries in a case of severe epidemics are only ten per cent. Of 126 cases reported from Manila from January 20 to March 30, 1900, 112 cases resulted fatally. In India, where the plague has been the most severe, the deaths from this cause have averaged 5,000 a week of recent years, a considerable amount of study has been devoted to the various phases of the plague, by physicians in Europe and the East especially, and a number have given their lives to the cause of medical science in attempts to find some method of successfully combating it. It is needless to say that no specific has as yet been discovered in its treatment, and ordinary curative measures have but little effect on its course.

In Chinatown, San Francisco, where it made its appearance, a rigid "cordon sanitaire" was established, and all outer intercourse prohibited. It is not believed that conditions are inviting in North America, although "the wish may be father to the thought."

The following brief expression relative to Madagascar and comment on Negro status in the following letter to the "Colored American," published in Washington City, may be in place:

Tamatave, Madagascar, Aug. 5, 1900.

Dear Friend Cooper: I have your favor June 14th last, in which you say you would like to have a line from me, that you "may let the friends over here know what you are doing." Well, here it is, line upon line, if not precept, etc. I am "still doing business at the same old stand," and doubt if I have anything to say regarding this "faraway post" that would particularly interest your readers, engrossed as I perceive they are in domestic phases and in the alignment of our recent acquisitions.

Regarding the physical development or moral progress of Madagascar, as you know it is now a French province, with a Governor General and staff, all appointees from France. The Government is doing considerable to open up the country by means of telegraphs, railroads, turnpikes and canals. At Paris they recently voted sixty millions francs (12 million dollars) for a railroad from here to Tananarivo, the capital, 200 miles from here, over a mountainous and broken country. The cap-

ital is situated on a plateau 5,000 feet
above sea level, with a climate cool and
bracing. Here at Tamatave a fireplace or
heating stove in a house are unknown ap-
pendages. The Hovas for a long period
were the rulers previous to the conquest
and occupation by the French, who by
diplomacy—"force and iron will"—the
means usually adopted by the strong when
a coveted prize looms in the distance, added an immense territory to their colonial
possessions. But perhaps in the interest
of civilization the change is not to be de-
plored. The Hovas were a superior class
of Madagascan people the rulers being
men of education and ability, but not
equal in quality or quantity to cope with
the energy, wealth and military prowess of
a power like France.

The mental and physical conditions of
the great bulk of the natives were not, and
are not, inviting; they were held by a mild
system of slavery, a system that in sub-
stance still exists under French rule as to
forced labor on public works. The severity of tasks and bad rum are said by a
friendly society at Paris in its protest "to
be fast decimating their number." The
French Government, however, are establishing an extension of schools for the natives, where industrial training will be the
marked feature, and which on yesterday,
the occasion being an official visit the Governor was pleased to pay me, I took pains
to extol; as you know industrial training

is my pet. The General wisely remarking, "we wish first to place the present generation in a position to earn more money, so they will be able to give their offspring a higher education if they wish." The English, Norwegians from America, the Friends and other missions, are doing something for their educational and moral progress, but the appliances are meager compared with the herculean task that awaits them.

There is, however, this difference in the problem here. There are colored men occupying places of prominence as officials, as tellers in banks, clerks in counting-houses and merchant stores. Here it is condition, and not color, wealth and position, the "open sesame." On social occasions the brother in black is in evidence, without special notice of the fact, and, strangest of it all, on the following day the sun and other heavenly bodies seem to stand or revolve in their accustomed orbits. My health has been good, although the bubonic pest, periodical in its visitations, has been alarming in the suddenness of its destruction of life, In the spring it is again expected to alight without "healing in its wings." But I will not longer dwell on Madagascan peculiarities, many of which, as elsewhere, are not chastening. What I am interested in, and want to know about is, how you are getting on with the "old grudge?" If I judge correctly from the journals that reach me, that during my near three years' absence, its status, unlike renowned grape-juice, has neither dissipated or improved by lapse of time, and that lynching and disfranchisement still have the right of way.

The expansion of our sovereignty is fraught with complications, and onerous duties from the statesman, the zeal of the humanitarian, and of reformers and friends of equitable government, unflinching determination are required, that kindness and justice shall be ceded to the people thereof. But is the prospect for the dissemination or ascendancy of these virtues either bright or promising? If the exercise and enjoyments of these attributes are not granted to millions of the American household, is it reasonable to expect they will dominate abroad? There is reason for apprehension that our cousins in the East will find little change of despotic tendencies amid the rank and file of American adventurers. The philosophy of our system of government seems out of balance. Cicero wrote "that excessive liberty leads both nations and individuals into excessive slavery."

But amid the lights and shadows that environ the Negro, he is neither undeserving of the assistance rendered, and indispensable for educational development, which has been generous, and for which he is grateful, although handicapped by a prejudice confronting on so many avenues of industry, and forbidding his entry. Not undeserving for patient and non-anarchist in the realms of labor, his right to possess and enjoying equality of citizenship is written with blood and bravery on the battlefield of every war of the Republic where he "fell forward as fits a man." Munificent contributions of Christians and philanthropists, for missionary work abroad, are greatly in evidence, given with a self-complacency of duty done; but, however, fail to vivify the declining pulse-beat for equality before the law and justice at home. Manifestly there is an absence of that arraignment and condemnation of wrong done the weak, that contributed so largely to abolish the "corn laws of England" and slavery in the United States. History is the record that it is the men of moral courage and heroism who by pen and voice, that sociality and gain cannot intimidate and combat evil in their very midst that "leave footprints in the sands of time."

I must close this letter, already too long. Don't regard me as a pessimist. I know that Bacon wrote that "men of age object too much," but the fact is, Cooper, it has been so long since I heard a Fourth of July hallelujah chorus that I am getting out of tune.

McKinley has been again nominated, I see, and doubtless will be elected, with a Congress in harmony, thus giving the party another lease of power, which, God grant, let us hope, may redound to the wel-

fare of all the people. Say to my many
friends that they are, "though lost to sight
to memory dear."   Truly your friend,

M. W. GIBBS.

CHAPTER XXII.

The Island of Madagascar was discovered in 1506 by Lawrence Almeyda, a Portuguese; but the Persians and Arabs are said to have known it from time immemorial. The island is divided into 28 provinces and is said to contain two hundred millions acres of excellent land, watered on all sides by streams and large rivers. Its two highest mountains are Vigagora in the north and Batistmene in the south, said to contain in their bowels abundance of fossils and valuable minerals. This island, situated near the eastern coast of Africa, with 300 miles of the Mozambique Channel intervening, is 1,000 miles in length and varying from 200 to 400 miles in width, and is supposed to have been in remote ages a portion of the continent of Africa and that the progenitors of its people were to that "manor born;" others that the channel was crossed in canoes and Madagascar populated.

Rev. W. E. Cousins, an English missionary, in a late edition of "Madagascar of Today," says that "its people are not on the whole an African people, and much of its ora and fauna indicate a very long sep-

aration from the neighboring continent.
Particularly notable is the fact that Madagascar has no lions, deer, elephants or an-
telopes, which are abundant in Africa; the
people generally are not Africans, but be-
long to the same family as Malays and Ma-
layo Polynesians." How the Malayon came
to be the predominant language has exer-
cised the thoughts of many, Africa being
not more than 300 miles from the west
coast of Madagascar, whereas the nearest
point, Malayon Peninsula, is 3,000 miles
away. That the distinct type of African
presents itself in large numbers of native
population is beyond question.

For much of the following as to the religion, morals and customs of the Madagascar people, I am indebted to Rev. Cousins,
the missionary above referred to, and a
work entitled "Madagascar, or Drury's
Journal," edited by Pasfield Oliver and
published in 1729. Robert Drury was an
English lad that ran away from home, was
shipwrecked, and held in captivity by the
natives for 15 years, and redeemed by Captain Mackett, commanding the "Prince of
Wales" in the East India Company's service. Also to the "Island of Madagascar,"
by Abbe Alexis Rochon, a learned French-
man, who visited the island in 1767 and
made an extensive report.

Mr. Oliver mentions that there are authors who say that the religion of these
people is Mahometanism, but he is at a

loss to know from what they drew their conclusions, since their sacrifices and their antipathy to revelation; and, besides, at the only place where a Moorish ship (Mahometan) came, swines' flesh is eaten. These obviously show that there can be nothing in more direct opposition to it. There is no one circumstance like it, except circumcision, and that is well known to those learned in ancient history to have been common to some Eastern nations, even before the Jews had it, and where there is no reason to think the name of the Jews was ever heard, and we have more reason to think that the Jews derived a great deal from them instead of they from the Jews; that their religion is more ancient is evident for several obvious reasons.

First, by their regarding dreams and divining by them, which so early as the Mosaic law the Children of Israel were warned against.

Secondly, these people shave their hair all off in mourning for the dead. This Moses expressly commands the Israelites not to do, and the Jews do superstitiously observe this last and suffer their hair to grow in their mourning.

Thirdly, Moses commanded none but males to be sacrificed. On the contrary, these sacrifice cows for the most part. They have no burnt offerings but near their sepulchers, which with gum, burnt likewise,

BISHOP ABRAHAM GRANT.

Joined Church at an Early Age—Advanced Until he Was Elected Bishop of the
A. M. E. Church—An Able Pulpit Orator, and Among the Bishops He
is Known as the Politician of his Church—Having a Com-
petency, He is Devoting His Closing Years to Be-
nevolence and the Promotion of His Race.

may only arise from a defense of cadaverous scents.

Fourthly, but the most remarkable instance of all is, that the "owley," which these Madagascar people divine by and procure most extraordinary dreams, is evidently the Ephod and Teraphin which the Levites used who lived in Micah's house (see Judges 17) and which the Israelites could never be wholly brought off from, though contrary to their law. Some have taken these Teraphin for images like a man, and there seems a show of reason in it from Michah, Saul's daughter putting one in David's bed to deceive her father's messenger, while he escaped. This, it is possible, alludes to some divination by the Teraphin which she used in his behalf, for Teraphin is the plural number; therefore, could not signify only one image; neither could the gods which Rachel stole from her father, Labon, be one god as big as a man, for she sat on them and hid them. The word is here in the original "Teraphin," although translated gods. Then, in Hosea, chapter 3, verse 4, "an image, an Ephod and Teraphin," are all mentioned in one verse, plainly showing that they are distinct things. It is further to be remarked that by this Teraphin they invoked the dead, which is exactly the same as these people do by the "Owley" always invoking the spirits of their forefathers, which is expressly forbidden to Israelites, and often sharply inveighed against by the prophets.

That these people had not their religion
from any polite or learned nation is by
their retaining no notion or meaning of
letters, nor their having a horse among
them, either for carriage or other use,
which could never have been forgotten had
they ever had it.

Mr. Oliver positively asserts that these
Madagascar people came from Africa, and
is certain on account of their color, while
other writers think most of them to be descendants of Malays.

Captain Mackett, previously mentioned
as the redeemer of Robert Drury from his
15 years' captivity, states that Devon
(King) Toak, often told him they had a tradition of their coming to the island many
years ago in large canoes; "but," says Captain Oliver, "let them come from where they
will, it is evident that their religion is the
most ancient in the known world and not
much removed from natural religion, and
whether the Egyptians and Canaanites had
their religion from them, or that they are
Egyptians originally, it had its rise long
before the Children of Israel were in bondage, for Egypt was then a very polite
country, and although idolators, they were
not any more so than their neighbors before Abraham's time.

"The respect due from children to parents is taught them early by those parents
and grows with them, besides the gratitude naturally arising to those who have

fed and protected them when they were
helpless infants. So it is no wonder to find
a law there against cursing parents. The
notion of the Being of one Supreme Author of nature arises from natural reflec-
tion on the visible harmony and uniformity
of the universe and seeing that men and
things did not produce themselves. The
reverence due to this stupendous Being is
only of a pious and rightly amazement,
dread and respect. The testimony was
everywhere uniform that where Europeans
or Mahometans had not corrupted them
they were innocent, moral and humane.

"Physically the island has lost none of
its picturesque character, so vividly portrayed by Abbe Rochon more than a century ago, who wrote 'The Traveler,' who
in pursuit of knowledge traverses for the
first time wild and mountainous countries,
intersected by ridges and valleys, where
nature, abandoned to its own fertility, presents the most singular and varied productions, cannot help being struck with terror and surprise on viewing those awful
precipices, the summits of which are covered with trees as ancient perhaps as the
world. His astonishment is increased
when he hears the noise of immense cas-
cades which are so inaccessible that it is
impossible for him to approach them. But
these scenes, truly picturesque, are always
succeeded by rural views, delightful hills
and plains, where vegetation is never in-

terrupted by the severity and vicissitudes
of the seasons. The eye with pleasure be-
holds those extensive savannas which afford nourishment to numerous herds of
cattle and flocks of sheep. Fields of rice
and potatoes present also a new and highly
interesting spectacle. One sees agriculture
flourishing, while nature alone defrays almost all the expense. The fortunate inhabitants of Madagascar need not moisten
the earth with their sweat; they turn it up
slightly with a pick-axe, and this labor
alone is sufficient. They make holes in the
ground at a little distance from each other
and throw into them a few grains of rice,
over which they spread the mold with
their feet. And what proves the great fertility of the soil is that a field thus sown
produces an hundred-fold. The forests
contain a prodigious variety of the most
beautiful trees, such as palms of every
kind, ebony, wood for dyeing, bamboos of
an enormous size, and orange and lemon
trees." The Abbe's picture is quite en-
chanting, for it seems that "every prospect
pleases."

A view of Antananarivo, the capital of
Madagascar, in the word-painting of Cameron, a war correspondent of the London
Standard, is interesting. "Antananarivo
was in sight and we could plainly see the
glass windows of the palace glistening in
the morning sun, on the top of the long
hill upon which the city is built. It was

Sunday, and the people were clustering along the foot-paths on their way to church or sitting in the grass outside waiting for the services to begin, as they do in villages at home. The women, who appeared to be in the majority, wore white cotton gowns, often neatly embroidered, and white or black and white striped lambas, thrown gracefully over their shoulders. The men were clad also in cotton, white cotton pantaloons, cotton lambas, and straw hats, with large black silk band. In the morning sun the play of colors over the landscape was lovely. The dark green hills, studded with the brilliant red brick houses of the inhabitants, whose white garments dotted the lanes and foot-paths, contrasted with the brighter emerald of the rice fields in the hollows. The soil everywhere is deep red, almost magenta, in color, and where the roads or pathways cross the hills they shine out as if so many paint-brushes had streaked the country in broad red stripes. Above all, the spires of the strange city, set on top of its mountain with a deep blue sky for a background, added to the beauty of the scene.

"It was difficult to imagine that this peaceful country, with its pretty cottages, its innumerable chapels, whose bells were then calling its people to worship, and its troops of white-robed men and women answering the summons, was the barbarous Madagascar of twenty years ago."

(17)

Mention of the form of government had
by the Madagascar people and which is
now being superseded by occupancy of the
French and the introduction of laws of a
civilized nation, may not be out of place.
As far back as tradition will carry, there
existed in Madagascar a kind of feudalism.
Villages were usually built on the hilltops,
and each hilltop had its own chieftain, and
these petty feudal chiefs were constantly
waging war with each other. The people
living on these feudal estates paid taxes
and rendered certain services to their feudal lords. Each chief enjoyed a semi-inde-
pendence, for no strong over-lord existed.
Attempts were made from time to time
to unite these petty chieftains into one
Kingdom, but no one tribe succeeded in
making itself supreme till the days of Ra-
dam I, who succeeded in bringing the whole
of Imerina under his government, and to
his son, Radama, he left the task of subduing the rest of the island. By allying himself closely with England, Radama obtained military instruction and carried
war into distant provinces. He ultimately
succeded in conquering many of the tribes
and his reign marked the beginning of a
new era in Madagascar. Indeed, only from
his days could Madagascar in any sense be
regarded as a political unit.

In one direction, however, the results of
Radama's policy must be regarded as retro-
gressive. Before his reign no chief or
king was powerful enough to impose his

rule upon the people without their consent.

Opposition to rule, without the consent of the governed, has been the shibboleth with which liberty has rallied the votaries of constitutional government in all its reforms. It was the magna charter extorted from King John at Runnymead—the trumpet call echoing and re-echoing by hill and through valley in our Declaration of Independence. Before Radama, although rude and primitive in form, it was the basic principle cherished by the people of Madagascar. The principal men of each district had to be constantly consulted and Kabary, or public assemblies like the Greek or the Swiss Communal assemblies, were called for the discussion of all important affairs, and public opinion had a fair opportunity of making itself effective.

"A single tree does not make a forest, but the thoughts of many constitute a government," is handed down by tradition as one of the farewell sayings of their early kings, and is often quoted by the people. This was the spirit that existed in "ye olden time," but after Radama I. formed a large army and a military caste was created there was a strong tendency to repress and minimize the influence of civilians in public affairs, and men holding military rank have wielded the chief authority.

It was ever thus; for while the chiefs of victorious legions are received with strains of "conquering hero," have roses for a pathway canopied with waving flag and triumphant banner, there is not wanting a latent, reserved concern for the legitimate use of the franchise granted and whether vaulting ambition may not destroy the sacred inheritance they were commissioned to preserve. Military rank in Madagascar was strangely reckoned by numbers. The highest officers being called men of "sixteen honors," the men of twelve honors would be equal in rank to a field marshal, the men of nine honors to a colonel, and the man of three honors to a sergeant, and so on, through the whole series.

When any important government business had to be made known the men from 12 honors upward were summoned to the palace. Above all these officers stood the Prime Minister. His Excellency Ramiloi-arivony. The supreme head of the state was the Mpanjaka, or sovereign, and every proclamation was issued in her name and was generally countersigned and confirmed as a genuine royal message by the Prime Minister. For three reigns, namely, from the accession of Rasaherina in 1863, Mpanjaka had been a woman and the wife of the Prime Minister. A general impression exists in England that this is an old Madagascar custom, but such is not the case. The arrangement is of quite recent date. The last Prime Minister (not being of royal blood) was content to be Mpanjaka, or ruler, and while all public honor was shown to the Queen, and her authority fully acknowledged, those behind the scenes would have us believe that the Queen was supreme only in name.

As a matter of fact, the Prime Minister, and even his supposed wishes and preferences, were the most potent forces in Madagascar. No one seemed able to exercise any independent influence, and time after time the men who showed any special ability or gained popularity have been removed, swept away as it were, out of the path of the man who had assumed and by his ability and astuteness maintained for thirty years the highest position in the country. There was, no doubt, a large amount of latent rebellion against this "one-man government," but those who were the most ready to grumble in private were in public, perhaps, the most servile of any. It is conceded that in many ways the Prime Minister was an able ruler, and compared with those who went before him was deserving of great praise.

He made many attempts to prevent the corruption of justice, and strenuously endeavored to improve the administration, and for many years had managed to hold in check the ambitious projects of French statesmen, and had shown at many times his interest in the cause of education.

But his monopoly as a ruler, the idea of omnipotent control, refusal to allow his subordinates to take their share of responsibility, like many similar instances which history records, loosened the bond of patriotic interest, love and integrity for country, and made easy the ingress of the French in subduing and appropriating the Island of Madagascar.

It has been stated that no account of Madagascar government would be complete that did not include a description of their system of "fanompoana," or forced service, which answers very nearly to the old feudal service, and to the system known in Egypt as "corvee." The tax-gatherer is not the ubiquitous person in Madagascar he is generally supposed to have been.

There were a few taxes paid by the people, such, for example, as a small tax in kind on the rice crop, and occasionally a small poll-tax, and money paid the sovereigns as a token of allegiance on many occasions.

Taxes of this kind were not burdensome. The one burden that galled and irritated the people was the liability to be called upon at any moment to render unrequited service to the government.

Every man had something that was regarded as "fanompoana." The people of one district might be required to make mats for the government, in another pots, the article required. From one district certain men were required to bring crayfish to the capital, charcoal from another, iron from another, and so on through all the series of wants. The jeweler must make such articles as the Queen would desire, the tailor use his needle and the writer his

HON. JOHN E. BUSH,
Receiver of United States Lands at Little Rock, Arkansas.

Former Principal of Public Schools of Little Rock—Clerk in Railway Mail Service
—Grand Scribe of "Mosaic Templars of America"—An Able
and Leading Republican of Arkansas.

pen, as the government might need. The system had in it some show of rough-and-ready justice, and was based on the idea that each must contribute to the needs of the state according to his several abilities; but in the actual working it had a most injurious influence on the wellbeing of the country. Each man tried to avoid the demands made upon him, and the art "how not to do it" was cultivated to a very high degree of perfection. Many of the head men made this "fanompoana" system a means of enriching themselves, compelling the subordinates to serve them as well as the government. History does but repeat itself, as there are not wanting instances in our own country where certain heads of department "fanomponed" subordinates for private service.

In many ways are recorded the product of the fertile brain of these head men. For instance, the centurion, or head man of a certain district, gave out a notice in the church yard, on Sunday morning, or at a week-day market, that a hundred men would be required next morning to carry charcoal for the government. As a matter of fact, he required only twenty, but he knew that many would come to him to beg off, and as none would come empty-handed, his profit on the transaction was considerable. Another illustration was given Mr. Cousins by the British Consul. It was customary to send up mails from the coast by government runners, but Eng-

lish ideas being adverse to demanding unrequited service, the Consul had always
sent the usual wages for the runners to the
Governor, who pocketed the dollars and
"fanomponed" the mail. But enough of
this, as it has a flavor of our "Star Route
Mail" disclosures, which startled the country some years ago, and conclude with a
tribute to Tammany, as:

We arise to remark, and our language is
      plain,
That the Tweeds and the Crokers are of
      Malagash fame.

CHAPTER XXIII.

The introduction and perpetuation of the Christian religion in Madagascar has been attended with vicissitudes, hopeful, discouraging, and finally permanent. The Catholics were the first to attempt to gain a footing on the southeast corner of the island. A French mission settled and commenced to instruct the natives in the Roman Catholic faith, and maintained a mission in spite of many discouragements for twenty years, and then came to an end. Protestants who a century and a half later carried the Gospel to Madagascar found it virgin soil. They found a people without a written language or knowledge of the Christian faith. Both in their literary and evangelical labors they had to revive a work that was not dying out, but to start de novo, and the London Missionary Society had to seek its own way to carry out its objects.

The men to whom it appears that the Madagascar people are indebted for their written languages and the first translation of the Scriptures were two Welshmen.

David Jones and David Griffiths—these

two men were the pioneers of Protestant
missions in Madagascar—the first in 1820,
the second a year later. The main strength
of these early missionaries was devoted to
educational work, in which they were vigorously supported by King Radama I, and
Mr. Hastie, the British agent. Besides
this they began very early to make a translation of the Scriptures, and in ten years
after the arrival of Mr. Jones in Antananarivo the first edition of 3,000 copies of the
New Testament was completed, in March,
1830. At this time much progress had
been made in the translation of the Old
Testament. The account of the completion
of it is interesting. Soon after the death
of King Radama I, in 1828, the missionaries saw clear indications of the uncertainty of their positions; ominous clouds
began to gather until the storm burst.

The edict of Queen Ranavalona I against
the Christian Church was published March
1, 1835. A portion of the Old Testament
translation was uncompleted. The missions were deserted by their converts, and
they could procure no workman to assist;
so with trembling haste they proceeded
with their task, and at the end of June
they had joy in seeing the first bound copies of the completed Bible. Most of these
were secretly distributed, and seventy remaining copies were buried for safety in
the earth—precious seed over which God
watched and which in due season produced
a glorious harvest. The translators were

driven away, but the book remained.
Studied in secret, and at the risk of life, it
served during more than a quarter of a
century of persecution to keep alive faith
in the newly received religion; for, during
all this time, to use the familiar native
phrase, "the land was dark." At its commencement Queen Ranavalona (the Queen
Mary of Madagascar), with all the force of
her strong will, set herself to destroy the
new religion. "It was cloth," she said, "of
a pattern she did not like, and she was determined none of her people should use it."
The victims of her fury form a noble
army of martyrs, of whom Madagascar is
justly proud. The causes that led to the
persecution are not far to seek. On the one
hand, they were intensely conservative,
clinging to ancestral customs; and on the
other hand, a suspicious and jealous fear
of foreign influence. The zealous work of
the missionaries was believed by many of
the Queen's advisers to be only a cloak to
conceal political designs. The teachings
of the foreigners were proving so attractive
that their chapels were crowded, and the
influence of this new religion was making
itself felt in many families. Whither
would all this lead? Was it to pave the
way to annex the island to the English
Government? The word "society" to a native ignorant of English would suggest a
phrase of their own which sounds alike,
viz: "sosoy-oty"—"push the canoe over this
way." This to the ingenuous or suspi-

cious mind of the hearers suggested the idea of pushing over the Government of Madagascar to those across the ocean who were supposed to be greedily seeking to seize it. This is seemingly absurd, but not too ridiculous to obtain credence with a people excited and suspicious.

The former King Radama showed his shrewdness in giving permission to the missionaries to reside in his country, for he expressly stipulated that some of them should be skilled artisans, so that his people might be instructed in weaving, smith-work, carpentry, etc. To this the society wisely assented, and a number of Christian artisans were sent out. The influence of these were of immense value, and to them is to be attributed much of the skill of the Madagascar workman of today.

There is no doubt that the manifest utility of their work did much to win for the mission a measure of tolerance from the heathen rulers of the country. One of the missionaries with great mechanical skill, in his "Recollections," states that Queen Ranavalona in 1830 was beginning to feel uneasy about the growing influence of foreign ideas and wished to get rid of the missionaries. She sent officers to carry her message, and the missionaries were gathered together to meet the messengers, and were told that they had been a long time in the country and had taught much, and that it was time for them to think of returning to their native land. The mission-

aries, alarmed at this message, answered
that they had only begun to teach some
of the elements of knowledge, and that
very many more remained to be imported,
mentioning sundry branches of education,
among which were Greek and Hebrew languages, which had already been taught to
some. The messengers returned to the
Queen, and soon came back with the answer: "The Queen does not care much for
Greek and Hebrew. Can you teach how to
make soap?" (And if cleanliness is akin to
godliness she was evidently groping in the
right direction.) This was an awkward
question to address theologians; almost as
much so as "Do you know enough to come
in out of the rain?" to some college graduates; but after a moment's pause Mr.
Griffith turned to Mr. Cameron and asked
him if he could answer it. "Give me a
week," and it was given, and when the
messengers again met at the close of the
week a bar of tolerable good white soap,
made from materials found in the country,
was presented. This was entirely satisfactory, and the manufacture of soap was
forthwith introduced, and is still continued
to the present day. This bar of soap gained
the missionaries a respite of five years, the
Queen tolerating their presence on account
of material advantage derived from the
work of the artisans. In believing that industrial training, the knowledge to make
things in demand, was the first necessary

step for the elevation of her people, the
Queen was eminently correct.

During the fifteen years (from 1820 to
1835) the mission was allowed to exist it
was estimated that 10,000 to 15,000 children passed through school, so that when
the missionaries were compelled to leave
the island there were thousands who had
learned to read, and thereby raised far
above the mass of their heathen fellow-
countrymen.

Dark Days—January, 1835, a formal
complaint was presented to the missionaries by one of the Queen's officers against
the Christian religion under six different
heads. Excitement increased and opposition to the new teaching grew bolder. The
Queen, in passing a native chapel and hearing singing, was heard to say: "They will
not stop till some of them lose their
heads."

On the first of March, 1835, the edict
publicly prohibiting the Christian religion
was delivered in the presence of thousands
of people who had been summoned to hear
it. The place of meeting was a large open
space lying to the west of the long hill on
which the city of Antananarivo is built,
and large enough to contain two or more
thousand people. In the middle of the plain
crops up a large mass of granite rock, on
which only royal persons were allowed to
stand; hence probably the name "Imo-
hamosine," which means "having power to
make sacred." There from time to time

large public assemblies have been held, but
never one of greater significance or of more
far-reaching issues than that. Of this
great "kabary," or meeting, notices had
been sent far and wide. All possible measures had been taken to inspire the people
with awe and to make them feel that a
proclamation of unusual importance was
about to be published. Queen Ranavalona
semed anxious to make her people feel that
her anger was burning with an unwonted
fury. It is stated that morning had scarcely dawned when the report of the cannon
intended to strike terror and awe into the
hearts of the people ushered in the day on
which the will and power of the sovereign
of Madagascar to punish the defenseless
followers of Christ was to be declared. Fifteen thousand troops were drawn up, part
of them on the plain and the rest in two
lines a mile in length along the road leading to the place. The booming of artillery
from the high ground overlooking the
plain and the reports of musketry of the
troops, which was continued during the
preparatory arrangements, produced
among the multitude the most intense and
anxious feelings. At length the Chief Justice, attended by his companions in office,
advanced and delivered the message of the
Sovereign, which was enforced by Rami-
haro, the chief officer of the Government.
After expressing the Queen's confidence in
the idols, and her determination to treat as

criminals all who refused to do them homage, the message proceeded:

"As to baptism, societies, places of worship, and the observance of the Sabbath—how many rulers are there in the land? Is it not I, alone, that rule? These things are not to be done. They are unlawful in my country," said the Queen, "for they are not the customs of our ancestors."

As a result of this "kabary" 400 officers were reduced in rank and fines were paid for 2,000 others, and thus was ushered in a persecution which lasted a quarter of a century.

The Rev. William Ellis, on English missionaries, in his book entitled "Madagascar Revisited," states that the first martyr for Christ who suffered there in 1836 was "Rosolama." She was a Christian woman, between twenty and thirty years of age, bearing no common name, for Rosolama signifies peace and happiness. She was imprisoned at Ambotonakonga, the site of the first house built exclusively for Christian worship in the country. A memorial church has been erected on the spot. When brought to the place she knelt down and asked a few minutes to pray. This was granted, and then her body fell, pierced with the spears of her executioners.

The second martyr, Rayfarolahy, a young man, suffered on the same place some time after. At the request of Rosolama when she was taken forth to death he had walked by her side to the place of execu-

REV. J. P. ROBINSON.
Pastor of First Baptist Church, Little Rock, Arkansas.

Eminent as a Successful Preacher, with Much Originality of Thought
and Strength of Convictions.

tion and offered words of encouragement
to her to the last. When brought to the
place himself the executioners seized him
and were about, as was their custom, to
forcibly throw him down, he said to them
calmly, "There is no need to do that; I
will not cause any trouble." He also asked
to be allowed to pray, and then gently laid
himself down and received the executioners' spears. The measures taken to destroy
Christianity were not at all times equally
severe. The years that stand out with
special prominence are 1835, 1837, 1840,
1849 and 1857. Of what took place in 1840
was depicted at the time in a letter written by Rev. D. Griffiths, who was then re-
siding at Antananarivo. The nine condemned Christians were taken past Mr.
Griffiths' house. "Ramonisa," he says,
"looked at me and smiled; others also
looked at me, and their faces shone like
those of angels in the posture of prayer and
wrestling with God. They were too weak
to walk, having been without rice or water
for a long time. The people on the wall
and in the yard before our house were
cleared off by the swords and spears of
those leading them to execution. That we
might have a clear, full and last sight of
them, they were presented opposite the bal-
cony on the road and at the entrance of the
yard for about ten minutes, carried on
poles by the executioners, with merely a
hand breadth of cloth to cover them, they

(18)

were then led away to execution. The cannon fired to announce their death was shattered to pieces, and the gunners' clothes burnt, which was considered ominous, many whispering 'Thus will the kingdom of Ranavalona Manjaka be shattered to pieces.'"

In 1849 what may be called the great persecution took place; not less than 1,900 persons suffered persecution of various kinds—fines, imprisonment, chains, or forced labor in the quarries. Of this number 18 suffered death, four, of noble birth, by being burned, and 14 by being thrown over the great precipice of Ampomarinona. It is not easy to estimate exactly the number of those who suffered the punishment of death in these successive outbursts of persecution. It is most probable the victims were between seventy or eighty. But these form only a small portion of the total number of sufferers. Probably hundreds of others died from their heavy irons, chains, or from fevers, severe forced labor, or privations during the time they were compelled to hide in caves or in the depths of the forests.

Notwithstanding the severe persecution much quiet Christian work was carried on in the lulls between storms—sometimes on hilltops, sometimes in caves, or even in unfinished tombs. Thus the story of the Covenanters was repeated, and the impossibility of destroying the Christian faith by persecution again shown. Through

CHRISTIAN MARTYR,

In Madagascar in chains—Receiving consolation.

these long years of persecution the Christians were constantly receiving accessions
to their ranks, and the more they were opposed "the more they multiplied and
grew."

The year 1861 will ever be a period from
which date results momentous in behalf of
civil and religious liberty for the Negro.
It was the beginning of the end of Negro
slavery in the United States and the permanent establishment of religious freedom
in Madagascar. Queen Ranavalona had a
long reign of thirty three years, but in that
year it became evident she could not reign
much longer. Natives give details of her
last days. The aged Queen had for some
time been suffering in health; diviners had
been urgently consulted, charms and potent herbs had been empdoyed, with no
avail. Late in the summer of 1861 it became generally known that the fatal moment could not long be delayed. Mys-
terious fires were said to be seen on the
tops of mountains surrounding the capital,
and a sound like music was rising from
Iatry to Andohalo. The Queen eagerly
questioned those around her as to the
meaning of these portents. But while the
dying Queen was anxiously praying to the
idol in which she placed her trust, there
were those who whispered to the prince
that the fire was the sign of jubilee to bring
together the dispersed, and to redeem the
lost, and so the event proved.

The aged Queen passed away during the night of August 15, 1861, and early on the morning of August 16 the news spread rapidly through the capital, and her son was proclaimed as Radama II. One of the first acts of the new sovereign was to proclaim religious liberty. The chains were struck off from the persecuted Christians and the banished were recalled. Many came back who had long been in banishment or in hiding, and their return seemed to friends who had supposed them to be dead like a veritable resurrection.

The joy of the Christian was intense. The long season of repression had at last come to an end. Now it was no longer a crime to meet for Christian worship, or to possess Christian books. On that first Friday evening some of the older Christians met and spent the night in prayer, and Sunday services were begun in eleven private houses; but these were soon consolidated into three large congregations. Radama II eagerly welcomed intercourse with foreigners and gave Christians permission to write at once, urging that missionaries be sent out, himself writing to the London Missionary Society making the same request. The society responded promptly with a large band of men and women missionaries, twenty or thirty thousand copies of the Bible, New Testament and tracts.

The result of three-quarters of a century of Christian work in Madagascar has been that the Christian religion has taken firm hold on the people. Manifest and noticeable are the number and prominence of church buildings in and around the capital. There are four stone memorial churches, built by the friends of the London Missionary Society to remind coming generations of the fidelity of the martyrs, and a very fine and well situated Roman Catholic cathedral in Ambodin Audaholo. Prominent as Christian agencies in Madagascar are "The Society for the Propagation of the Gospel," who sent out Bishop Kestel Cornish and James Coles; "The Norwegian Missionary Society," "The Roman Catholic Missionary Society," and "The Society of Friends in England."

To summarize, approximately there are now 110 foreign missionaries on the island; over 2,000 congregations, with a total of 400,000 adherents, which include 100,000 church members; while the Protestant schools contain 150,000 children. No statement of the Christianizing agencies and influences would be just or correct that did not include that of the Roman Catholic Church. "No one," it has been truly said, "can be long in Madagascar without learning to admire the self-denial, patience and heroic fortitude with which its work is carried on." It has been thus fittingly described, a few years ago, by an English visitor: "In 1861, when Catholic missionaries landed on the shores of Tamatave there was not a Catholic on the island; but little by little, by dint of unwearied labor, suffering and preaching, they won over not hundreds but thousands of pagans to the love and knowledge of our Lord and His truth, so that their pagan converts number over 130,000. They have built a magnificent cathedral, which is the glory and pride of Antananarivo. They have also 300 churches and 400 or more Catholic stations scattered over the island, where 18,000 children are taught and trained by a large and elevated staff of Christian brothers and sisters of St. Joseph, and 641 native teachers. They have also created industrial schools, where various trades are taught by two devoted brothers, Benjamin and Arnoad, and at Ambohipo they have a flourishing college for young Malagash. They have also on the island four large dispensaries, where thousands of prescriptions are distrubuted gratis to all who seek to relieve their sufferings. They have also established a leper hospital at Ambohivoraka, where the temporal and spiritual wants of 150 poor lepers are freely administered to, and have already opened another such establishment, in Betsilio land. Prison visitation, dispensing rice, clothing, and spiritual instruction to half-starved and naked prisoners under the Madagascar rule; their catalogue of books devotional, literary and scientific; a dictionary, all of which have been edited and published in the Madigascan language, are among the

golden contributions for civilization by the
Catholics in this far-off island continent in
the Indian seas."

In referring to their labors, and to which,
comparatively, I have made but brief reference, Mr. Cousins says: "To much in the
Roman Catholic system we may be strenuously opposed; but to their zeal, their
skill, their patience, their self-denial, we
render the homage of an ungrudging admiration."

The foregoing were the labors and results of missionary effort up to the date of
the French taking absolute possession of
the island. It is to be hoped there will be
no retrograde movement lessening the efficiency of these civilizing agencies. Although it is alleged that French control
and influence in Tahiti and other South Sea
islands have been averse to both morality
and evangelical Christianity, and hence
there are not wanting those who predict
incumbrances in missionary work, now
French authority is established. But in
this age of progress along all the lines of
human endeavor the French Government
will undoubtedly see the justice and utility
of governing with a regard to the advancement of these wards that the prowess of
its arms have committed to its care. It is
not unreasonable to expect, and the promise should be flattering, that with the
European ideas of the proper functions of
government, the incipient steps for the
mental culture of the natives, present evi-

dence of large expenditure and introduction of the most modern applications for the physical development of the island, the Madigascan people will attain in the future a higher degree of human advancement from contact with the civilization of the French than it was possible they could have under "Hova rule." And in this connection it is gratifying to note that "The Native Race Protection Committee," headed by Mr. Paul Viollet, of the Paris Institute, in June, 1899, addressed an appeal to the Colonial Minister in behalf of the Malagash, entreating him to shorten the forced labor, to reduce the taxes, and to annul decrees, which greatly re-established slavery.

The appeal dwelt on the fearful mortality occasioned by forced labor on the roads, which threatened to reduce the most robust population of the highlands as to debar colonists from commercial and agricultural enterprises, and very pertinently asks "Is it not better to be without roads than without a healthy population?" The appeal also denounced arbitrary acts. "The native," it is said, "is arrested and imprisoned for months without a trial, and this with all the less forbearance, as the prisoner is always utilized as an economic laborer." The justice of this appeal and prompt reception and accord with the French conscience was evidenced in the public announcement to the natives by Gen. Galliena, the Governor of Madagascar, a few months later, that forced labor would be discontinued after January 1, 1900, and thereafter they could work for whom they pleased, and if for government they would be paid wages agreed to. It is needless to say that this proclamation was received by the natives with tumultuous rejoicing. Forced labor is now abolished, and the natives rejoice in a jubilee from a servitude the most galling.

CHAPTER XXIV.

The adaptability of the Negro to conditions that are at the time inevitable has been the paladium that has sustained and multiplied him amid the determined prejudice that has ever assailed him. The Indian, unassimilating, combatted the prejudice of caste by physical force, and has been well nigh extinguished, while the Negro has bowed to the inevitable with the mental reservation to rise to a higher recognition by a persistent assimilation of the forces that disenthralled and exalted the Saxon.

The foregoing chapter, indicating the policy of the French in their occupation and dealing with Madagascar, the planting of a nation's authority and establishing a colony on the ruins of a weaker power, or of subject races, under the plea of humanity, or through the chicanery of diplomacy, has ever been the rule when territory has been desired by a stronger power. The proximity of Cuba to the States, and Spanish misrule of that island, and also of the Philippines, were the "open sesame," it is alleged, that beckoned the armed force of the United States to take possession. But in truth the Spanish jewel, Cuba, shone in

the distance, "so near, and yet so far"—so
near for mischievous complication, and so
far for material and diplomatic control.
With a vicious administration by a nation
of decaying prestige were all elements
promising success to the invader. The
covert and dastardly destruction of the U.
S. warship "Maine" in Cuban waters, the
offspring of Spanish suspicion of American
designs, was all, and more than required,
to inaugurate a "causi belli" and complete
the conquest of the island. To claim that,
these movements had their inclpiency in
a consensus of desire of the American people for justice to subject races, and was
solely, or even mainly, on account of Spanish tyranny, is a statement that will not
bear investigation for moral consistency.
It being the very antipodes of their current
behavior to a large class of citizens born
beneath the pinions of their eagle of freedom at home.

For how does it happen that the alien
Cuban and Filipino colored brothers are so
much more entitled to protection and
the enjoyment of civil and political rights
than the colored American brother, that
thousands of lives and millions of treasure
must be expended to establish that humanity and justice abroad denied by these
"world reformers" to millions of their citizens at home? Really, it would seem that
to duty and the bestowal of justice 'tis "distance that lends enchantment to the view."
"Wherever you see a head, hit it," was the

slogan of Pat, at Donnybrook Fair, and wherever there has been a territorial plum ripe in its loneliness, and tempting in its lusciousness, there has not been wanting a "grabber." It was the French in Madagascar, the English in Africa, and the Americans in the Antilles. "O! civilization; what crimes are committed in thy name!" The record of our stewardship is in the tomb of the future for the coming historian to "point a moral or adorn a tale."

The acquisition of new territory, when honorably acquired, is ever attended with peculiar conditions and vicissitudes. The transformation of the population of which into a desirable element of the body politic depends much upon the wisdom of the statesman, and the insistence of moral rectitude on the part of the Christian and philanthropist whether it shall be a blessing or an evil to both parties in interest.

It is no secret that in many minds the motive and manner of acquiring the Philippines are open to much disparaging comment. We are charged with wresting by superior force that independence that a weak but heroic people were and had been for ten years struggling to attain from the Spanish yoke; that we, whom they hailed as an assistant and in good faith co-operated with in turn, became their hostile enemies and destroyed that identity as an independent entity for which they fought.

The conditions which confronted Agui-

CHESTER W. KEATTS,

Grand Master "Mosaic Templars of America."
Born in Pulaski County, Arkansas, in 1860—For Many Years Prominent in the
Mail Service of that State—Broad in His Sympathies, and Strong as
an Advocate for the Beneficent Principles of the Institution of which He is the Head.

naldo as the leader of the Philippine revolution have been vividly described by a writer of English history: "With the statesman in revolutionary times, it is not through decisive moments that seemed only trivial, and by important turns that semed indifferent; for he explores dark and untried paths; groping his way through a jungle of vicissitudes, ambush and strategem; expedient, a match for fortune in all her moods. Regardless of what has been called 'history's severe and scathing touch,' we cannot forget the torrid air of revolutionary times, the blinding sand storms of faction, the suspicions, jealousies and hatreds, the distinctions of mood and aim, the fierce play of passions that put an hourly strain of untold intensity on the constancy, the prudence, and the valor of a leader."

No one can read the state papers and proclamations of Aguinaldo without being impressed with his ability as a leader, the intensity of his patriotism and honesty of purpose depicted for the independence of his country from Spanish rule. The statesmanship he displayed, the intelligent and liberal conception of constitutional government, and the needs and aspirations of his people, are at variance with the allegation that the Filipinos were unfit for self-government.

Hence it is that men ask, "Would it not have been national nobility of a high order if as a protector we should have given them a protectorate instead of the ignoble action of shooting them down in their patriotic attempt?" Indeed, it remains to be seen whether absolute authority obtained by such means, together with current American usage of colored races, will not evolve the fact that they have bnt changed masters. For here in our own hemisphere our country's history continues to be rife with lawlessness at the bidding of a vicious sentiment, and in some sections it is the rule and not the exception. Free from the restraint of law-abiding localities in the States, the American adventurer of lawless propensity will have free reign in bullying and oppressing, and probable partiality in the administration of the law.

George E. Horr, the able editor of the "Watchman," under "Treatment to Subject Races," is pointed and timely when he says: "The Englishman who emigrates to an English colony finds that he comes under the same laws that apply to the natives; he is not a privileged personage, by virtue of the fact that he is an Englishman. Law is enacted and executed with absolute impartiality. In India a native and an Englishman stand exactly on the same plane before the law. Indeed, in many cases, an Englishman will be tried by an Indian judge. The British have not succeeded in winning the affections of the natives, but the natives are thoroughly conviced the Englishman will act justly. There will not be (in practice) one law for European and another for the native, as in too many cases in our own country there is one law for the white man and another for the black man."

But let us all work, hope and trust that the best of American Christianity and civilization may be equal to the emergency, giving the Filipinos a larger measure of liberty and civil rights than they had under the erstwhile rule of Spain.

Under a constitutional government it is premised that sustenance and valor for "amor patria" proceeds from the fact that its institutions are designed as bulwarks for the citizen's liberty, and that its political and economic features are such as guarantee equality before the law and promote an equal chance in the race of life.

That there is a degree of selfishness in his patriotism, and that government is revered only as a means to an end, is evidenced by revolutionary tendencies ever uppermost when there are reasons to believe that these benign purposes are being thwarted. But if for wrongs, the return be fidelity, for obloquy patience, for maltreatment loyalty, be a high type of Christian ethics, the reflex influence of which, we read, are God-like; surely the Negro has virtues "not born to die," presaging an endurance that must evolve out of this nettle discomfort, justice and contentment. For, as heretofore, in the last war with Spain, putting behind him his century of oppression in slavery, and the vicious discrimination since his emancipation, forgetful of all

else save the honor and glory of the flag,
there, as, always, he wrote his name high
up on the roll of his country's heroes.
"Our's not to ask the reason why; our's to
do or die." To read the reports of commanders and other officers, and the narratives of bystanders, all attesting to a
bravery invincible, causes the blood to tin-
gle and the patriot heart to leap. We are
making history replete with self-abnegation as we continue to bring to our country's altar an unstinted devotion and brilliant achievement. These take their places
fittingly, and we should keep them in the
forefront of our claim for equality of citizenship.

For it is declared that "not the least valuable lesson taught by the war with Spain
is the excellence of the Negro soldiery. In
the battle of San Juan, near Santiago, a
Negro regiment is said to have borne the
brunt of the battle. Three companies suffered nearly as seriously, yet they remained steady under fire without an officer. The war has not shown greater heroism. In the battle of Guasimas it is said
by some of the "Rough Riders" themselves
that it was the brilliant supporting charge
of the Tenth Cavalry that saved them from
destruction. George Rennon writes: "I
do not hesitate to call attention to the
splendid behavior of the colored troops."
It is the testimony of all who saw them under fire that they fought with the utmost
courage, coolness and determination; and

Colonel Roosevelt said to a squad of them in the trenches in my presence that he never expected to have and could not ask to have better men beside him in a hard fight. If soldiers come up to Colonel Roosevelt's standard of courage, their friends have no reason to be ashamed of them. His commendation is equivalent to a medal of honor for conspicuous gallantry, because, in the slang of the camp, he is himself a fighter "from way back." I can testify, furthermore, from my own personal observation in the hospital of the Fifth Army Corps, Saturday and Sunday night, that the colored regulars who were brought in there displayed extraordinary fortitude and self-control. There were a great many of them, but I cannot remember to have heard a groan or complaint from a single man.

General Miles is quoted as favoring an increased number of colored soldiers in the United States service. He said that "in no instance had they failed to do their full duty in this war, or in the campaigns in the West; in short, they were model soldiers in every respect; not only in courage have they done themselves credit, but in their conduct as well."

When the Second Volunteer regiment of Immunes (white) became so disorderly in Santiago that they had to be sent outside to the hills for better discipline, General Shafter ordered into the city the Eighth

Illinois regiment of colored troops, who had an unsullied name for sobriety and discipline, and enjoyed the thorough confidence of those in command. And the following brief compendium of Spanish war mention from a few of the leading press of the country is good reading. A soldier writing home to friends in Springfield said: "You want to see the Negroes; they let out a yell and charge, and the fight is over." Arthur Partridge, of Co. B, writes: "At first we got the worst of it, but we received reinforcements from the two regiments of colored infantry, who walked right up to the block house, against their whole fire; they lost heavily, but it put heart into everybody, and the way we drove those Spaniards was a caution. A colored man can have anything of mine he wants. When storming they yelled like fiends." Corporal Keating of Co. B writes: "The Negroes are fighters from their toes up. They saved Roosevelt at the first battle, and took one of the forts in the battle a few days ago."

Thomas Holmes, a Rough Rider, who hails from Newkirk, Oklahoma, was the magnet of attraction at St. Paul's Hospital, says a writer in the New York Tribune. "He is a handsome, stalwart fellow, full of anecdote and good humor, and popular all around. He was sitting next to Corporal Johnson, of the Tenth Cavalry, a Negro who still carries a Mauser bullet somewhere 'inside of me inside,' as he expressed

it. 'The colored cavalry fought well, eh?'
interjected the clergyman. 'Indeed they
did,' said Holmes, fervently. 'That old idea
about a "yellow streak" being in a Negro
is all wrong. No men could have fought
more bravely, and I want to tell you that
but for the coming up of the Tenth Cavalry
the Rough Riders might have been cut to
pieces.' 'Oh, he is just talking,' said the
colored man, who smiled like a happy child
nevertheless."

Says the "Philadelphia Daily Press:" "At
every forward movement in our national
life the Negro comes to the front and
shares in the advance with each national
expansion. He does his part of the work,
and deserves equal recognition. At Santiago two Negro regiments—the Ninth, in
General Sumner's Brigade, and the Tenth,
in General Bates'—were at the front in the
center of the line. With the rest they
crested the heights of San Juan; with the
rest they left their men thickly scattered
on the slope, and since they shared in
death every member of the race has a right
to ask that in life no rights be denied and
no privileges curtailed. The white regiments that connected them in that thin
blue line, that slender hoop of steel which
hemmed in more than its opposing number, may have held men who hesitate about
this and that, contact with color; but on
that Saturday afternoon and Sunday
morning, when risk and peril hung heavy
over the line, there was no hesitation in

closing up on the Ninth and Tenth Regiments, because the men in them were colored. All honor to the black troops of the gallant Tenth."

Says the "New York Mail and Express:" "No more striking example of bravery and coolness has been shown since the destruction of the Maine than by the colored veterans of the Tenth Cavalry during the attack on Fort Caney of Saturday. By the side of the intrepid 'Rough Riders' they followed their leader up the terrible hill from whose crest the desperate Spaniards poured down a deathly fire of shell and musketry. They never faltered; the rents in their ranks were filled as soon as made. Firing as they marched, their aim was splendid, their coolness superb, and their courage aroused the admiration of their comrades. Their advance was greeted with wild cheers from the white regiments, and with an answering shout they pressed onward over the trenches they had taken close in pursuit of the retreating enemy. The war has not shown greater heroism. The men whose freedom was baptised in blood have proven themselves capable of giving their lives that others may be free. Today is a glorious 'Fourth' for all races of people in this great land."

The "New Orleans Item" gives its contemporary, the "States," the following spanking (with the usual interrogation, "Now will you be good?"): "The 'States' has evidently failed to profit by the beneficial lesson taught since the opening of the Santiago campaign. Had our esteemed contemporary been present in Richmond a few days since, when the form of a Negro soldier pierced by nine Mauser bullets was tenderly borne through the streets by four stalwart white infantry men, he would have heard the lustiest cheers that ever went up from the throats of the residents of the former capital of the Confederacy. Perhaps our anti-Negro friend would have learned wisdom from the statement of a member of Roosevelt's regiment, who declared in an interview with a press representative, that had it not been for the valiant conduct of the Negro cavalry at Baguiri the Rough Riders would have found the routing of the Spaniards almost a hopeless task. The attack of the 'States' on the Negro soldier is vicious and unpardonable. There is no more intrepid or hardy fighter to be found anywhere than the much-abused descendant of Ham. He has dogged persistence and a determination to conquer which triumphs over all obstacles. He is aware of his social inferiority and never seeks to attain positions of eminence to which his valor and his spirit of daring do not entitle him. The 'States' presents one of the most rabid cases of negrophobia extant. It should seek an immediate cure."

Such indorsements from the white press of the country is not only timely, but for

all time.   History of his endurance and
endeavor in peace, and his valor in war,
stimulates his demand and strengthens his
claim for equal justice.   Such and kindred
books as "Johnson's School History of the
Race in America" should be prominent as
household gods in every Afro-American
home, that along the realm of time the
vista of heroic effort "bequeathed from sire
to son" may gladden hearts in "the good
time coming;" for it is display in endurance, a vigorous courage, a gladsome self-
control, a triumphant self-sacrifice, that
mankind applaud as supreme for exalta-
tion, and the highest types of self-abnegation for human advancement; for "before
man made us citizens, Great Nature made
us men."

Equally as in the realm of war has
the race produced its noblemen in the
arena of peace and mental development.
For, if it be true that "the greatest names
in history are those who in the full career
and amid the turbid extremities of political
action, have yet touched the closest and at
most points the ever-standing problems of
the world and the things in which the interests of men never die," our industrial
educators are fittingly placed.

Of the ever-standing problem of the
world, and in which mankind is ever alert,
is the struggle for survival, and he that by
inspiring word and untiring deeds leads
the deserving poor and destitute to prosperity and contentment, is entitled to un-

HON. JOSIAH T. SETTLE, A. B. A. M.

Born in Tennessee, September, 1850—Entered Oberlin College in 1868—Graduated
From Howard University, 1872—A Leading Member of the Bar—Member of State Legislature of 1883—Assistant Attorney-General
—For Integrity as a Man, Learning as a Jurist,
and Eloquence of Appeal, He Has Made
an Honorable Record.

stinted praise as a great human force directed to a high moral purpose. While an advocate for the higher education of as many of the race who have the will or means to obtain it, for the majority, after obtaining a good English education, it should be immediately supplemented by a trade, to labor skillfully, is its great want today.

The question has been asked: "Can any race safely exist in any country composed only of unskilled laborers and professional men? Must not the future leaders of our people come from the middle classes, from those who work and think?" Education to be of practical advantage must not only sharpen the intellect, but it must be of that sort that will enable them to engage in pursuits and avocations above those of mere drudgery; those that are more lucrative, and from which accumulate wealth. The school room must be the stepping stone to a good trade. The statement has been made (which may be problematical) that we have fewer, comparatively, very many fewer, mechanics of all kinds now than we had in the days of slavery. The master knew that the money value of the slave was increased in the ratio of his efficiency as a skilled laborer.

To the credit of Kentucky, Alabama, Arkansas and other Southern States, they have made generous provisions for industrial education by supplying machinery and the most modern appliances to teach

skilled labor to those who prefer them to
the white apron of the waiter or the grub-
bing hoe of the plantation. Of the students that graduate from our high schools
and colleges there are those who have not
the qualities of head and heart essential
for teaching and preaching, including a
love and devotion to those callings, and
possibly would have been shining marks
had their studies fitted them to graple with
the mercantile or industrial factors that
promise a future more independent and
lucrative.

The advancement of any race in morals
and culture is retarded when poor and dependent. It is indispensable to progress
that it has the benefit of earnings laid by.
It is therefore to these industrial features
that we must look for the foundation of
advancement for the race. It will not be
found at either extreme of our present avocations; neither the attainment of the professions, nor devotion to menial labor will
solve the problem of the "better way." A
greater number must be fitted to obtain
work more lucrative in character and more
ennobling in effect. Institutions of applied
science and business pursuits seem to me
the great doorway to ultimate success.
Economy and industries of this kind will
more rapidly produce the means to achieve
that higher education for the race so desirable. Morality, learning and wealth are
a trio invincible.

To content ourselves with denouncing injustice is to fail to enlist the economic features so necessary as assistants. For amid all our disadvantages we are to a large extent arbiters of our fortunes, for we can by an indomitable will dispel many, many seeming mountains that encumber our way. But we have much to unlearn, and especially that the road to financial prosperity is not chiefly the dictum of the facile mouth, but through the manifestation of skilled hands and routine of business methods, however much the mouth may attempt to compete, conscious of its wealth of assertion and extent of capacity. While it is eminently proper we should strive for the administration of equitable laws for our protection, it should be ever remembered that while local laws under our constitutional government are supposed to be the equity of public opinion, for us they are not sustained unless in harmony with feelings and sentiments of their environments. Our work as a dependent element is plainly to use such, and only such, methods as will sustain or create the sentiment desired by a fraternization of business and material interests. This we cannot do either in the arena of politics or the status of the menial laborer. For in the one, when the polls are closed, we are continuously reminded of "Othello's occupation gone." In the other, the abundance of raw and uncouth labor robs it of its vitality as a force to compel conditions.

CHAPTER XXV.

The spirit in which these "schools of trade" have been conceived, and the success of their conduct, indicate they have struck a responsive chord in the communities where local approval is a necessity. Constituting an agreeable counterpoise to the fixed determination of the white people of the South that within its purview the Negro, however worthy, shall not occupy political prominence. This, while diametrically opposed to the genius and spirit of republican government, may yet be the boomerang, beneficent in its return, redounding to his advantage by turning the current of his aspirations to trades and business activities rich with promise of material and ennobling fame. From this point of view history records the Jew as a shining example. The Negro, constitutionally buoyant, should be energetic and hopeful, for "there is a destiny that shapes our ends," blunt them however much by damning with faint praise" or apology for oppression from whilom friends. In the darkest hour of slavery and ignorance came freedom and education. When lynchings became prevalent, lynching of whites made it unpopular; when disfranchisement

came, debasing him in localities as a factor
in civil government, came elevation and
high honor ungrudgingly bestowed for heroic deeds by commanders of the national
armies.

President McKinley, in his order for the
enlistment and promotion of the colored
soldier in the Spanish war, added additional luster to his page in history, it being
an act the result of which has been of inestimable value to the race. Just and inspiring is the speech of Hon. Charles H.
Grosvenor, of Ohio, delivered at the close
of the 56th Congress, entitled "The
Colored Citizen; His Share in the Affairs
of the Nation in the Years of 1897 to 1900.
Fifteen thousand participated in the war.
The President's generous treatment of colored men in the military and civil service
of the Government."

General Grosvenor commences with an
exordium eloquent in succinctness and noble in generosity. "I cannot let pass this
opportunity at the close of a long session
of Congress, and at the end of three years
of this Administration, without putting on
record to enlighten future generations the
history of the part which the colored citizen has had in the stirring events of this
remarkable period. It is a period in the
history of the country of which future generations will be proud, as are those of today, and as the colored citizens of the
United States have participated nobly in

it, it is but just to them that the facts be put on record.

"I want to speak of his part in the war in Cuba, in Porto Rico, in the Philippines. Would a war with Spain benefit the Negro? was a popular question for debate. Some thought it would benefit, others thought not. In many respects it has been a God-send and beyond dispute a great benefit. If in no other way, 15,048 privates have shown their patriotism and their valor by offering their bared breasts as shields for the country's honor; 4,114 regulars did actual, noble and heroic service at El Caney, San Juan and Santiago, while 266 officers (261 volunteers and five regulars) did similar service and demonstrated the ability of the American Negro to properly command ever so well, as he does readily obey."

General Grosvenor then pertinently adds: "When we learn to appreciate the fact that three years ago the Negro had in the army only five officers and 4,114 privates, and that one year ago he had 266 officers and 15,048 privates, we must know that inestimable benefit has come to the race. Among the officers are to be found many of the brightest minds of the race. Fully 80 per cent of those in authority come from the best known and most influential families in the land. Their contact with and influence upon their superior officers will be sure to raise the Negro in the popular esteem and do an incalculable good."

Reference is made to disbursements to
Negro officers and soldiers during the
Spanish war, which he colates to be
$5,000,000; adding the salaries of those em-
ployed in the civil service brings up to a
sum exceeding $6,000,000 paid the Negro
citizen. This, coupled with the high honor
attached to such military designations as
colonels, lieutenants and captains conferred upon him, shed a halo of generosity
over President McKinley's Administration.

General Grosvenor is richly entitled to
and received a just meed of praise for the
great service he has done by putting this
grand array of fact and heroic deed in popular form, and thereby strengthening the
Negro appeal for justice and opportunity,
while its pages are a noble contribution to
a valor that will illumine Negro history
for all time. It was most opportune, for
the then pressing need to strengthen the
weak and recall the recalcitrants who indiscriminately charge the party with being
remiss in requiting and acknowledging
the Negro's devotion. The well-earned
plaudits for his bravery on the battlefield
should widen the area of his consciousness, intensify conviction that mediocrity
is a drug in every human activity, for
whether in the professions, literature, agriculture or trades, it is excellence alone that
counts and will bring recognition, despite
the frowning battlements of caste. As we
become more and more valued factors in
the common cause of the general welfare,

that the flexibility of American sentiment
on conviction of merit will be more apparent we cannot but believe; for conditions
seem to have surmounted law and seek
their own solution, since the supreme law
of the land seems ineffectual and local sentiment the arbiter, when the Negro is
plaintiff.

In the first section of Article 14 of the
Constitution we have: "All persons born
or naturalized in the United States and
subject to the jurisdiction thereof are citizens of the United States and of the several States wherein they reside. No State
shall enforce any law which shall abridge
the privileges or immunities of citizens of
the United States." To neutralize this pronounced and unequivocal legislation we
have the dictum of the Supreme Court of
the United States that this constitutional
right, so plainly set forth, can be legally
abrogated by a State convention or legislature. While from the premises stated the
conclusion may be evident to a jurist, to
the layman it is perplexing; and while bow-
ing in obeyance to this court of last resort,
he cannot but admire the judicial agility
in escaping the problem. He is reminded
of a final response touching the character
and standing of a church member of whom
the inquirer wishes to know. The reply
was: "Brother B. is quite prominent and
well known here." "Well, what is his standing?" "Oh, very high; he is the elder of our
church and superintendent of the Sunday

JOHN MARSHALL HARLAN,

Chief Justice of the United States.
Born in Kentucky—A Colonel in the Union Army—Candidate for Vice-President
of the United States—One of the Foremost Authorities on Constitutional Law—Learned and Impartial.

school." "Yes, but as I am thinking of having some business dealings with him, what I want to know is, how does he stand for credit and promptness?" "Well, stranger, if you put it that way, I must say that heavenward Bro. B. is all right, but earthward he is rather twistical." Ordinaryward, the Supreme Court is all right; but Negroward, twistical.

For the law-abiding citizens of these Commonwealths we have this other, the second section of the same article: "When the right to vote at any election for the choice of electors for President or Vice-President of the United States, Representatives in Congress, the executive or judicial officers of a State, or the members of the legislature thereof, is denied to any one of the male inhabitants of such State being twenty-one years of age and a citizen of the United States, or in any way abridged, except for participation in rebellion or other crimes, the basis of representation thereon shall be reduced in the proportion which the number of such male citizens shall bear to the whole number of male citizens twenty-one years of age in such State."

If, as avowed, that it is for the welfare of such Southern States that they desire to banish the Negro from politics, can welfare be promoted or national integrity sustained by such rank injustice, as their Members of Congress occupying seats therein, or having representation in the electoral college based upon an apportionment in which the Negro numerically is so prominent a factor, and in the exercise of rights pertaining thereto, he is a nonentity.

"The Baptist Watchman" takes this unassailable position of this misrule: "Ex-Governor Northen, of Georgia, in his address before the Congregational Club the other evening, declared that the status of the black race in the South was that of permanent dependence upon the white race. The central point of his contention is that capacity to rule confers the right to rule. The white man can give the black man a better government that he can give himself; therefore, the black man should be glad to receive the blessing at the hands of the white man. For our part, we believe that, whatever specious defense on the ground of philanthropy, civilization and religion may be made for this position, it is radically repugnant to the genius of American institutions. If the men of the nation who are best qualified to rule have a right to rule, they themselves being the judge of their qualifications, England or Russia would be justified in attempting to impose their sovereignty on the United States, if they thought they could give us a better government than we are apt to give ourselves. Unless the doctrine is vigorously maintained that governments 'derive their just powers from the consent of the governed,' and not from the conceit of an aristocracy as to its own capacity, then we of the North will not find it easy to protest effectively against the disfranchisement of the Southern Negroes."

But the issue will not be made in opposition to a great national party that draws a large measure of its strength from the South till disaster from material issues compel. With the Republican party (as of a Christmas morning) "everything is lovely and the goose hangs high;" but discomfiture, sometimes laggard, is ever attendant on direlection of duty. This usurpation, which should have been throttled when a babe, has now become a giant seated in its castle, compelling deference and acquiescence to an anomaly, reaching beyond the Negro in its menace to representative government.

And now, while from inertia the Republican party has been privy to this misrepresentation, prominent Northern leaders are trying to take advantage of their own neglect in an attempt to reduce representation in national conventions from Southern States, irregularly Democratic. But the friends of just government need not despond, for the political and industrial revolution which the war for the perpetuation of the Union and the basic principle of equity it evolved will continue to demand and eventually secure equal rights for all beneath the flag.

(20)

CHAPTER XXVI.

Now, on the eve of my departure from Madagascar, and approaching four years of consular intercourse, I have only pleasant memories. My relations with Gen. eral Gallieni, Governor-General of the Island, and his official family, have ever been most cordial. On learning of my intended departure, he very graciously wrote me, as follows:

Madagascar and Dependencies.

Governeur-General.

Tananirivo, 19th Mch., 1901.

My Dear Consul:

I learn with much displeasure of your early departure from Madagascar, and would have been very glad to have met you again at the beginning of May, when going down to the coast. But I always intend to take a trip to America, and perhaps may find an opportunity to see you again in your powerful and flourishing country, which I wish so much to know. I thank you very much for your kind letter, and reciprocate. I had always with you the best relations, and I could appreciate your friendly and highly estimable character, and regret your departure. I have read with great pleasure your biographical sketch, and I see that you have already rendered many valuable services to your country, where your name is known very honorably. Yours faithfully,

GALLIENI.

Socially, as a member of the "Circle Francais" (a club of the elite of the French residents, a constant recipient of its sociability, the urbanity and kindness of Messrs. Proctor Brothers, Messrs. Dadubhoy & Co., and Messrs. Oswold & Co., representing, respectively, the leading English and German mercantile firms in the island, contributed much in making life enjoyable at that far-away post. My official life in Madagascar was not without its lights and shadows, and the latter sometimes "paled the ineffectual rays" of belated instructions. Of an instance I may make mention. I was in receipt of a cablegram from the Department of State advising me that the flagship "Chicago," with Admiral Howison, would at an early date stop at Tamatave and instructing me to obtain what wild animals I could indigenous to Madagascar and have them ready to ship thereby for the Smithsonian Institute, at Washington, D. C. How I responded, and the result of the response, is attempted to be set forth in the following dispatch to the Department of State:

Consulate of the United States,

Tamatave, Madagascar, July 3, 1899.

Mr. Gibbs to the Department of State.
Subject:

Madagascar Branch of Smithsonian Institute.

A Consul's "Burden."

———

Abstract of Contents:

Procuration of Live Animals, as per Order
of the Department, and Declination of
the Admiral to Receive Them on Board.

Honorable Assistant Secretary of State,

Washington, D. C.

Sir:—Referring to your cablegram under
date of May 22d last, directing me to secure
live animals for the Smithsonian Institu-
tute, to be sent home on the flagship "Chicago" on its arrival at this port, I have to
report that I proceeded with more or less
trepidation to accomplish the same, the
wild animals of Madagascar being exceedingly alive. With assistance of natives I
succeeded, after much trouble and expense,
in obtaining twelve, had them caged and
brought to the consulate weeks before the
arrival of the ship. This, I regret to say,
was a misadventure. I should have located them in the woods and pointed them
out to the Admiral on his arrival. At first
they seemed to agree, and were tractable
until a patriotic but unlucky impulse in-

duced me to give them the names of a few
prominent Generals in the late war. After
that, oh, my!

The twelve consist of different varieties.
One of the twelve seems a cross of panther
and wild cat, and rejoices in the appela-
tion of "Aye Aye."

On the arrival of the "Chicago," forthwith I reported to Admiral Howison my
success in capturing "these things of beauty," and eternal terrors, and my desire
that they change domicile. He received
me with such charming suavity, and my
report with so many tender expressions of
sympathy for the monkeys that I got a little mixed as to his preference. Still joy-
smitten, I was ill-prepared for the announcement "that it was unwise to take
them, as it was impossible to procure food
to keep them alive until the termination of
the voyage."

It was then, Mr. Secretary, that I sadly
realized that I was confronted by a condition. Over seventy years of age, 10,000
miles from home, a beggarly salary, with
a menagerie on my hands, while bankruptcy and a humbled flag threatened to
stare me in the face. There remained
nothing for me, but to "bow to the inevitable," transpose myself into a committee
of ways and means for the purpose of securing sleep for my eyelids and a saving to
the United States Treasury. For while
ever loyal to "the old flag and an appropriation," a sense of duty compels me to

advise that this branch of the Smithsonion Institute is of doubtful utility.

With a desire to avoid, if possible, "the deep damnation of their taking-off," by starvation, several plans promising relief suggested themselves, viz: Sell them, turn them loose, or keep them at Government expense. I very much regret that the latter course I shall be compelled to adopt. My many offers to sell seemed not understood, as the only response I have yet received has been: "I get you more like him, I can." As to turning them loose, I have been warned by the local authorities that if I did so I would do so at my peril. A necessary part of diet for these animals is condensed milk, meat, bread, jam, and bananas, but they are not content. Having been a member of the bar, and retaining much veneration for the Quixotic capers of judicial twelve, on their desire to leave I "polled" them and found a hung jury, swinging by their tails; eleven indicated "aye," but the twelfth, with his double affirmative cry of "Aye, Aye," being equal to negative, hung them up. Meanwhile, they bid fair to be a permanent exhibit.

Under cover of even date I enclose account for animals' food and attention to June 30, and beg to say regarding the item of food, that I anticipate a monthly increase of cost, as the appetite of the animals seem to improve in captivity. I conclude, Mr. Secretary, with but a single solace: They may possibly eat off their heads, but their tails give abundant promise of remaining in evidence. Patiently awaiting instructions as the the future disposition of these wild and wayward wards of the Government, I have the honor to be,

Your obedient servant,

M. W. GIBBS,

U. S. Consul.

How and when "I got rid of my burden" and the joyous expressions of a long-suffering Government on the event, will (or will not) "be continued in our next."

Having asked for leave of absence, and leaving Mr. William H. Hunt, the Vice-Consul, in charge of the consulate, on the 3d of April, 1891, I took passage on the French steamer, "Yantse," for Marseilles, France.

CHAPTER XXVII.

April 3, 1901.—It was not without regret, that found expression at a banquet
given me on the eve preceding my departure, by Mr. Erlington, the German Consul
at Tamatave, that I took my leave of Madagascar, when the flags of the officials of
the French Residency and flags of all the
foreign consuls were flying, honoring me
with a kindly farewell. A jolly French
friend of mine, who came out to the steamer to see me off, said: "Judge, don't you be
too sure of the meaning of the flags flying
at your departure from Tamatave, for we
demonstrate here for gladness, as well as
for regret." "Well," I replied, "in either
event I am in unison with the sentiment
intended to be expressed; for I have both
gladness and regret—gladness with anticipations of home, and with regret that, in
all human probability, I am taking leave
of a community from whom for nearly four
years I have been the recipient, officially,
of the highest respect; and socially of unstinted friendliness."

I found Vice-Consul Hunt had secured
and had had my baggage placed in a desirable state room. The ringing of the bell

CHARLES W. CHESNUT.

A Distinguished Colored Writer—Author of "The House Behind the Cedars,"
"The Wife of My Youth," "The Conjure Woman," "The Morrow of
Tradition"—All Sparkling with Justice, Wisdom, and Wit.

notified all non-passengers ashore. After
hearty handshakes from the Vice-Consul,
German, French, and other friends, taking
with them a bottle or two of wine that had
been previously placed where it would do
the most good, they took the consular boat,
and with the Stars and Stripes flying,
and handkerchiefs waving a final farewell, they were pulled ashore. The anchor
weighs, and the good ship "Yantse" in-
hales a long, moist, and heated breath and
commences to walk with stately strides
and quickened pace—weather charming
and the sea as quiet as a tired child. The
next day a stop at the Island of St. Maria,
a French possession, and on the fifth day
at Deigo Suarez, on the north end of Madagascar.

On the ninth day from Tamatave we entered the Gulf of Aden, and after some
hours dropped anchor at Camp Aden, in
Arabia. Mr. Byramzie, a Tamatave friend
of mine, and of the London firm of Dadab-
hoy & Co., with a branch at Aden, came off
to meet me and accompany me ashore.
Camp Aden is a British fortification I cannot readily describe with reference to its
topography or the heterogenous character
and pursuits of its inhabitants. Nature
was certainly in no passive mood when
last it flung its constituents together; for,
with the exception of a few circling acres
forming a rim around the harbor, high,
broken, and frowning battlements of rock,
ungainly and sterile, look down upon you

as far as the eye can reach. No sprig, or tree, or blade of grass takes root in its parched soil or stony bed, or survives the blasting heat. Scattered and dotted on crag, hilltop or slope, in glaring white, are the many offices and residence buildings of the camp. While in hidden crevices and forbidden paths are planted the most approved armament, with its "dogs of war" to dispute a passage from the Gulf.

In a dilapidated four-wheeler, drawn by one horse, after considerable time spent by my friend in agreeing on terms (concerning which I pause to remark that these benighted Jehus can give a Bowery cabman points on "how not to do it"), over a macadam road of five miles we reach Aden proper—the site of hotels, stores and residences with little pretensions to architectural beauty; the buildings are quite all constructed of stone, that material being in superabundance on every intended site; their massive walls contributing to a cool interior indispensable as a refuge from the blistering heat. Pure water for drinking is a luxury, spasmodic in its supply. I once heard an hilarious Irish song that stated:

"We are jolly and happy, for we know
    without doubt,
That the whisky is plenty, and the water
    is out."

This, I learn is the normal condition at Aden as to the relative status of whisky and water—a very elysium for the toper

who could not understand why whisky
should be spoiled by mixing it with water.
Rains are infrequent and well water un-
palatable. Sea water is distilled, but the
mineral and health-giving qualities are
said to be absent. The water highly prized
and sold is the rainwater caught in tanks.
Hollowed out at the foot of the rock hills,
there are numbers of peculiar construction,
connected and on different elevations. But
for the last three years the non-rainfall has
kept them without a tenant. As I looked
in them not a drop sparkled witthin their
capacious confines; they are seldom filled,
and the supply is ever deficient. The population is from 6,000 to 8,000, amid which
the Parsee, the Mohammedan, Jew,
Portuguese, and other nationalities compete for the commerce of the interior. The
natives are of varied castes, the Samiles
the most energetic and prevailing type.
The inferior classes go about almost naked
and live in long, unprepossessing struc-
tures, one story high, divided into single
rooms, rude and uncleanly.

While at Aden I availed myself of the
honor and pleasure of a visit to the American Consulate, and received a warm, jolly,
and spiritual welcome from the incumbent,
the Hon. E. T. Cunningham, of Knoxville,
Tenn. Mr. Cunningham intended to stay
at Aden for six months. Like "linked
sweetness long drawn out," that period has
extended to three years, and is now "los-
ing its sweetness on the desert air." He

stated that he was not infatuated with
those "scarlet days" and "Arabian nights,"
and is seeking relief or placement amid
more congenial surroundings, where distance (does not) "lend enchantment to the
view." But I assured him the Department
was as astute as selfish. It knows when it
has a good thing, and endeavors to keep it.
Mr. Cunningham has proved himself to be
an efficient and trusted official. We parted
with mutual hope of again meeting in "the
land of the cotton and the corn."

On my way to the landing I passed many
convoys of camels and asses, laden with
coffee, it being one of the main articles of
export. Arriving at the steamer and bidding my Parsee friend a last, long farewell, shortly we weighed anchor and away
for a five days sail to Suez.

On the 17th of April, eventful to me, being my birthday, we arrived at Suez for a
short stay, without time or inclination to
go ashore. But, seeing the Stars and
Stripes flying from a ship lying in the distance, I could not withstand the temptation. Jumping into a native sailboat that
described every point of the compass with
oars and adverse wind, I reached the
United States cruiser, "New York." Capt.
Rodgers and his gentlemanly officers gave
me a very cordial reception, ensuring an
enjoyable visit. Capt. Rodgers informed
me that Lieutenant Poundstone was
aboard, who knew me as a "promoter" for
the Smithsonian Institute at Washington,

he having been aboard the "Chicago"
when it visited Tamatave, and when Admiral Howison declined to convey my "gay
and festive" collection of wild animals to
America. I would be most happy to see
him. He soon appeared with pleasant
greetings and recollections of Tamatave
incidents. My stay from ship being limited, after a chat, mingled with sherry and
cigars and an expression of regret from
Capt Rodgers that, not being in our "bail-
iwick," he could not give me a consular salute from his guns, he ordered the ship's
steam launch, and, escorted by the Lieutenant, under our national banner, I soon
boarded my ship. I was much indebted to
Capt. Rodgers and officers for their charming courtesy.

Leaving Suez at mid-day, we shortly enter the Suez Canal—85 miles, with numerous tie-ups to allow other ships the right of
way.

At 8 o'clock the following morning we
dropped anchor at Port Said, a populous
city of Arabia with 30,000 inhabitants,
much diversified as to nativities, Turks,
Assyrians, Jews, and Greeks being largely
represented. The city is quite prepossessing, and seems to have improved its sanitary features since my visit four years ago.
There are many charming views; an interesting place for the tourist, alike for the
virtuous and the vicious, for those so in-
clined can see human nature "unadorned."
Wide streets pierce the city, the stores on

which are a continuous bazaar, lined with
many exquisite productions of necessity
and Eastern art. But I have previously
dwelt on Port Said peculiarities.

Leaving Port Said on the 18th, our good
ship soon enters the Mediterranean, and
with smooth seas passes through the
Straits of Messina, with a fine view of Mt.
Etna, as of yore, belching forth flames and
smoke, with Sicily on our left and Italy
and her cities on our right. Again entering the Mediterranean, we encounter our
first rough seas and diminution of guests
at the table.   Neptune, who had been len-
ient for 17 days, now demanded settlement
before digestion should again be allowed
to resume its sway. For myself, I was like
and unlike the impecunious boarder, who
"never missed a meal nor paid a cent," but
like him only in constant attendance, for
I could ill-afford to miss any part of the
pleasure of transit or menu costing $10 a
day—happy, however, that I was minus
"mal de mer," seasickness. But this temporary ailment of the passengers was soon
banished by another phase of ocean travel,
that of being enveloped in a fog so dense
that the ship's length could not be seen
ahead from the bow—every officer of the
ship alert, the fog horn blowing its warn-
ings at short intervals, answered by the
"ships that pass in the night" of fogs. The
anxiety of the passengers that the fog
would lift was relieved after 36 hours, and
our ship hied away and reached Marsielles

on the 23d. From there by rail to Paris.
Ensconced again at the "Hotel Binda," the
next day I visited the site of the great
Paris Exposition. Few of the buildings
were in their entirety, but what remained
of the classic beauty of their construction
shone the more vivid amid the debris of
demolition that surrounded them. The
French were not enthusiastic in relation to
the financial benefit of the exposition.

A few days in Paris, and thence to Cher-
bourg to cross the English Channel to
Southampton, London. This channel,
which has a well-merited reputation for
being gay and frolicsome, was exteremely
gracious, allowing us to glide over its
placid bosom with scarce a tremor.

CHAPTER XXVIII.

This was my first visit to the land of Wilberforces and Clarksons of the seventeenth century, whose devotion and fidelity to liberty abolished African slavery in Britain's dominion and created the sentiment that found expression in the immortal utterance of Judge Mansfield's decision: "Slaves cannot breathe in England; upon touch of its soil they stand forth redeemed and regenerated by the genuis of universal liberty." With my English friend, C. B. Hurwitz, as an escort, I enjoyed an excursion on the Thames, and visited many places of note, including England's veteran bank, designated as the "Old Lady of Threadneedle Street," and the Towers of London. One of these, the Beauchamp Tower, is supposed to have been built in the twelfth or thirteenth century, the architecture corresponding with that in use at that period, and lately restored to its original state. Herein are many inscriptions, some very rude, others quite artistic. It was during the restoration that these inscriptions were partially discovered and carefully preserved. They were cut in the stone walls and partitions by the unhappy occupants, confined for life or execution for their religion or rebellion in the thirteenth to the sixteenth century. Many are adorned with rude devices and inscriptions denoting the undying faith of the martyr; others the wailing of distress and despair. Five hundred years have elapsed, yet the sadness of the crushed hearts of the unhappy occupants still lingers like a funeral pall to point a moral that should strengthen tolerance and cherish liberty.

Leaving Southampton, London, on the steamship St. Louis, after an uneventful passage I arrived in New York, and from thence to Washington, D. C. After my leave of absence had expired, I decided not to return to Madagascar. For after nearly four years' dalliance with the Malagash fever in the spring and dodging the bubonic plague in the fall, I concluded that Madagascar was a good place to *come from*.

W. H. Hunt, the Vice-Consul, who had filed application for the Consulship, conditioned upon my resignation, was appointed. An admirable appointment, for the duties pertaining thereto, I have no doubt, will be performed with much credit to himself and to the satisfaction of the Government.

I was honored as a delegate to a very interesting assembly of colored men from 32 States, designated the "National Negro Business Men's League," which met in Chicago, Ill., Aug. 27, 1901. Of its object and labors my conclusions were: That no better evidence can be produced that the negro has a good hold on the lever which will not only give a self-consciousness of latent powers, but will surely elevate him in the estimation of his fellw-citizens, than the increasing interest he is taking and engaging in many of the business ventures of the country, and the popular acquiescence manifested by the crowded attendance at every session of the meeting.

The President of the League, Booker T. Washington, expressed the following golden thoughts in his opening speech:

"As a race we must learn more and more that the opinion of the world regarding us is not much influenced by what we may say of ourselves, or by what others say of us, but it is permanently influenced by actual, tangible, visible results. The object-lesson of one honest Negro succeeding magnificently in each community in some business or industry is worth a hundred abstract speeches in securing opportunity for the race.

"In the South, as in most parts of the world, the Negro who does something and possesses something is respected by both races. Usefulness in the community where we live will constitute our most lasting and potent protection.

"We want to learn the lesson of small things and small beginnings. We must not feel ourselves above the most humble occupation or the simple, humble beginning. If our vision is clear, our will strong, we

will use the very obstacles that often seem
to beset us as stepping-stones to a higher
and more useful life."

The enrollment of the members present
was not completed at the first session, but
the hall was crowded and 200 of those
present were visitors in Chicago. Pictures
and some of the product of Negro concerns
decorated the walls, as evidence that the
black man is rising above the cotton plantation, his first field of labor in this country. Pictures of brick blocks, factories,
livery stables, farms and shops of every
description owned by Negroes in many different States of the Union were in the collection, but the greater evidence of the Negro's development were the men taking
part in the deliberations of the sessions.
They are clean cut, well-dressed, intelligent, and have put a business method into
the organization.

The Governor of the State and Mayor of
Chicago were represented with stirring addresses of welcome. The convention was
singular and peculiar in this: The central
idea of the meeting was scrupulously adhered to; there was present no disposition
to refer to grievances or deprivations. A
feeling seemed to permeate the participants of confidence and surety that they
had fathomed the depths of much that
stood in the way of a just recognition of
Negro worth and a just appreciation and
resolution to "fight it out on that line if it
took all summer," or many summers.

There were so many expressions so full of wisdom; so many suggestions practical and adaptable, I would, had I space, record them all here.

Theodore Jones, of Chicago, a successful business man, in concluding an able paper, "Can a Negro Succeed as a Business Man," said:

"The tone of this convention clearly indicates that the Negro will succeed as a business man in proportion as he learns that manhood and womanhood are qualities of his own making, and that no external forces can either give or take them away. It demonstrates that intelligence, punctuality, industry, and integrity are the conquering forces in the business and commercial world, as well as in all the affairs of human life."

Giles B. Jackson, Secretary of the Business League of Virginia, read a paper on "Negro Industries," showing what had been done toward the solution of the so-called "Negro problem." The Negroes, he stated, had $14,000,000 invested in business enterprises in Virginia.

William L. Taylor, President of the "True Reformers' Bank," of Richmond, Va., gave interesting details in an able and intelligent effort, of the aims and accomplishments of that successful institution, presenting many phases of the enterprise —its branch stores, different farms, hotel and printing department, giving employ-

ment to more than 100 officers, clerks, and
employees. Dr. R. H. Boyd, of Nashville,
Tenn., the head of the "Colored Publishing
Company, of Nashville," employing 123 assistants, delivered an able address on the
"Negro in the Publishing Business,"
which was discussed with marked ability
by the Rev. Dr. Morris, of Helena, Ark.

All the paticipants are worthy of a meed
of praise for their many helpful utterances
and manly deportment. Prominent among
them were Charles Banks, merchant and a
large property owner of Clarkesdale, Miss.,
who spoke on "Merchandizing"; William
O. Murphy, of Atlanta, Ga., on the "Gro-
cery Business"; Harris Barrett, of Hampton, Va., on "The Building and Loan Association of Hampton, Va."; A. N. Johnson, publisher and editor, of Mobile, on
"The Negro Business Enterprises of Mobile"; F. D. Patterson, of Greenfield, Ohio,
on "Carriage Manufacturing"; Martin Fer-
guson on "Livery Business," small in stat-
ure, light in weight, but herculean in size
and heavy in force of persistency, told how
by self-denial he had gained a fair compe-
tency; L. G. Wheeler, of Chicago, Ill., on
"Merchant Tailoring"; Willis S. Stearns,
a druggist, of Decatur, Ala., in his address
stated that 14 years ago there was not a
Negro druggist in that State; now there
are over 200 such stores owned by colored
men in various cities of that State, with an
invested capital of $500,000. Walter P.
Hall, of Philadelphia, Pa., an extensive

dealer in game and poultry, spoke on that subject.

And possibly as a fitting wind-up, as all sublunary things must come to an end, George E. Jones, of Little Rock, Ark., and G. E. Russel, of St. Louis, Mo., under-takers, spoke pathetically to their fellow-members of the League (I trust not expec-tantly) of the advance in the science of em-balming and other facilities for conveying them to that "bourne from which no trav-eller returns." The session was "a feast of reason and a flow of soul" from its com-mencement until its close. And, as ever has been the case on our upward journey, there were women lighting the pathway and stimulating effort; for during the ses-sions Mrs. Albreta Smith read a very in-teresting paper on "The Success of the Ne-gro Women's Business Club of Chicago"; a delightful one was read by Mrs. Dora Miller, of Brooklyn, N. Y.; "Dressmaking and Millinery" was entertainingly present-ed by Mrs. Emma L. Pitts, of Macon, Ga., the ladies dwelling on the great good that was being done by their establishments by teaching and giving employment to scores of poor but worthy girls, and there-by helping them to lead pure and useful lives.

I have given this exhibition of what the Negro is doing the foregoing space for en-couragement and precept, because I be-lieve it to be the key to unlock many doors to honorable and useful lives heretofore barred against us.

WILLIAM McKINLEY,

Late Martyred President of the United States.
With a Record for Statesmanship, Patriotism, and Justice Imperishable—"His
Life Was Gentle and the Elements so Mixed in Him, that Nature
Might Stand Up and Say to all the World, 'This is a Man.'"

CHAPTER XXIX.

Leaving Chicago, and having business with the President, I visited him at Canton, was kindly received, and accomplished the object of my visit, little thinking that, in common with my countrymen I was so soon to be horrified and appalled by an atrocity which bathed the country in tears and startled the world in the taking-off of one of the purest patriots that had ever trod his native soil.

The tragedy occurred at 4 o'clock p. m., on the 6th of September, 1901, in the Temple of Music on the grounds of and during the Exposition at Buffalo, N. Y. Surrounded by a body-guard, among whom was Secret Service Detective Samuel R. Ireland, of Washington, who was directly in front of the President, the latter engaged in the usual manner of handshaking at a public reception at the White House. Not many minutes had expired; a hundred or more of the line had passed the President, when a young-looking man named Leon Czolgosz, said to be of Polish extraction, approached, offering his left hand, while his right hand contained a pistol concealed under a handkerchief, fired two shots at the President.

James Parker, a colored man, a very hercules in height, who was next to have greeted the President, struck the assassin a terrific blow that felled him to the floor, preventing him (as Czolgosz himself avers in the following interview) from firing the third shot:

"Yesterday morning I went again to the Exposition grounds. Emma Goldman's speech was still burning me up. I waited near the central entrance for the President, who was to board his special train from that gate, but the police allowed nobody but the President's party to pass where the train waited. So I stayed at the grounds all day waiting.

"During yesterday I first thought of hiding my pistol under my handkerchief. I was afraid if I had to draw it from my pocket I would be seen and seized by the guards. I got to the Temple of Music the first one, and waited at the spot where the reception was to be held.

"Then he came, the President—the ruler —and I got in line and trembled and trembled until I got right up to him, and then I shot him twice through my white handkerchief. I would have fired more, but I was stunned by a blow in the face— a frightful blow that knocked me down— and then everybody jumped on me. I thought I would be killed, and was surprised the way they treated me."

Czolgosz ended his story in utter exhaustion. When he had about concluded he was asked:

"Did you really mean to kill the President?"

"I did," was the cold-blooded reply.

"What was your motive; what good could it do?"

"I am an anarchist. I am a disciple of Emma Goldman. Her words set me on fire," he replied, with not the slightest tremor.

During the first few days after he was shot there were cheering bulletins issued by the medical fraternity in attendance, all typical of his early recovery, and the heart of the nation was elated, to be, a week later, depressed with sadness at the announcement that a change had come and that the President was dying. Never was grief more sincere for a ruler. He was buried encased with the homage and love of his people. William McKinley will live in history, not only as a man whose private life was stainless, and whose Administration of the Government was beyond reproach, but as one brilliant, progressive, wise, and humane.

Pre-eminent as an arbiter and director, developing the nation as a world power, and bringing to the effete and semi-civilized peoples of the Orient the blessings of civilized Government; as a leader and protector of the industrial forces of the country, William McKinley was conspicuous. With strength of conviction, leading at one

time an almost forlorn hope, by his statesmanship and intensity of purpose, he had
grafted on the statute books of the Nation
a policy that has turned the wheels of a
thousand idle mills, employed a hundred
thousand idle hands, and stimulated every
manufacturing industry.

This accomplished, in his last speech,
memorable not only as his last public utterance, but doubly so as to wise statesmanship in its advocacy of a less restrict-
ive tariff, increased reciprocity, and interchange with the world's commodities. His
love of justice was imperial. He was noted
in this, that he was not only mentally eminent, but morally great. During his last
tour in the South, while endeavoring to
heal animosities engendered by the civil
war and banish estrangement, he was positive in the display of heartfelt interest in
the Negro, visiting Tuskegee and other
like institutions of learning, and by his
presence and words of good cheer stimulating us to noble deeds.

Nor was his interest manifest alone in
words; his appointments in the bureaus of
the Government of colored men exceeded
that of any previous Executive—a representation which should increase in accordance with parity of numbers and fitness
for place.

The following excerpts from the Washington Post, the verity of which was
echoed in the account of the crime by the

JAMES B. PARKER.

Who, Inspired by Patriotism and Fidelity, Struck Down the Assassin of
President McKinley.

New York and other metropolitan journals on the day following the sad occurrence, gives a sketch of the manner and expressions of the criminal, and throws light on a peculiar phase of the catastrophe, that for the truth of history and in the interest of justice should not be so rudely and covertly buried 'neath the immature "beatings of time."

Washington Post: In an interview Secret Service Detective Ireland, who, with Officers Foster and Gallagher, was near the President when the shots were fired, said:

"A few moments before Czolgosz approached a man came along with three fingers of his right hand tied up in a bandage, and he had shaken hands with his left. When Czolgosz came up I noticed he was a boyish-looking fellow, with an innocent face, perfectly calm, and I also noticed that his right hand was wrapped in what appeared to be a bandage. I watched him closely, but was interrupted by the man in front of him, who held on to the President's hand an unusually long time. This man appeared to be an Italian, and wore a short, heavy, black mustache. He was persistent, and it was necessary for me to push him along so that the others could reach the President. Just as he released the President's hand, and as the President was reaching for the hand of the assassin, there were two quick shots. Startled for a moment, I looked and saw the

President draw his right hand up under his coat, straighten up, and, pressing his lips together, give Czolgosz the most scorn and contemptuous look possible to imagine.

"At the same time I reached for the young man, and caught his left arm. The big Negro standing just back of him, and who would have been next to take the President's hand, struck the young man in the neck with one hand, and with the other reached for the revolver, which had been discharged through the handkerchief, and the shots from which had set fire to the linen.

"Immediately a dozen men fell upon the assassin and bore him to the floor. While on the floor Czolgosz again tried to discharge the revolver, but before he could point it at the President, it was knocked from his hand by the Negro. It flew across the floor, and one of the artillerymen picked it up and put it in his pocket."

Another account : " Mr. McKinley straightened himself, paled slightly, and riveted his eyes upon the assassin. He did not fall or make an outcry. A Negro, named Parker, employed in the stadium, seized the wretch and threw him to the floor, striking him in the mouth. As he fell he struggled to use the weapon again, but was quickly overpowered. Guard Foster sprang to the side of Mr. McKinley, who walked to a chair a few feet away."

Washington Post, Oct. 9: James Par-

ker, the six-foot Georgia Negro, who
knocked down the assassin of President
McKinley on the fatal day in the Temple
of Music, after the two shots were fired,
gave a talk to an audience in the Metropolitan A. M. E. Church last night. He was
introduced by Hon. George H. White.
Parker arose, and after a few preliminary
remarks, in which he thanked the crowd
for its presence, he said he was glad to see
so many colored people believed he did
what he claimed he did at Buffalo.

"When the assassin dealt his blow," said
Parker, "I felt it was time to act. It is no
great honor I am trying to get, but simply what the American people think I am
entitled to. If Mr. McKinley had lived
there would have been no question as to
this matter. President McKinley was
looking right at me; in fact, his eyes were
riveted upon me when I felled the assassin
to the floor.

"The assassin was in front of me, and as
the President went to shake his hand, he
looked hard at one hand which the fellow
held across his breast bandaged. I looked
over the man's shoulder to see what the
President was looking at. Just then there
were two flashes and a report, and I saw
the flame leap from the supposed bandage.
I seized the man by the shoulder and dealt
him a blow. I tried to catch hold of the
gun, but he had lowered that arm. Quick
as a flash I grasped his throat and choked
him as hard as I could. As this happened

he raised the hand with the gun in it again as if to fire, the burnig handkerchief hanging to the weapon. I helped carry the assassin into a side room, and helped to search him."

Parker told of certain things he was about to do to the assassin when one of the officers asked him to step outside. Parker refused. He declared the officers wanted to get him out of the way. He said he helped to carry the assassin to the carriage in which the wretch was taken to jail.

"I don't know why I wasn't summoned to the trial," he said.

Parker said Attorney Penney took his testimony after the shooting.

"I was not at the trial, though," concluded Parker in an injured tone. "I don't say this was done with any intent to defraud me, but it looks mighty funny, that's all."

The above interviews with officers present agree with Parker's version of the affair, and whether the afterthought that further recognition of his decisive action would detract from the reputation for vigilance which they were expected to observe is a fitting subject for presumption.

At the time of the occurrence Parker was the cynosure for all eyes. Pieces of the clothing that he wore were solicited and given to his enthusiastic witnesses of the deed, to be preserved as trophies of his action in preventing the third shot. No one present at that perilous hour and witnessing doubted or questioned that Parker was the hero of the occasion. This, the better impulse, indicating a just appreciation was destined soon to be stifled and ignored. At the sittings of the coroner's jury to investigate the shooting of the President, he was neither solicited nor allowed to be present, or testimony adduced in proof of his bravery in attempting to save the life of the Chief Magistrate of the Republic. Therefore, Parker, bereft of the well-earned plaudits of his countrymen, must content himself with duty done.

Remarkable are the coincidences at every startling episode in the life of the Nation. Beginning at our country's history, the Negro is always found at the fore. He was there when Crispus Attacks received the first of English bullets in the struggle of American patriots for Independence; there in the civil war, when he asked to be assigned to posts of greatest danger. He was there quite recently at El Caney; and now Parker bravely bares his breast between the intended third shot of the assassin and that of President McKinley.

If this dispensation shall awaken the Nation to the peril of admitting the refuse of nations within our borders, and clothing them with the panoply of American citizenship; if it shall engender a higher appreciation of the loyalty and devotion of the Negro citizens of the Republic by the extension of justice to all beneath the flag, William McKinley will not have died in vain.

CHAPTER XXX.

Taking up the reins of the Administration of the Government, with its complex statesmanship, where a master had laid them down, President Roosevelt, heretofore known for his sterling worth as an administrator, and his imperial honesty as a man, has put forth no uncertain sound as to his intended course. The announcement that the foreign policy of his illustrious predecessor would be chiefly adhered to has struck a responsive chord in every patriotic heart. The appointment of ex-Gov. Jones; of Alabama, to a Federal judgeship was an appointment in unison with the best of popular accord. The nobility of the Governor in his utterances on the subject of lynching should endear him to every lover of justice and the faithful execution of law. For he so grandly evinced what is so sadly wanting in many humane and law-abiding men—the courage of his convictions.

"For when a free thought sought expression,
  He spoke it boldly, spoke it all."

It is only to the fruition of such expressions, the molding of an adverse senti-

THEODORE ROOSEVELT,

President of the United States.
Civil Service Commissioner—Police Commissioner of New York—Assistant Sec-
retary of War and Vice-President of the United States—
A Hero in War, a Statesman in Peace.

ment to such lawlessness that we can look
for the abolishment of that crime of crimes
which, to the disgrace of our country, is
solely ours.

This appointment is considered eminently wise, not only for the superior ability of the appointee as a jurist, but for his
broad humanity as a man, fully recognizing the inviolability of human life and its
subjection to law. For the Negro, his pri-
mal needs are protection and the common
liberty vouchsafed to his fellow-country-
men. To enjoy them it is necessary that he
be in harmony with his environments. A
bulwark he must have, of a friendship not
the product of coercion, but a concession
from the pulse-beat of justice. Such appointments pass the word down the line
that President Roosevelt, in his endeavor
to be the exponent of the genius of American citizenship, will recognize the sterling
advocates of the basic elements of constitutional Government, those of law and order, irrespective of party affiliation.

This appointment will probably cause
dissent in Republican circles, but it may be
doubted if the Negro advances his political
fortunes by invidious criticism of the efforts of a Republican Administration to
harmonize ante-bellum issues. For while
he in all honesty may be strenuous for the
inviolability of franchises of the Republican household, and widens the gap between friendly surroundings, each of the

(22)

political litigants meet with their knees under each other's mahogany, and jocularly discuss Negro idiosyncrasies, and tacitly agree to give his political aspirations a "letting alone." For, with character and ability unquestioned for the discharge of duties, the vote polled for him usually falls far short of the average of that polled by his party for other candidates on the ticket.

The summary killing of human beings by mobs without the form of law is not of late origin. Ever since the first note of reconstruction was sounded, each Administration has denounced lynching. All history is the record that it is only through discussion and the ventilation of wrong that right becomes a valued factor. But regard for justice is not diminishing in our country. The judiciary, although weak and amenable to prevailing local prejudices in localities, as a whole is far in advance on the sustenance of righteous rule than in the middle of the last century, when slavery ruled the Nation and its edicts were law, and its baleful influence permeated every branch of the Government.

Of the judiciary at that period Theodore Parker, an eminent Congregational divine and most noted leader of Christian thought, during a sermon in 1854, said:

"Slavery corrupts the judicial class. In America, especially in New England, no class of men has been so much respected as

the judges, and for this reason: We have
had wise, learned, and excellent men for
our judges, men who reverenced the
higher law of God, and sought by human
statutes to execute justice. You all know
their venerable names and how reveren-
tially we have looked up to them. Many of
them are dead, and some are still living,
and their hoary hairs are a crown of glory
on a judicial life without judicial blot. But
of late slavery has put a different class of
men on the benches of the Federal Courts
—mere tools of the Government creatures
who get their appointments as pay for
past political service, and as pay in advance for iniquity not yet accomplished.
You see the consequences. Note the zeal
of the Federal judges to execute iniquity
by statute and destroy liberty. See how
ready they are to support the Fugitive
Slave Bill, which tramples on the spirit of
the Constitution and its letter, too; which
outrages justice and violates the most sacred principles and precepts of Christianity. Not a United States Judge, Circuit or
District, has uttered one word against that
bill of abominations. Nay, how greedy
they are to get victims under it. No wolf
loves better to rend a lamb into fragments
than these judges to kidnap a fugitive
slave and punish any man who desires to
speak against it. You know what has happened in Fugitive Slave Bill courts. You
remember the 'miraculous' rescue of a
Shadrach; the peaceable snatching of a

man from the hands of a cowardly kidnap-
er was 'high treason;' it was 'levying
war.' You remember the trial of the res-
cuers! Judge Sprague's charge to the jury
that if they thought the question was
which they ought to obey, the laws of man
or the laws of God, then they must 'obey
both,' serve God and Mammon, Christ and
the devil in the same act. You remember
the trial, the ruling of the bench, the
swearing on the stand, the witness coming back to alter and enlarge his testimony and have another gird at the prisoner.
You have not forgotten the trials before
Judge Kane at Philadelphia and Judge
Greer at Christiana and Wilkesbarre.

"These are natural results from causes
well known. You cannot escape a principle. Enslave a negro, will you? You
doom to bondage your own sons and
daughters by your own act."

At the death of Theodore Parker, among
the many eulogies on his life was one by
Ralph Waldo Emerson, highly noted for
his humanity, his learning and his philosophy. It contains apples of gold, and
richly deserves immortality; for in the
worldly strife for effervescent wealth and
prominence, a benign consciousness that
our posthumous fame as unselfish benefactors to our fellow-men is to live on
through the ages, would be a solace for
much misrepresentation. Emerson said:
"It is plain to me that Theodore Parker
has achieved a historic immortality here.

HON. GEORGE B. CORTELYOU.

Secretary to the President.
Born July, 1862, in State of New York—Has Made Mark in Literature and
Art—His Promotion Has Been Rapid, From Stenographer to Executive
Clerk, Thence to Secretary to Presidents McKinley and
Roosevelt, an Office Now Grown to the Dignity
of a Cabinet Position.

It will not be in the acts of City Councils
nor of obsequious Mayors nor in the State
House; the proclamations of Governors,
with their failing virtue failing them at
critical moments, that generations will
study what really befel; but in the plain
lessons of Theodore Parker in this hall, in
Faneuil Hall and in legislative committee
rooms, that the true temper and authentic
record of these days will be read. The next
generation will care little for the chances
of election that govern Governors now; it
will care little for fine gentlemen who be-
haved shabbily; but it will read very intel-
ligently in his rough story, fortified with
exact anecdotes, precise with names and
dates, what part was taken by each actor
who threw himself into the cause of humanity and came to the rescue of civilization at a hard pinch; and those who
blocked its course.

"The vice charged against America is the
want of sincerity in leading men. It does
not lie at his door. He never kept back
the truth for fear of making an enemy.
But, on the other hand, it was complained
that he was bitter and harsh; that his zeal
burned with too hot a flame. It is so hard
in evil times to escape this charge for the
faithful preacher. Most of all, it was his
merit, like Luther, Knox, and Latimer and
John the Baptist, to speak tart truth when
that was peremptory and when there were
few to say it. His commanding merit as a
reformer is this, that he insisted beyond all

men in pulpit—I cannot think of one rival
—that the essence of Christianity is its
practical morals; it is there for use, or it is
nothing.   If you combine it with sharp
trading, or with ordinary city ambitions to
glaze over municipal corruptions or private intemperance, or successful frauds,
or immoral politics, or unjust wars, or the
cheating of Indians, or the robbing of
frontier natives, it is hypocrisy and the
truth is not in you, and no love of religious
music, or dreams of Swedenborg, or praise
of John Wesley or of Jeremy Taylor, can
save you from the Satan which you are."

CHAPTER XXXI.

The accord so generally given to the appointment of ex-Governor Jones, of Alabama—a Gold Democrat, having views on domestic order in harmony with the Administration to a Federal judgeship was destined to be followed by a bitter arraignment of President Roosevelt for having invited Booker T. Washington to dine with him at the White House. As a passing event not without interest, in this era of the times, indicative of "shadow and light," I append a few extracts from Southern and Northern Journals:

SHADOW.

In all parts of the country comment has been provoked by the fact that President Roosevelt, on Wednesday night last, entertained at dinner in the White House, Booker T. Washington, who is generally regarded as the representative of the colored race in America. Especially in the South has the incident aroused indignation, according to the numerous news dispatches. The following comments from the editorial columns of newspapers and from prominent men are given:

New Orleans, Oct. 19.—The Times-Dem-ocrat says:

"It is strange news that comes from Washington. The President of the United States, for the first time in the history of the nation, has entertained a Negro at dinner in the White House. White men of the South, how do you like it? White women of the South, how do you like it?

"Everyone knows that when Mr. Roosevelt sits down to dinner in the White House with a Negro he that moment declares to all the world that in the judgment of the President of the United States the Negro is the social equal of the white man. The Negro is not the social equal of the white man. Mr. Roosevelt might as well attempt to rub the stars out of the firmament as to try to erase that conviction from the heart and brain of the American people."

The Daily States: "In the face of the facts it can but appear that the President's action was little less than a studied insult to the South adopted at the outset of his Adminstration for the purpose of showing his contempt for the sentiments and prejudices of this section."

Richmond, Va., Oct. 19.—The Dispatch says:

"With many qualities that are good—with some, possibly, that are great—Mr. Roosevelt is a negrophilist. While Governor of New York he invited a Negro (who, on account of race prejudice, could not obtain accommodation at any hotel) to be his guest at the Executive Mansion, and, it is said, gave him the best room in the house.

"Night before last the President had Prof. Booker T. Washington to dine with him at the White House. That was a deliberate act, taken under no alleged pressure of necessity, as in the Albany case, and may be taken as outlining his policy toward the Negro as a factor in Washington society. We say 'Washington society,' rather than 'American society,' because the former, on account of its political atmosphere, is much more 'advanced' in such matters than that of any other American city of which we know anything. The President, having invited Booker T. Washington to his table, residents of Washington of less conspicuous standing may be expected to do likewise. And if they invite him they may invite lesser lights—colored lights.

"When Mr. Cleveland was President he received Fred Douglass at some of his public entertainments — 'functions,' so-called—butwe do not remember that Fred was singled out for the distinguished honor of dining with the President, as Booker Washington has been.

"We do not like Mr. Roosevelt's negrophilism at all, and are sorry to see him seeking opportunities to indulge in it. He is reported to have rejoiced that Negro children were going to school with his children at Oyster Bay. But then, it may be said, too, that he has more reasons than the average white man to be fond of Negroes, since it was a Negro regiment that saved the Rough Riders from decimation at San Juan Hill. And but for San Juan Hill it is quite unlikely that Mr. Roosevelt would be President to-day.

"Booker Washington is said to have been very influential with the President in having Judge Jones put upon the Federal bench in Alabama, and we are now fully prepared to believe that statement.

"With our long-matured views on the subject of social intercourse between blacks and whites, the least we can say now is that we deplore the President's taste, and we distrust his wisdom."

Birmingham, Ala., Oct. 19.—The Enterprise says:

"It remained for Mr. Roosevelt to establish a precedent humiliating to the South and a disgrace to the nation. Judge Jones owes a duty to the South, to his friends and to common decency to promptly resign and hurl the appointment back into the very teeth of the white man who would invite a nigger to eat with his family."

Augusta, Ga., Oct. 19.—The Augusta Chroncile says, in its leading editorial, to-day:

"The news from Washington that President Booker T. Washington, of Tuskegee

Institute, was a guest at the White House at a dinner with President and Mrs. Roosevelt and family, and that after dinner there was the usual social hour over cigars, is a distinct shock to the favorable sentiment that was crystallizing in the South for the new President.

"While encouraging the people in the hope that the Negro is to be largely eliminated from office in the South, President Roosevelt throws the fat in the fire by giving countenance to the Negro's claims for social equality by having one to dine in the White House.

"President Roosevelt has made a mistake, one that will not only efface the good impression he had begun to create in the South, but one that will actively antagonize Southern people and meet the disapproval of good Anglo-Saxon sentiment in all latitudes.

"The South does not relish the Negro in office, but that is a small matter compared with its unalterable opposition to social equality between the races. President Roosevelt has flown in the face of public sentiment and precipitated an issue that has long since been fought out, and which should have been left in the list of settled questions."

Nashville, Tenn., Oct. 19.—The Evening Banner says:

"Whatever justification may be attempted of the President's action in this instance, it goes without saying that it will tend to chill the favor with which he is regarded in the South, and will embarrass him in his reputed purpose to build up his party in this section."

Louisville, Ky., Oct. 19.—The Times of yesterday afternoon says:

"The President has eliminated the color line from his private and official residences and with public office is hiring white Democrats to whitewash it down South."

Atlanta, Ga., Oct. 19.—Governor Candler says:

"No self-respecting white man can ally himself with the President after what has occurred. The step has done the Republican party no earthly good, and it will materially injure its chances in the South. The effect of the Jones appointment is largely neutralized. Still, I guess it's like the old woman when she kissed the cow. As a matter of fact, Northern people do not understand the Negro. They see the best types and judge of the remainder by them."

LIGHT.

Philadelphia, Oct. 19.—The Ledger this morning says:

"Because President Roosevelt saw fit, in his good judgment, to invite Booker T. Washington to dinner, strong words of disapproval are heard in the South. Mr. Washington is a colored man who enjoys

the universal respect of all people in this
country, black and white, on account of attainments, character and deeds. As the
President invited him to be ·his private
guest, and did not attempt to enforce the
companionship of a colored man upon any
one to whom the association could possibly be distasteful, any criticism of the
President's act savors of very great im-
pertinence. But, considered in any light,
the invitation is not a subject for criticism.
Booker T. Washington is one of the most
notable citizens of the country, just because he has done noteworthy things. He
is the founder and the successful executive
of one of the most remarkable institutions
in the United States, the Tuskegee (Alabama) Institute, which not only aims, but
in fact does, educate and train the youth
of the negro race to become useful, industrious and self-supporting citizens.

"Booker T. Washington is the embodiment of common sense and, instead of in-
citing the members of his race to dwell
upon their wrongs, to waste their time
upon politics and to try to get something
for nothing in this life, in order to live
without work, he has constantly preached
the gospel of honest work, and has founded a great industrial school, which fits the
young Negroes for useful lives as workers
and teachers of industry to others. This is
the man who was justly called by President McKinley, after he had inspected
Tuskegee, the "leader of his race," and in

the South no intelligent man denies that
he is doing a great service to the whole
population of both colors in this land. It
is evident that the only objection that
could be brought against association with
such a man as that is color alone, and
President Roosevelt will not recognize
that prejudice."

The Evening Bulletin says:

"President Roosevelt night before last
had Booker T. Washington, the worthy
and much-respected colored man who is
at the head of the Tuskegee Institute, as a
guest at his private table in the White
House. This has caused some indignation
among Southerners and in Southern newspapers.

"Yet all the President really seems to
have done was an act of courtesy in asking
Mr. Washington to sit down with him to
dinner and have a talk with him. As
Booker T. Washington is an entirely reputable man, as well as an interesting one.
the President doubtless enjoyed his company. Many Presidents in the past have
had far less reputable and agreeable men
at their table. If Mr. Roosevelt shall have
no worse ones among his private guests,
the country will have no cause for complaint.

"The right of the President to dine with
anyone he may please to have with him is
entirely his own affair, and Theodore
Roosevelt is not a likely man to pick out

bad company, black or white, for his personal or social companionship. The rumpus which some indiscreet Southerners are trying to raise because he has been hospitable to a colored man is a foolish display of both manners and temper."

Boston, Oct. 19.—Commenting on President Roosevelt's action in extending hospitality to Booker T. Washington, President Charles Eliot, of Harvard, said:

"Harvard dined Booker Washington at her tables at the last commencement. Harvard conferred an honorary degree on him. This ought to show what Harvard thinks about the matter."

William Lloyd Garrison: "It was a fine object lesson, and most encouraging. It was the act of a gentleman—an act of unconscious natural simplicity."

Charles Eliot Norton: "I uphold the President in the bold stand that he has taken."

NO SYMPATHY WITH PREJUDICE.

New York Herald: "The President has absolutely no sympathy with the prejudice against color. He has shown this on two occasions. Once he invited to his house at Oyster Bay, Harris, the Negro half-back of Yale, and entertained him over night. The other occasion was when he took in at the Executive Mansion at Albany, 'Bringham, the Negro baritone of St. George's Church, who was giving a con-

cert in Albany and had been refused food
and shelter by all the hotels.

WASTING THEIR BREATH.

Philadelphia Press: President Roosevelt's critics are wasting breath and spill-
ing ink. There is an obstinate man in the
White House. The cry of "nigger" will neither prevent him from continuing to appoint to any office in the Southern States
the best men, under whatever color of politics, who can be found under current conditions, or recognizing in the hospitalities
of the White House the best type of American manhood, under whatever color of
skin it can be found.

THAT DINNER.

New York Tribune: The Southern politician who criticises President Roosevelt's
action in inviting Prof. Booker T. Washington to dine at the White House is likely
to raise the query whether the manager of
the Tuskegee Institute or himself is really
the more deserving and genuine friend of
the South.

DEMOCRATS HAVE CHANGED ATTITUDE.

Glad of Booker T. Washington's Help in Securing Office.

NOW JEER ROOSEVELT.

Berate President for Dining With a Negro.

Some Noted Occasions When the Alabama Educator Has Received the Plaudits of the South.

Washington, D. C., Oct. 19.—President Roosevelt has a fine sense of humor, and while he regrets that he has without malice stirred up a tempest in a teapot for the Southern editors by entertaining Professor Booker T. Washington at dinner, he cannot put aside the humorous side of the situation. It is only a few weeks since a number of white Democrats co-operated with Booker Washington in regard to the appointment of ex-Governor Jones to the vacancy on the Federal bench in Alabama, and Washington spoke for these white Democrats when he came to the capital and assured President Roosevelt that Jones would accept the appointment and that it would be satisfactory to all classes.

(23)

Washington had seen the President and had acted as his agent in interviewing Governor Jones and others as to the appointment. The Southern Democrats applauded the appointment of Jones, and they praised Washington for using his influence at the White House to secure such an appointment for a Democrat. Then they all spoke of Washington as a gentleman of culture, who had the refined sense to cut loose from the Republican leaders of the Negro party in the South and work in harmony with the best class of whites. Now they are abusing the President for dining with a "nigger."

Washington has entertained more distinguished Northern men and more distinguished Southern men at the Tuskegee Institute than any other man in the State, if not in the South. President McKinley and his Cabinet, accompanied by many other distinguished gentlemen, were the guests of Washington at Tuskegee two years ago, and they lunched at his table. Washington was the guest of honor at a banquet in Paris three years ago, when Ambassador Porter presided and ex-President Harrison and Archbishop Ireland were among the guests. This same "nigger" was received by Queen Victoria and took tea in Buckingham Palace the same year.

INVITATION FROM WHITE HOUSE.

When he returned to this country Washington received invitations from all parts of the South to deliver addresses and at-

tend receptions given by white people. He
was received by the Governors of Georgia,
Virginia, West Virginia and Louisiana. He
spoke to many mixed audiences in the
South, where whites and blacks united to
do him honor. When the people of Atlanta
wanted an appropriation from Congress
for their Exposition in 1895 they sent a
large committee of the most distinguished
men in the South to the National Capital
to plead their cause. Booker T. Washington was one of these distinguished Southern men. Congressman Joseph E. Cannon,
Chairman of the Committee on Appropria-
tions in the House, says that Washington
by his force and eloquence secured that appropriation of $250,000 for the Atlanta Ex-
position.

The Southern people had only praise for
him when he was arranging to take Vice-
President Roosevelt to Tuskegee and Montgomery and Atlanta this fall, and they
were eager to co-operate with him in entertaining such a distinguished visitor. They
still hope to have President Roosevelt visit
the South, and if he goes he will go as the
guest of Booker T. Washington.

The President knows, too, that the real
leaders of the South, white Democrats, do
not sympathize with this hue and cry of
Southern editors because Washington was
a guest at the White House. Today the
President has received many messages
from Southern men, urging him to pay no
attention to the yawp of the bourbon edi-

tors, who have not been able to get over the old habit of historical discussion of "social equality." Southern men called at the White House today as usual to ask for favors at the hands of the President, and they are not afraid of contamination by meeting the man who "ate with a nigger."

AMUSES THE PRESIDENT.

President Roosevelt cannot help seeing the humorous side of the situation he has created by asking his friend to dinner, and he is pursuing the even tenor of his way as President without worrying over the outcome. He has, in the last two weeks, given cause for much excitement in the South. The first was when he appointed a Democrat to office and ignored the professional Republican politicians, who claimed to carry the "nigger" vote in their pocket. He was not disturbed by the threats of the Southern Republican politicians over that incident, and he is not disturbed by the threats of the Southern Democratic editors over this incident.

As to the Southern objection to dining with a Negro, Opie Read, of Chicago, tells a story about M. W. Gibbs, who has just resigned his position as United States Consul at Tamatave, Madagascar. Gibbs is now in Washington on his way home to Little Rock. He resigned to give a younger man a chance to serve his country as a Consul. Here is the story Opie Read told about Gibbs dining with white men at a banquet in honor of General Grant in Little Rock:

"In the reconstruction days a Negro by the name of Mifflin Wistar Gibbs located in Little Rock, Ark. He showed the community that he was keener than a whole lot of its leading citizens, who had kept the offices in their families for generations. Under the new order of things he was appointed Attorney of Pulaski County. His ability and the considerate manner in which he conducted his relationship with the whites gave him a greater popularity than any other colored man had ever before enjoyed in that place. His influence increased, until General Grant, then President, appointed him Register of the United States Land Office at Little Rock.

GIBBS' SPEECH THE BEST.

"When General Grant visited our city a banquet was prepared, and it was finally decided that for the first time in the history of the 'Bear State' a Negro would be welcomed at a social function on terms of absolute equality. I was then editor of the Gazette, and my seat was next to that of Gibbs. The speaker who had been selected to respond to the toast, 'The Possibilities of American Citizenship' was absent. I asked Gibbs if he would not talk on that subject. He consented, and I arranged the matter with the toastmaster. The novelty and the picturesqueness of the thing appealed to me. Every guest was spellbound, and General Grant was astonished. Not only was the speech of the Negro the best one delivered on that occasion, but it was one of the most remarkable to which I have ever listened.

"The owner of the Gazette was a Democrat of the Democrats, and a strict keeper of the traditions of the South. Moreover, his paper was the official organ of the Democratic party, and we were in the heat of a bitter campaign. In spite of all this, however, I came out with the editorial statement that Gibbs had scored the greatest oratorical triumph of the affair. Perhaps this didn't stir things up a little. But the gratitude of Gibbs was touching. He is now United States Consul at Tamatave, Madagascar. In my opinion he is the greatest living representative of the colored race. We have been close friends ever since that banquet."

BOOKER WASHINGTON THE VICTIM.

(From the Washington (D. C.) Post, October 23, 1901.)

Quite the most deplorable feature of the Booker Washington incident is, in our opinion, the effect it is likely to have on Washington himself; yet this is an aspect of the case which does not seem to have occurred thus far to any of the multitudinous and more or less enlightened commentators who have bestowed their views upon the country. Criticisms of the Presi-

·dent are matters of taste. For our part, we hold, and have always held, that a President's private and domestic affairs are not proper subjects of public discussion. A man does not surrender all of his personal liberties in becoming the Chief Executive of the Nation. At least, his purely family arrangements are not the legitimate concern of outsiders. The Presidency would hardly be worth the having otherwise. The country, however, has a right to consider the incident in the light of its probable injury to Washington and to the great and useful work in which he is engaged.

In closing this page of "Shadow and Light" I am loath to believe that this extreme display of adverse feeling regarding the President's action in inviting Mr. Washington to dine with him, as shown in some localities, is fully shared by the best element of Southern opinion. Few Southern gentlemen of the class who so cheerfully pay the largest amount of taxation for the tuition of the Negro, give him employment and do much to advance him along educational and industrial lines, fear that the President's action will cause the obtrusion of his bronze pedals beneath their mahogany. Trusting that he will be inspired to foster those elements of character so conspicuous in Mr. Washington and that have endeared him to his broad-

minded countrymen both North and South.
The best intelligence, the acknowledged
leaders of the race, are not only conservative along political lines, but are in accord
with those who claim that social equality
is not the creature of law, or the product
of coercion, for, in a generic sense, there
is no such thing as social equality. The
gentlemen who are so disturbed hesitate,
or refuse such equality with many of their
own race; the same can be truthfully said
of the Negro. Many antibellum theories
and usages have already vanished under
the advance of a higher civilization, but
the "old grudge" is still utilized when
truth and justice refuse their service.

CHAPTER XXXII.

Washington, the American "Mecca" for political worshipers, is a beautiful city, but well deserving its "nom de plume" as "the city of magnificent distances;" for any one with whom you have business seems to live five miles from every imaginable point of the compass; and should you be on stern business bent, distance will not "lend enchantment to the view." It is here that the patriot, and the mercenary, the ambitious and the envious gather, and where unity and divergence hold high carnival.

Dramatists have found no better field for portraying the vicissitudes and uncertainties, the successes and triumphs of human endeavor. The ante-room to the President's office presents a vivid picture, as they wait for, or emerge from, executive presence, delineating the varied phases of impressible human nature—the despondent air of ill success; the pomp of place secured; the expectant, but hope deferred; the bitterness depicted in waiting delegations on a mission of opposition bent; the gleam of gladness on success; homage to the influential—all these figure, strut or bemoan in the ratio of a self-importance or a dejected mein. There is no more humorous reading, or more typical, than the ups and downs of office-seekers. Sometimes it is that of William the "Innocent," and often that of William the "Croker." The trials of "an unsuccessful," a prototype of "Orpheus C. Kerr," the nom de plume of that prince of writers, on this subject, is in place:

Diary of an office-seeker, William the "Innocent":

March 2d—Just arrived. Washington a nice town. Wonder if it would not be as well to stay here as go abroad.

March 4th—Saw McKinley inaugurated. We folks who nominated him will be all right now. Think I had better take an assistant secretaryship. The Administration wants good men, who know something about politics; besides, I am getting to like Washington.

March 8th—Big crowd at the White House. They ought to give the President time to settle himself. Have sold my excursion ticket and will stay awhile. Too many people make a hotel uncomfortable. Have found a good boarding house.

March 11th—Shook hands with the President in the East Room and told him I would call on a matter of business in a few days. He seemed pleased.

March 15th—Went to the Capitol and found Senator X. He was sour. Said the whole State was there chasing him. Asked me what I wanted, and said, "Better go for something in reach." Maybe an auditorship would be the thing.

March 23d—Took my papers to the White House. Thought I'd wait and have a private talk with the President, but Sergeant Porter said I'd have to go along with the rest. What an ill-natured set they were. Elbowed me right along just because they saw the President wanted to talk with me. Will have to go back and finish our conversation.

March 27—Got some money from home.

March 29th—Went to the White House, but the chap at Porter's door wouldn't let me in. Said it was after hours. He ought to be fired.

April 3d—Saw Mark Hanna, after waiting five hours. Asked him why my letter had not been answered. He said he was getting 400 a day and his secretaries would catch up some time next year. I always thought Hanna overestimated. Now I know it.

April 5th—Had an interview with the President. Was last in the line, so they could not push me along. When I told him of my services to the party, he replied: "Oh, yes;" and for me to file my papers in the State Department. Said he had many good friends in Indiana and hoped they would be patient. Can he have forgotten I am not from Indiana? Probably the tariff is worrying him. Shameful the way the Senate is acting.

April 7th—Borrowed a little more money. Washington is an expensive town to live in.

April 11th—Senator X. says all the auditorships were mortgaged before the election, but he will indorse me for a special agency or a chief clerkship, if I can find one that is not under the civil service law.

April 12th—D—n the civil service law.

April 17th—Didn't know there were so many good positions abroad. Ought to have gone for one of them in the first place. That State Department is a great thing. Think I'll start with Antwerp and check off a few which will suit me. Wonder where I can negotiate a small loan?

April 19th—Got in to see the President and told him I could best serve the Administration and the party abroad. He said, "Oh, yes," and to file my papers in the Post-office Department, and he hoped his friends in Massachusetts would be patient. What made him think I was from Massachusetts? I suppose he gets mixed sometimes.

April 20th—Senator X. says there is one chance in a million of getting a Consulate; but if I will concentrate on Z town he and the delegation will do what they can. Salary, $1,000; fees, $87.

April 21st—Have concentrated on Z town. Got in line today just for a moment to tell the President it would suit me. He

said, "Oh, yes," and to file my papers in the
Treasury Department, and he hoped his
friends in Minnesota would be patient till
he could get around to them. Queer he
should think I was from Minnesota.

April 26th—The ingratitude of that man
McKinley! He has nominated Jones for
Z town, when he knew I had concentrated
on it. After my services to the party, too!
Who is Jones, anyhow?

April 27th—I am going home. Senator
X has got me a pass. Will send for my
trunk later. It is base ingratitude.

William the "Croker," the other appli-
cant for official favor, wanted "Ambasador
to Russia," and while not attaining the full
measure of his ambition, was nevertheless
rewarded for his pertinacity. His sojourn
in Washington had been long, and was becoming irksome, particularly so to the Senators and Members of Congress from his
State, who had from time to time ministered to his pecuniary wants. But Seth
Orton was noted at home and abroad for
his staying qualities. He came from an
outlying district in his State that was politically pivotal, and Seth had been known
on several occasions by his fox-horn contributions to rally the "unwashed" and
save the day when hope but faintly glim-
mered above the political horizon. For his
Congressional delegation Seth was both
useful at home and expensive abroad. That
the mission for which he aspired was be-

yond his reach they were fully aware; that he must be disposed of they were equally agreed. After having adroitly removed the props to his aspirations for Ambassador, Minister Plenipotentiary and Consul, they told him they had succeeded in getting him an Indian agency, paying $1,000 a year. He was disgusted, and proclaimed rebellion. They appeased him by telling him that the appropriation for supplies and other necessaries the last year was ten thousand dollars, and they were of the opinion that the former agent had saved half of it. A gleam of joy and quick consent were prompt! Walking up and down his Congressman's room, pleased, then thoughtful, then morose, he finally exclaimed to his patron, "Look here, Mr. Harris; don't you think that $5,000 of the $10,000 too much to give them d—n nigger Indians?"

On the official side of colored Washington life, we see much that is gratifying recognition. The receipt by us of over a million dollars annually, on the one side, and the rendering of a creditable service on the other, while our professional and business status in the District is equally commendable, and much more prolific in the bestowal of substantial and lasting benefit. And on the domestic side we have much that is cheering, comprising a large representation of wealth and intelligence, living in homes indicating refinement and culture, and with a social contact the most desirable.

WILLIAM CALVIN CHASE,
Lawyer, and Editor of "Washington Bee."

Born in Washington, D. C., February, 1854—Leaving the Public School entered
Howard University and there Graduated—As Editor or Lawyer He is
Tireless in His Adherence to well-formed Convictions—The
"Bee" Hums no Uncertain Sound.

Mr. Andrew F. Hilyer, editor and compiler of "The Twentieth Century Union League Directory," in his introduction to that able and useful publication, says: "This being the close of the nineteenth century, after a generation of freedom, it was thought to be a good point at which to stop and take an account of stock, and see just what is the actual status of the colored population of Washington, the Capital of the Nation, where the colored population is large, and where the conditions are the most favorable, to see what is their actual status as skilled workmen, in business, in the professions, and in their organizations; in short, to make a study, at first hand, of their efforts for social betterment."

This publication contains the names, character and location of 500 business men and women. It is creditable to the compiler and encouraging for the subjects of its reference.

The colored newspapers of the District, several in number, are of high order, and maintain a reputation for intelligent journalism, and for energy and devotion to the cause they espouse are abreast with those of sister communities. The growth of Negro journals in our country has been marked. We have now three hundred or more newspapers and magazines, edited and published by colored men and women. The publisher of a race paper early finds that it is not a sinecure nor a bed of roses. If he is zealous and uncompromising in the defense of his race, exposing outrages and injustice; advertisements are withdrawn by those who have the most patronage to bestow. Should he "crook the pregnant hinges of the knee, that thrift may follow fawning," and fail to denounce the wrong, the paper loses influence and subscriptions of those in whose interest it is professedly established, and hence, as an advertising medium, it is deserted.

So, as for the publisher (in the words of that eccentric Puritan, Lorenzo Dow), "He'll be damned if he does, and be damned if he don't." He is between "Scilla and Carribdes," requiring versatility of ability, courage of conviction and a wise discretion, that he may steer "between the rocks of too much danger and pale fear," and reach the port of success. The mission of the Negro press is a noble one, for "Right is of no sex, and Wrong of no color," and God, the Father of us all, with these as its standard, to be effectual it must give a "plain, unvarnished tale, nor set down aught in malice." The white journals of the country often quote the Negro press as to Negro wants and Negro aspirations, and as time and conditions shall justify it will necessarily become more metropolitan and less exclusive, dealing more with economic and industrial subjects on broader lines and from more material standpoints.

HON. WILLIAM H. HUNT.

United States Consul to Madagascar.
Born May, 1860, in Louisiana—Graduated at Groton Academy, Massachusetts,
and Studied at Williams' College—Secretary and Vice-Consul to the
Consulate—Appointed Consul by President McKinley
August 27, 1901—Competent an Worthy.

CHAPTER XXXIII.

HOWARD UNIVERSITY.

Howard University was established by a special act of Congress in 1867. It takes its name from that of the great philanthropist and soldier, Gen. O. O. Howard, who may be called its founder and greatest patron. It was through the untiring efforts of General Howard that this special act passed Congress to establish a university on such broad and liberal lines as those that characterize Howard University.

This University admits students of both sexes and any color to all of its departments. The great majority of its students, however, are colored, and some of its graduates are the most distinguished men of the Negro race in America. It has splendid departments of law, medicine, theology and the arts and sciences.

Howard University is situated on one of the most beautiful sites of the Capital of the Nation.

Having two members of my family as teachers in the public schools of Washington City, I have learned considerable about them. They are said to rank among our

(24)

best public schools, and are constantly improving, under the careful supervision of a highly competent superintendent, and a paid board of trustees. There are 112 school buildings in the city—75 for white and 37 for colored, the number being regulated according to population, about one-third being colored. New manual training schools have just been erected, for both races, and a growing disposition exists to provide equal (though separate) accommodation and opportunity. The colored schools are taught exclusively by colored teachers, the grade schools being conducted by the graduates of the Washington Normal School almost entirely. The M Street High School, a leading sample of the best public schools of the country, has a teaching faculty of twenty teachers, most of them graduates of our best colleges, such as Howard, Yale, Oberlin, University of Michigan, Amherst, Brown and Cornell.

R. H. Terrill, the present principal, is a graduate of Howard, with the degree of "Cum laude," and, after having won golden opinions from the board and attaches of the school for his scholarship and supervising ability, has been appointed by President Roosevelt to a judgship of the District, and will assume the duties thereof in January, 1902.

All such appointments are helpful, coming from the highest ruler, and for place, at the fountain head of the Government, have a reflex influence upon much which is

JUDGE ROBERT H. TERRILL.

Was born in Virginia in 1857—A Graduate of Harvard College—A Chief of Division in the United States Treasury and Principal of the Colored High School—Appointed one of the Judges of the District of Columbia November, 1901.

unjust. With each success we should beware of envy, the offspring of selfishness,
which is apt to creep insiduously into our
lives. We should crown the man who has
achieved distinction and advise him as to
pitfalls. "No sadder proof," Carlisle has
said, "can be given by a man of his own
littleness than disbelief in great men."
There is no royal road to a lasting eminence but the toilsome pathway of diligence, self-denial and high moral rectitude;
surely not by turning sharp corners to follow that "will-o'-the wisp" transient success, at the expense of upright conduct.
Neither suavity of manner nor the gilding
of education will atone for disregarding
the sanctity of obligation, the violation of
which continues to wreck the lives and
blast the promise of many. By sowing the
seed of uprighteousness, by unceasing effort and rigid frugality, the harvest,
though sometimes tardy, will be sure to
produce an hundred fold in Christian virtues and material prosperity. The latter is
a necessity for our progress; for, say what
you will about being "just as good as anybody," the world of mankind has little use
for a penniless man. The ratio of its attention to you is largely commensurate with
your bank account and your ability to further ends involving expenditure. Whether
this estimate is in accord with the highest
principle, the Negro has not time to investigate, for he is up against the hard fact
that confronts the great majority of man-

kind, and one with which each for himself must grapple. Opportunity may be late, but it comes to him who watches and waits while diligent in what his hands may find to do. For, with all that may be said, gracious or malicious, of the "Negro problem," we are unmistakably on the upward grade, educationally and financially, while these bitter criticisms and animadversions will be the moral weights to steady our footsteps and give surety to progress.

Granting no excuse for ignorance or unfitness in a political aspirant, or for a religious ministry at the present day, we cannot but remember that our present lines in more pleasant places, both in Church and State, had impetus through the trying ordeal of toil, suffering and massacre during the era of reconstruction. Many, though unlettered, with a nobility of soul that oppression could not humble, were martyrs to their Christian zeal for the right and finger boards and beacon lights on the dark and perilous road to our present advanced position.

In concluding this imperfect autobiography, containing mention of "men I have met" in the nineteenth century, absence of many co-laborers, both white and colored, will be observable, whose ability, devotion and sacrifice should be treasured as heirlooms by a grateful people.

And now, kind reader, who has followed me in my wanderings—

"Say not 'Good night,' but in some brighter clime bid me 'Good morning.'"

In the *Blacks in the American* West series

SHADOW AND LIGHT: AN AUTOBIOGRAPHY
by Mifflin W. Gibbs

BORN TO BE
by Taylor Gordon

THE LIFE AND ADVENTURES OF NAT LOVE
by Nat Love